DINERS

OF **PENNSYLVANIA**

D1028614

0 11557 02878 2

DINERS OF PENNSYLVANIA

Brian Butko and Kevin Patrick

STACKPOLE
BOOKS

Published by
STACKPOLE BOOKS
5067 Ritter Road
Mechanicsburg, PA 17055
www.stackpolebooks.com

Printed in the United States of America

10 9 8 7 6 5 4 3 2

FIRST EDITION

Cover design by Caroline Stover

Front cover: Late in 1953, the DeRaffele Company delivered the shiny
By-Pass Diner to Herr Street in Harrisburg to replace an old
dining car. It was named for the U.S. Route 22
bypass at its front door. It's now called
the American Dream Diner.
Owner Fred Jenkins
says, "I cook everything
that goes out the door."
PHOTO BY BRIAN BUTKO

Back cover: Huge neon signs
still stand in front of some
diners, beckoning highway
travelers to stop in for a bite.
This one is at the Decoven Diner
in Duncannon.
PHOTO BY KYLE WEAVER

Library of Congress Cataloging-in-Publication Data

Butko, Brian A.
 Diners of Pennsylvania / Brian Butko and Kevin Patrick. — 1st ed.
  p.   cm.
 Includes bibliographical references and index.
 ISBN 0-8117-2878-1
 1. Diners (Restaurants) — Pennsylvania. I. Patrick, Kevin Joseph. II. Title.
TX945.B884 1999
647.95748—dc21

99–18350
CIP

Contents

Foreword

Diners are not all created equal. And despite what big-time restaurateurs may tell you, consistency is not always charming. At any diner, there are a lot of variables: the architecture, the food, the waitresses, the regulars, the shared conversations, the time of day, your mood.

When you're on the road, it's nice to know where to find some great grub, local flavor, and perhaps some unusual characters. And it also can be fun to discover places near your home that you've somehow missed. There may be more diners in New Jersey, but as a well-fed native and current resident of Pennsylvania, I find that its diners are among the most beautiful and often have the tastiest food.

My eyes were opened to many of the joys of motoring in Pennsylvania by Brian Butko, co-author of this book. I met him while researching for the public-television series "Pennsylvania Road Show," and his enthusiasm for the Lincoln Highway, the Ship Hotel, tourist cabins, and cool old places to eat made him an essential part of our production team, as well as a stellar on-camera personality. When we decided to make the documentary "Pennsylvania Diners and Other Roadside Restaurants," Brian became our most important guide. One day he took me to Pip's Diner, a Pittsburgh landmark that I never knew existed, but was sure glad to find out about.

Since then, Brian wrote the book *The Lincoln Highway*, and now he's teamed up with the talented and much-traveled Kevin Patrick to put this volume together. It's a book to keep in the car, to refer to before and during all Pennsylvania road trips, and great fun to travel through anytime. It incorporates helpful maps and a new way of learning about history and geography. It has lots of diners I haven't visited yet, and it makes me yearn for new trips, new encounters, and new daily specials.

Rick Sebak
Producer
WQED-TV, Pittsburgh

Acknowledgments

Our biggest thanks go to Richard J. S. Gutman, for offering unprecedented access to his thirty-year collection of diner information; Daniel Zilka, for sharing the files of the American Diner Museum; Carol Ingald and Kevin and Lori Butko, for tracking down diners in the far reaches of the state; Randy Garbin, of *Roadside Magazine,* for offering his knowledge and diner listings; Kyle Weaver, of Stackpole Books, for his editing and on-the-road research; and Larry Cultrera, Steve Harwin, Bernie Heisey, Jeff Lee, Rick Sebak, and Bob Viguers, for generously sharing their expertise and materials.

We greatly appreciate the support of friends and family who helped to ferret out diners and put us up while we were away from home, including Theresa Patrick and the girls, Kaitlyn and Veronica; the extended Patrick and Angst families; and Chuck and Suzanne Yula.

Hundreds of others helped, including John Axtell and Diana Ames; Jack "The Scribbler" Brubaker; Sarah Butko; Ron Dylewski; Marilyn Erwin; Michael Groff; David Hebb; Cy Hosmer; Gerry Juran; Rick Kriss; Curt Miner; Harold L. Myers; Bill Plack Jr.; Paul Roberts; Richard Leaman Smith; George Smurlo; Gordon Tindall; the many people involved in the book's production, including Joyce Bertsch, Eileen Connors, Kerry Handel, Ann Harrison, Richard King, Beth Oberholtzer, Tracy Patterson, and Caroline Stover; and the many diner owners throughout the state.

Many staff members at libraries and historical societies also gave their assistance, including Steve Doell, David Grinnell, JoAnn Kartsonas, Art Louderback, Jane Moffitt, Renee Savits, and Sharon Watson-Mauro, Historical Society of Western Pennsylvania Library & Archives; Marjory Blubaugh, Franklin County Library, Chambersburg; Luanne Eisler, Butler Area Public Library, Butler; Robert Fuhrman, Mercer County Historical Society, Mercer; Edward Hahn, Westmoreland County Historical Society, Greensburg; Audrey Iacone, Carnegie Library of Pittsburgh, Oakland; Deborah Toomey Rutledge, Reading Public Library, Reading; Edith Serkownek, Warren County Historical Society, Warren; and Marianne Squyres, Delaware County Historical Society, Chester.

A Word about
Diner Manufacturers

Throughout this book are references to manufacturers that shipped diners to Pennsylvania. No diners are believed to have been built in Pennsylvania; the closest the state came was the J. G. Brill Company in Philadelphia, a streetcar maker that had subsidiaries in other states produce the all-steel Brill Steel diners from 1927 to 1932. Those plants—G. C. Kuhlman Car Company of Cleveland, Ohio, and Wason Manufacturing Company of Springfield, Massachusetts—made the firm's boxy diners with monitor roofs. Some reportedly were shipped to Pennsylvania, but none are known to exist here today. Modern Diner Builders, a Philadelphia company, did not manufacture diners but reconditioned them in the 1940s and early '50s. Mountain View was selling so many diners here that a branch office opened in Philadelphia in 1953.

Learning to identify a diner's make takes work, as diners from a particular era all look similar. Dating is not an exact science, as styles and model years overlapped and the time between placing an order and delivery could stretch over three years. Also, many diners are older models reconditioned in a newer style. The market for diners was so hot at midcentury that most of them were traded in and refurbished for resale. Many diners, therefore, are a decade older than they appear, and some trade-ins were rehabbed more than once. Here are some general (and unscientific) exterior clues for identification:

DeRaffele. 1933–present. Vertical fluting in the 1940s, fluted corners combined with streamline style in the 1950s, angular vestibule overhang starting about 1960, zigzag rooflines in the 1960s, arched windows with orange tile mansard in the 1970s.

Fodero. 1933–81. Either horizontal stainless or flat vertical porcelain fluting in the 1940s, both having rounded corners with stainless sunburst. The company used the name **National** from 1940 to 1945 and thereafter referred to those models as Foderos. Vertical stainless ribs below roofline in the 1950s.

Kullman. 1927–present. Vertical fluting in the 1940s, picture windows beginning in 1950, 5-foot-wide canopy starting in 1955. The company began making other structures in 1969, and by 1990 only 7 percent of its output was diners.

CARNEGIE LIBRARY OF PITTSBURGH

Diners often left little evidence of their make, locations, or owners. This Ward & Dickinson was snapped by Abram Brown, a photographer of Pittsburgh-area railcars who was intrigued by what he thought was a converted streetcar. No record exists of where this 1943 picture was taken.

Mountain View. 1939–57. Distinctive rolling roofline and glass block corners after war, cowcatcher corners in the late 1940s to early 1950s, square roof corners in the early 1950s, and thin scrolls at roofline in the late 1950s. A lot of these diners were shipped to Pennsylvania.

O'Mahony. 1913–56. Flat porcelain panels in the 1940s, rounded end windows from the late 1930s through 1950s.

Paramount. 1932–present. Completely stainless with burnished circles or vertical fluting in the 1940s, balls on wedding-cake or waterfall corner tops in the early 1950s, zigzag rooflines in the 1960s.

Silk City. 1927–64. This is the only make that was not custom built. Old-style monitor roofs till the early 1950s. Siding look until the mid-1950s. Corners in the 1950s were slim with stainless early, glass later. Zigzag stainless pattern in the 1960s.

Swingle. 1957–88. Vertical stainless fluting along roofline on early models.

Ward & Dickinson. 1923–circa 1940. Many W&Ds were shipped from their Buffalo, New York–area factory to western and central Pennsylvania. Their railcar style was topped by a high clerestory.

In addition, a few diners in Pennsylvania were made by **Bixler** (1931–circa 1937), **Comac** (1947–circa 1951), **Tierney** (1905–33), **Manno**

(1949–78), **Musi/Sunshine** (1966–present), **Master** (1947–circa 1955), **Rochester Grills** (circa 1940s), and **Sterling** (1936–42).

A number of manufacturers used serial numbers, including Mountain View, O'Mahony, Silk City, Sterling, Swingle, and Worcester. Only a couple of numbers are known for O'Mahony and Sterling.

Mountain View diners were numbered consecutively, apparently indicating when an order was placed. By the 1940s, numbers had reached the 200s, and by time the company folded in 1957, among the last diners completed was #525, Marie's (later Serro's) in Greensburg.

On most Silk City tags, the first two digits are the year, followed by the job number. The Windmill in Ono, #46101, was the one hundred and first diner made in 1946, and the Airport Diner in Kutztown, #6027, was the twenty-seventh diner made in 1960.

But a few numbers don't fit that pattern: Baby's in State College (#3071), Cadillac Diner in Downingtown (#6671), Coventry Diner in Pottstown (#2471), Ray's Diner in Jeffersonville (#5471), and the demolished Turf Club Diner in State College (#7271). Though they may seem like random numbers, the last two digits of all these diners are the same. The numbers could indicate a reconditioned car or, more likely, a new numbering system that was adopted between 1961 and the factory's close in 1964. All five diners appear to be of early-sixties vintage and are the same style, with angular ceilings and a zigzag pattern in their stainless exteriors.

Swingle produced its first diner, Twaddell's in Paoli, in 1957 and its last, the American Diner in Philadelphia, thirty-one years later. The digits of the serial numbers indicate the date of delivery and the letters give information about the product: D = diner, L = L-shape, V = vestibule outside, U = used, K = kitchen, R = reconditioned, and DR = dining room. So Twaddell's Diner, #1157DKLV, was delivered in November 1957 and was a diner with a kitchen, was L-shaped, and had a vestibule.

A Word about Diner Styles

The following are general categories of diner styles developed by the authors, based on traits typical for the era. Not all features are listed, and some styles overlap periods. Years are also approximate.

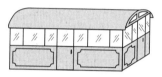

Barrel Roof (1910–35)

Exterior: Wood and porcelain enamel; sliding doors at front center and side.

Interior: Marble counter; porcelain enamel ceiling with vents; honeycomb tile floor; walls of 2-by-4-inch off-white and green tiles. Booths and restrooms are introduced. Cooking is done behind the counter.

Note: This category also includes the few monitor roof diners from the 1930s (usually Ward & Dickinsons).

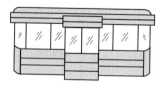

Modern Stainless (1935–55)

Exterior: Large porcelain panels or vertical fluting in early years, stainless facade later; glass block, corners rounded in early years then getting squarer; monitor-style or rounded roof.

Interior: Booths at one end; stainless steel backwall behind counter, with sunburst pattern; Formica countertops and ceilings; 4-inch square-tile walls of yellow, pale blue, pink, or gray. Cooking is done behind the counter or in an attached kitchen or both.

Exaggerated Modern (1955–65)

Exterior: Stainless steel with colored horizontal bands of flexglas or anodized aluminum; large, canted windows; wide, flared canopies with zigzag shape and recessed lights; flat roof.

Interior: Booths at both ends and along front windows; terrazzo floor of pink or green; tiered ceiling with mirror strip. Cooking is seldom done behind the counter.

Environmental (1965–85)

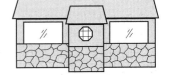

Exterior: Stone or brick facade; brown or red mansard roof; colonial traits, such as coach lamps, or Mediterranean traits, such as pillars or arched windows.

Interior: Wood grain; curtains and carpeting; brown or avocado upholstery; stools with backrests; wagon-wheel or chimney-flue chandeliers; acoustic tile ceilings with faux wooden beams; copper fixtures. No cooking is done behind the counter.

Note: Many older diners have been remodeled in this style, some retaining their original interiors.

Postmodern (1985–present)

Exterior and interior: Reinterpretation of classic diner elements: quilted stainless steel, neon trim, black-and-white-checkered walls, chrome fixtures, glass block, boomerang Formica on tables and counters. No cooking is done behind the counter.

Note: The category also includes the late-modern style, a transition between environmental and postmodern typified by black or mirrored glass exteriors. Some older diners have been remodeled with postmodern elements.

PENNSYLVANIA AS DINERLAND

I f America were regionalized by restaurants, the roads into the northeast United States would be marked, "Welcome to Dinerland." The diner here is taken for granted, assumed to exist everywhere, and not given much thought by the average person on the street. At the national level, however, diners are a novelty, part of the whole nostalgia industry. Newly manufactured stainless steel diners sporting neon, fifties paraphernalia, and black and white checked tiles are showing up all over the country in places that never had diners before. The Northeast is certainly not immune to the recent infatuation with diners, but here it is just the latest in a long history of attitude and style changes.

The tale of the Birmingham Grille is the quintessential Pennsylvania diner story. It began serving customers south of Philadelphia in 1949 and was moved a few miles north in the 1960s. A customer in 1990 could still order a Mexican omelet or meatloaf sandwich or even a full turkey dinner for $5.25. But diners do not stay put long, and the Birmingham Grille left for more profitable pastures. Diners are leaving Pennsylvania all too often these days, but this story has an added twist: The diner is now in two states. Its dining room, a 1965 Kullman-built annex, was joined to Ruthie and Moe's Diner in Cleveland, and the original part was moved to Truckee, California, and was redone in 1930s style. Such is the nature of mobile restaurants.

Now there is a story in all this. Not the nostalgia-laced one that waxes poetic about a hot cuppa joe, "Adam and Eve on a raft," gum-cracking waitresses who call you "Hon," and the good ol' days when Potsie and the gang cruised their hot rods down to the diner. That story has been told too often. The untold story is about the diner as a unique American form shaped by the sweeping changes of industrialization, urbanization, and the rise of the automobile as the dominant means of transportation. It is the untold story of the diner as an integral element in the cities, towns, and neighborhoods of the Northeast and in the lives of its middle-class inhabitants. This is the story of the diner as a place, rather than nostalgic history, and the setting for this story is Pennsylvania.

A book on Pennsylvania diners should start with some basic questions: How many diners are there? Where are they located? What do they look

STEVE HARWIN

Above: The Birmingham Grille, a 1949 Kullman, started life south of West Chester at Painters Crossroads, Routes 1 and 202. Louise Menna's dad, Joseph, opened the diner in 1949: "He was always the first one to hand out a meal to anyone who needed one. People loved him." In the mid-1990s, the diner was separated from its annex, a 1965 Kullman, which now does duty in Cleveland. Below: The original portion of the Birmingham now serves locals and tourists as Andy's Truckee Diner in Truckee, California.

RICHARD J. S. GUTMAN

like? Sounds simple, but it isn't. As for the first question, the number we have settled on is 260. It might be more, but it's probably not less. We kept busy checking on restaurants that call themselves diners but are not, and on authentic diners that look nothing like the classic form. So what *is* a diner? For our purposes, *a diner is a factory-built restaurant transported to its site of operation.* People can get very touchy about whether an assumed diner is "real" or not. Our criteria is not a value judgment about the restaurant, just a way of distinguishing diners from other eateries.

Yes, we had to leave out some great non-factory-built places like the Keystone Diner in New Oxford, Del-Kid near Pittsburgh, Tom and Joe's in Altoona, Ernie's Texas Lunch in Gettysburg, Red's in Lewistown, Russ's Dinor in Erie, the South Street Diner (second best food in Philadelphia, they told us), and a thousand other places. There's a book waiting to be written on all the non-factory-built diners, places like the Midtown IV Diner & Bar at 2013 Chestnut Street in Philadelphia, where co-owner Vivian G. Hionas said, "We have all the characteristics of a real diner. Open twenty-four hours, seven days—even Christmas!" But as when choosing wedding guests, we had to cut somewhere.

One of the draws of a factory-built diner to an operator is the ease of upgrading to a newer, larger, and more modern diner. If not destroyed, the old diner can be sold and moved to a different location or be sent back to a manufacturer's lot for reconditioning and resale. Many diners have been completely covered or converted to other uses. Some of these are obvious like HL's Live Bait and Tackle Shop, formerly the Transit Diner, in Morrisville; Country Food Market, formerly Ed's Diner, in Doylestown; or Bloomers Flower Shop, formerly the Congress Street Diner, in Bradford. Others really hide what's underneath, like Weiland's Flowers, formerly the Dutch Diner in Palmyra.

All the moving and remodeling can make identifying diners pretty difficult, but we had help. Our most useful sources were the diner lists generated and maintained by such experts as Richard J. S. Gutman in *American Diner: Then and Now*, Randy Garbin of *Roadside Magazine,* and Daniel Zilka at the American Diner Museum. We combined these leads with library searches, many miles on the road, and a lot of diner food.

Contrary to a widely held misconception, the diner did not evolve from the railroad dining car, but from the lowly lunch wagon. In 1872, Walter Scott pioneered the "night lunch" business by loading up a horse-drawn wagon with sandwiches, hard-boiled eggs, and pies and peddling them on the streets of Providence, Rhode Island, to the staffs of the town's three dailies, who toiled nightly to get out the morning edition. Scott—and his soon-to-appear competitors—found that the nighttime streets were filled with potential customers eager for a bite to eat.

The mobility of diners has helped their survival; when they're threatened by obsolescence, road widenings, or land development, they can be moved. Here, in 1963, Feiler's Diner (1948 DeRaffele) leaves Baum Boulevard in Pittsburgh for its new home in Butler.

It's not surprising that the diner originated in southern New England. Folks in rural America worked in the daylight and slept at night, but in industrial New England production ran full-tilt twenty-four hours a day. Employees worked in shifts, and hundreds were on the streets at odd hours. Walter Scott and many competitors soon were operating around the clock just like the twenty-four-hour factory system.

As the concept spread, the skilled workers needed to build "lunch" wagons were readily available in the towns that most appealed to operators. During the industry's early period in the 1880s and '90s, all six lunch wagon manufacturers were located in Massachusetts. But two developments around the turn of the century transformed the fledgling lunch wagon business into the diner industry. First, wagon owners began settling onto permanent sites to satisfy licensing requirements and to save wear on wheels and horses. Wagons could be situated on odd plots where rents were low, and could be moved if business fell off.

Second, cities were changing over from horse-drawn trolleys to electric cars, and for $15, one could purchase a trolley, remove its wheels, and convert it into a makeshift lunch wagon. Already worn-out from years of service, these dilapidated cars left a long-lasting stigma on the diner industry. A 1948 *Saturday Evening Post* article noted that when Patrick Tierney started making lunch wagons in 1905, "diners were about as easy to sell as rattlesnake pits." Typical of early wagon owners was one profiled in the article

COLLECTION OF BRIAN BUTKO

Lunch wagons are quite elusive even to discerning historians, but the one at lower left was caught serving Gettysburg tourists in the teens.

who amassed $50 in 1904 to open his first diner. "His place seated seven customers, and could be moved by borrowing a horse somewhere. He carried water for coffee in a pail from the nearest house, and clambered to the roof of the car every night to fill the gasoline tank which fed fuel to his stove." His first week's profit was $4, but he was still in business (in a newer car) four decades later.

COLLECTION OF BRIAN BUTKO

As the diner industry flourished, some entrepreneurs took a less expensive route to ownership by co-opting discarded interurban cars. Such was the case with Pike's Peak Tourist Home and Dining Car, which once served patrons traveling on Route 422, near Indiana, Pennsylvania.

The Royal chain operated diners in Philadelphia. This car, pictured in O'Mahony's 1932 catalog, was a specially constructed 45-foot O'Mahony.

In the maturing industrial economy of the early twentieth century, building lunch wagons in the backyard became a thing of the past. Manufacturers like Tierney and Jerry O'Mahony standardized their models and expanded their offerings to include indoor toilets and full-length, marble-topped counters. Tierney's innovations helped save the reputation of diners, and his ambitiousness made him worth $2 million by time he died in 1917 (the equivalent of $30 million today). Yet the stigma remained. In a 1922 issue of *New York Times Magazine*, a bank clerk said about his mother, "When I told her I ate in a lunch wagon she nearly had a fit. . . .'Why mother,' I told her, 'the butter and eggs in that wagon—you can't get 'em any better anywhere.'" But mom wasn't convinced: "'It's degrading!'"

By then, a lunch wagon's wheels were used only to move the eatery to its operating site. Railcar styles and dimensions were adopted to accommodate transportation by rail and to emulate their fancier cousins, railroad dining cars. Most notably, lunch wagons adopted the monitor roof, a raised center portion running lengthwise with a strip of ventilation windows. The style endured until midcentury, mainly because the design cleverly provided both ventilation and rapid water runoff, something railroads had long before discovered. The wagons came to be called dining cars as a way of expressing the full menu of a twenty-four-hour restaurant, and by the 1920s, the name was shortened to diner. The term also alluded to the elegant meal accommodations of crack express trains like the Broadway and Twentieth Century limiteds.

Rail-delivered diners were commodious by lunch wagon standards but were still compact enough to easily fit on an in-town lot—sideways with the end facing the street if the lot was particularly narrow. It's this compactness that even today lends itself to a dynamic mix of customers: the lawyers, bikers, doctors, and families that diner owners like to brag about. A 1927 *New York Times* piece said a patron would find that "formality ceased when he had pushed back the sliding door, sidled up to a stool and given his order. The lunch wagons were redolent with the atmosphere of good fellowship."

The diner industry was also aided by the endless possibilities of serving a mobile clientele of motorists and truck drivers along an expanding network of publicly funded highways. One writer suggested in a 1926 *New York Times*

WHERE TO FIND DINERS

The Keystone State is home to a multitude of diners—we counted 260. They're usually found at one of six different locations. Diner distribution overwhelmingly favors edge-of-town highway sites (39%). Other highway sites include suburban commercial strips (11%) and isolated rural locations (9%). In-town diners are predominantly found at the edges of the business district (20%) or at commercial arterials (19%). A few may be found at the center of business districts (2%). In-town diners tend to be older and pedestrian oriented, highway diners newer and auto-oriented.

---

article that maybe it was the mobile nature of diners that made them so appealing: "One feels instinctively that no mere profit hunter could have dreamed the lunch wagon. A philosopher, with tincture of the psychologist, was required—one who understood the hereditary or original whimsicalities of human nature . . . its appeal to the primitive nomadic instinct." Or as we'd say, Americans like to keep moving.

As the industry matured, its center of production shifted from southern New England to the Mid-Atlantic states around New York. By the teens, two of the nation's five top diner builders operated in the shadow of New York City, and by the twenties, downstate New York and New Jersey had six diner manufacturers to Massachusetts's four. After 1942, the only New England diner manufacturer left was Worcester Lunch Car Company, while nearly a dozen companies produced diners from plants in northern New Jersey.

A secondary diner manufacturing center arose in western New York and Ohio to serve the sprawling food processing, steel mill, furniture, and metal fabricating cities along the Great Lakes. At least nine companies opened there in the 1920s and '30s, most notably Ward & Dickinson in Silver Creek, New York, which sent much of its output to Pennsylvania. The small town of Warren, for example, welcomed the American Dining Car in 1926 and Jackson's Diner in 1932, and nearby Youngsville greeted Riche's Dining Car in 1932—quite a concentration of diners away from big cities.

Factory gates were favorite locations for diners since lunch wagon days. A 1927 Atlantic Refining Company article even boasted of a lunch car *inside* Herman's Gate in Philadelphia. It was open to the public, but its twenty-four-hour schedule was to provide "shift men and men working overtime . . . a warm nourishing meal instead of cold sandwiches carried from home."

A 1920s O'Mahony catalog listed eighty-four of the manufacturer's dining cars, eight of those in Pennsylvania: one each in Allentown, Carbondale, Easton, Pottsville, Stroudsburg, and Wilkes-Barre, and two in Philadelphia. In 1927, the United Dining Car Operators' Association in Philadelphia estimated that some 350,000 residents ate in its diners every week. The association stressed just how sanitary dining cars could be: "Nothing is concealed. If the customer orders a steak, he sees it come fresh from a clean, tile-lined ice box; sees it sizzle and brown on a clean griddle. . . . Compare this with the ordinary 'hole in the wall' type of restaurant, where the cooking of food is a dark secret carefully hidden from the customer. Did anyone ever see the cook in that type of restaurant? Is he neat and in good health? Who knows?"

The effects of the Great Depression led to a restructuring of the diner industry, but to the amazement of all, it continued expanding. Even under economic hardship, Americans were loath to give up their automobiles, and diners rode out the hard times as a recession-proof haven that actually attracted investment. Both O'Mahony and Worcester Lunch Car survived the Depression, and although Tierney went under in 1933, its remains were recycled as DeRaffele Manufacturing Company, which continues to make diners. In fact, many of the great postwar diner manufacturers, such as Fodero, Kullman, Mountain View, Paramount, and Valentine got their start during the 1930s, frequently with personnel from earlier diner producers.

As with many other products during the Great Depression, diner styles were retooled to reflect an improved image of "machine age" efficiency, which had become tarnished when the mechanized economy put a quarter of the labor force out of work. A style subsequently tagged "streamline moderne" attempted to imply the feeling of movement by incorporating curved corners, horizontal banding, and slick surfaces. New building materials like stainless steel, glass block, and neon gave diners a modern, progressive look.

By 1937, an estimated 6,000 diners were feeding more than 2 million customers daily. In 1940, a trade magazine reported that there were 7,000 diners, 60 percent using the name "diner," the rest using "grill." The article urged operators to call them diners: "In fact, so well respected is the name 'Diner' among people who have to look for good food at fair prices that proprietors of the small, shoddy restaurant—the type we call 'greasy spoon'—insist on naming their establishment 'Diner' just in order to capitalize on the pulling power of that name."

After World War II, diner sizes increased and began to be shipped in sections. Booths were added along the front windows, and the backbar grill was replaced by a full-size kitchen entered through swinging doors behind the counter. Formica replaced marble, terrazzo replaced tile, and wood trim became a thing of the past.

The cubist style of the late 1940s and '50s led to a squaring off of the corners and edges of diners, most of which were now predominantly sheathed in stainless steel. This was a period of unprecedented prosperity and growth, especially within the nation's highway-dependent suburbs. Railroad imagery was out of step in this age of jets, spacecraft, and atomic energy, leading to a shift in diner styles. The monitor roof shape was retained in the ceiling, but recessed fluorescent lighting was used rather than monitor windows with their diffused natural light. Signs, fixtures, and the graphic patterns on countertops and terrazzo floors abandoned their streamlined forms and took on a sharp-edged and angular look inspired by a jet fighter's wing or rocket fin. Manufacturers were ready to satisfy the diner owner's desire to look up-to-date; a 1951 Silk City ad began, "Old friends and old songs may be best, but old diners cost you money."

In 1937, Al Hook opened his first diner on Route 22 in Easton, and four years later he opened Wilson's Diner (a 1941 National) there. In this January 1949 ad, his new Hook's Diner sports Paramount's distinctive roofline and use of glass block. Russell Saylor purchased it in 1966, renaming it Saylor's, and his oldest son, Michael, has run it since 1992.

Urban diner owners felt the need to accommodate their increasingly mobile customers. When Otto Grupp replaced his Croydon Diner, northeast of Philadelphia, in 1949, he located the new Comac-brand diner adjacent to a supermarket he'd just built—with matching exteriors. An announcement read, "All parties agree that the huge black macadam parking lot, big enough to handle both supermarket and diner traffic, is responsible for the sensational increase in business." Meanwhile, in downtown Philadelphia, five buildings were torn down on Girard Avenue to make room for the

new American Diner (also a 1949
Comac) when the original site
across the street couldn't provide
enough parking.

Diners could no longer depend
on shift workers or neighborhood
allegiance. Some owners turned
to advertising to draw customers.
When Harry Muchnik (operator of
the Willow Grove Diner) opened
his Godfrey Diner at Broad Street
and Godfrey Avenue in Philadelphia, he mailed 5,000 invitations
for the opening and was rewarded
with a huge opening-day crowd,
which consumed over 9,000 hot
dogs. Muchnik also was featured in
the cover story of a diner trade magazine, and his diner appeared in
a 1954 Paramount ad. Few diner
owners grasped the power of televi-
sion the way fast-food chains did,
but at least one tried: Lou Marino
in 1949 televised the opening cere-
monies at the Grove Diner, his sixth
and biggest diner.

Of the twenty-two diner manufacturers operating on the East
Coast during the 1950s, nineteen of them were in the Mid-Atlantic states,
with the suburbs of North Jersey being firmly established as Dinerland
ground zero. O'Mahony bought a factory in St. Louis in 1952 to accommodate midwestern expansion, but it was already too late—the trend in
food service was drive-ins and fast foods. The more conservative appearance of O'Mahonys and Worcester Lunch Cars led to a decrease in their
popularity, and they soon folded. Meanwhile, the relatively new Comac
was making inroads with long-time diner owners. And as the huge diner-
restaurants exceeded the needs and budgets of new owners, manufacturers
began building compact models with names like Dinette, Junior, and
Economite. A Quakertown, Pennsylvania, firm even began making what it
called "portable diners," which were really just shiny versions of the old
lunch wagons, still popular at carnivals today.

The most lucrative diner locations were now out on the commercial strips at the edges of towns, where dozens of enterprises with flashy signs all vied for the attention of an increasing number of motorists who zipped by at ever-higher speeds. Diner manufacturers responded by building even larger restaurants with dining rooms, oversize eaves, and canted plate-glass facades that shrank the exterior stainless steel down to a low base at the bottom of the window.

Beginning as just another style change, the roadside environmental movement of the 1960s favored earth tones and natural materials like stone, brick, and wood over stainless steel, pastel porcelain enamel, and plate glass brightly lit from within. Although a brick-face restaurant certainly is no more environmentally friendly than a steel-clad one, changing landscape sensibilities were altering the image of modernity. Local ordinances and planning regulations prohibited Space Age styles. Meanwhile, dinermen sought to distance themselves from a raft of flamboyant fast-food competitors.

Both styles were intermingled at the Summit Diner in Somerset, made by Swingle in 1960. Here can be found stainless steel and terrazzo, as well as mosaic tile, wooden beams, and wagon wheel lights. The counter area has a soda fountain, but the grill is hidden behind the backbar. A neon arrow snakes toward the facade, but walnut paneling lines the dining room's walls.

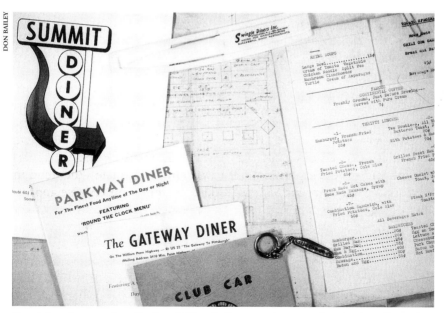

Blueprints and a menu from the Summit Diner in Somerset, plus menus from its sister diners, the Club Car, Parkway, and Gateway.

BRIAN BUTKO

By the 1970s, Swingle and the other manufacturers were producing Mediterranean-style diners, like Scotty's Diner in Monroeville. Owner Tom Scott recalled that the town council withheld approval until a member took a trip to the New Jersey factory to see the modern five-piece car. It's now Jaden's Family Dining, distancing itself even from the word "diner."

The North Jersey–New York center of diner production remained stable throughout the 1960s and '70s. Of the nine manufacturers that built restaurants in 1960, only Silk City Diners in Paterson, New Jersey, did not make it to 1970, but a new concern, Musi Dining Car, opened in nearby Carteret.

The late 1960s and '70s were the dark ages for diners, when *diner* became a dirty word banned from some roadsides and dropped from the names of a number of restaurants and manufacturers. The stainless steel image evoked by the word *diner* was yesterday's idea. This was a significant blow to an industry that had always tried to project a progressive, modernist image. Manufacturers now sought to craft a new identity for diners, using bricks, weather-vaned cupolas, shake-shingle mansard roofs, coach lamps, and imitation timber ceiling beams. These new "colonial" diners were indistinguishable from any other restaurant, which of course was the point. Diners had gone upscale, relinquishing their "inexpensive meals quickly" niche to the rapidly expanding fast-food chains.

With the rules of design relaxed, diners were open to influence from another quarter. As old dinermen retired, recently arrived Greek and Italian restaurateurs took over the reins of many a diner. As diner buyers and renovators, they began the Mediterranean modern movement, covering their diners in stone, decorating them with arches, and capping them with mansard roofs made of red clay pantiles rather than cedar shake shingles. Remodeling had been a constant theme in diner history, but now diners were subjected to complete makeovers that permanently changed the original atmosphere.

It seems like that should be the end of the story. Diners become restaurants, old dinermen retire, and everyone moves to the suburbs to live happily ever after. But then the 1980s arrived, and America's industrial economy went into a freefall. Blast furnaces toppled, manufacturers closed shop, and the auto industry teetered on the brink of ruin.

But while milltown—birthplace of the diner—came apart at the seams, downtown gleamed with the new office towers of corporations whose main product was money. The middle-class exodus toward the suburbs was joined by a migration from the snowy Rustbelt to the assumed prosperity of a high-tech economy spreading across the Sunbelt states.

Late-modern diners from the 1980s exemplified this new vision of a cyber future by taking on an irregular shape, bulging with greenhouselike atriums and encased in dark reflective glass, giving the buildings an intangible, ethereal quality. Old-style diners were thought to be dinosaurs, a disappearing breed long past its prime. The *Pittsburgh Post-Gazette* in an August 11, 1988, article on the failed attempts in Butler to give away Digger's Diner said, "There seems to be little sentiment for a relic from the 1940s."

RICHARD J. S. GUTMAN

Outdated looks and functions are primary reasons why diners are upgraded. Adding a mansard roof to the Peter Pan (1957 Mountain View #498) in Kuhnsville couldn't solve bigger needs, so it was replaced by a newer Swingle diner, Chris's Family Restaurant. The proprietor also owns Chris's in nearby Allentown, which itself replaced a fifteen-year-old O'Mahony in 1955.

But another diner look was also emerging. In 1981, Swingle Diners built The Dining Car for Joe and Joyce Morozin of Philadelphia. This six-section rendition of a 1930s O'Mahony dining car introduced postmodernism to the world of diners. Unlike modernism, which rejected historical and cultural influences, postmodernism not only embraced the past, but allowed for multiple interpretations of it, making it perfectly acceptable to mix classical columns with stylized Renaissance pediments trimmed in neon.

Enter the baby boomer with the money, inclination, and time to spend on nostalgic re-creations of lost childhoods. Whether it be antique collectibles, heritage parks, or old movie channels, nostalgia is big business in our postmodern economy, and the classic American diner style, in all its resplendent stainless steel glory, is popular once again. Manufacturers are not dusting off old blueprints to make historic reproductions of midcentury diners but are manipulating traditional diner materials—stainless steel, chrome, glass block, ceramic tile, and neon—in new ways to suggest the ambience of old diners. Remember, to profit on the roadside, the building form and function has to be up-to-date, even if the inspiration itself is forty years out of date.

In the late 1970s and '80s, the diner industry went through a period of restructuring that initiated a round of starts-ups and casualties. Diner manufacturing business deaths started with the Manno Dining Car (founded in 1949) in 1978, then Fodero Dining Car (founded in 1933) in 1981, and ironically, Swingle Diners (founded in 1957) in 1988, which folded despite its having pioneered retro diners. The restructuring came with a shift in the geography of production facilities, favoring lower-cost, higher-growth locations in the South and West. Of the numerous diner builders that opened since the 1970s, only Modular Designs (now Builders and Renovators Unlimited) of Fairfield, New Jersey, set up shop in the traditional heart of Dinerland. The wider distribution of production facilities is responsible for spreading postmodern retro diners to places that never had a diner culture—shopping centers and interstate interchanges in the suburban South and West. Some of the "dinerplexes" are coming to Pennsylvania. The Starlite Diner is scheduled to open soon on Route 30 in York. The new million-dollar DeRaffele will seat 175 in 5,000 square feet.

Today, for the most part, diners have been safely resurrected—they're restored, celebrated in splashy articles, and shipped overseas to appreciative customers. However, the greasy spoon image still exists somewhat, mostly because for every diner that's embraced cleanliness and home cooking, there are others that obviously have not.

But the diner name and image endures. America Online has been using a fifties diner and sign in its advertising. At the Eat at Joe's chain in Philadel-

STEVE BOKSENBAUM

When he was child, artist Steve Boksenbaum was told that art should be a sideline to a professional career. He's turned the tables, however, by spending his life painting and teaching art, while working part time as an operating room technician (see page 24).

"As a child in the 1950s, the imagery of the late Deco period sank into my subconscious even before I could speak. At age fifteen, I got a job as soda jerk at the Parkway Pharmacy in Pittsburgh, which had six round stools at the lunch counter, with soda fountain and Hamilton Beach milkshake makers, and stacks of china cups and dishes with a lime green line along the perimeter. I was already drawing habitually by then, and between customers, I drew the apparatus.

"I went to art school in Philadephia, a town full of good diners. I drank in the midnight diner atmosphere, sneaking out of the dorms past curfew and hiking to Littleton's or the Oak Lane. Later, from my apartment on Old York Road, I took breaks from painting at 2 A.M.; while the rest of the city slept, I found people awake at the Toddle House, flooded with warm light, clinking dishes, and loud conversations.

"In 1980, I took my wife and new baby out west. We got as far as Navajoland, snapping pictures along the way of cafés with hand-painted EAT signs and clientele representing all strata of society.

"When I returned to Pittsburgh, I took note of diners in particular. Out west there were few prefabricated diners, but back home I found Scotty's (now Charlie's) near Wilkinsburg; another Scotty's, on Route 8 (gone now); and the Venus in Gibsonia. In these places, all the imagery and atmosphere came together for me: the Deco sensibilities, the perpetual feeling of community, the unity of humanity.

"Then I took another road trip, this time going east to Massachusetts and Rhode Island, where diners were born. I returned with rolls and rolls of black-and-white photos, and in 1983, I had an exhibition of diner photos. There were a lot of negatives I couldn't use, for technical or aesthetic considerations, so I started to paint from these to circumvent my photographic deficiencies and preserve the design and atmosphere of those diners. In fifteen years of painting diners, I don't feel I have exhausted the imagery."

phia, walls are filled with memorabilia, jukeboxes spin fifties tunes, countermen wear soda jerk outfits, waitresses wear poodle skirts, and booths are built into replicas of a '57 Chevy. As one co-owner says, it's a 1990s version of what people believe the 1950s were like. He stressed that the plan is to keep customers coming back with good food once the novelty wears off.

The chain has ambitious expansion plans—sixty restaurants in five years. Thus, the diner—just a simple mid-twentieth-century northeastern building—has reached mythic status in mainstream American culture.

So how does Pennsylvania figure in all this? Imagine a tidal wave of diners flooding over Pennsylvania from the Southeast. The wave crashes at Philadelphia, leaving the greatest concentration of diners there; sweeps northwestward, depositing a thinning carpet of diners across Pennsylvania Dutch Country and just over the first few ridges of the Appalachians. A strong eddy swirls diners into the Lehigh Valley around Allentown and heaps them up against the Pocono Plateau and into the Wyoming Valley. Losing energy, the diner wave washes over the backbone of the Alleghenies and diffuses across hills and valleys of western Pennsylvania, where the remaining diners come to rest. Kooky though the analogy is, that's what diner geography in Pennsylvania looks like.

Fifty-five percent of the state's diners are in its ten southeasternmost counties. Arrayed around the city of Philadelphia, these counties make up megalopolitan Pennsylvania, part of the the high-density metropolitan sprawl that spreads from Boston to Washington, D.C., and cuts across the southeastern corner of the Keystone State.

New Jersey, New York, and Pennsylvania account for more than half of all the diners in the country. The expense of moving diners by rail or by truck lim-

Diners bridge the gap between mass-produced familiarity and hometown individuality, as the makeshift menu board—a staple of almost every diner—illustrates. This one was photographed in 1991 at Bob's Diner (1947 Mountain View #237), which sat along the Lincoln Highway in Columbia and now rests in a backyard in Maryland awaiting a new life.

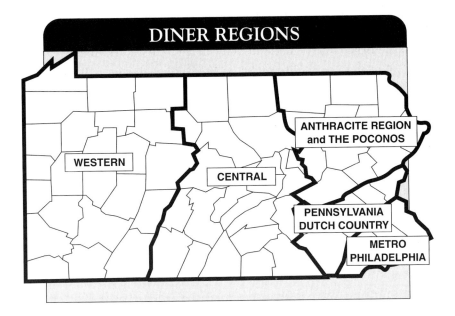

ited the range in which they could be effectively sold, so the industry naturally gravitated to the center of its market, building plants as close as possible to the greatest number of potential customers. This meant New York, North Jersey, and eastern Pennsylvania. Though New England was within the manufacturers' orb of delivery, it had already been blanketed by regional diner builders.

To illustrate the point, Fodero shipped forty-six diners into Pennsylvania between 1946 and 1959, compared with fifteen for all six New England states. During the 1950s, Mountain View built thirty-eight Pennsylvania diners, but only twenty-two New England diners. Nearly one-quarter of all Swingle Diners produced from 1957 to 1988 headed to Pennsylvania.

The state's diner map can be subdivided into five regions, each with its own unique set of characteristics that can be described as its "place identity." Diner distribution within each region is a little different, but there are some surprising similarities at the neighborhood level.

Metro Philadelphia consists of the five southeasternmost counties in Pennsylvania. Diner density for the region averages about fifteen per county.

Pennsylvania Dutch Country comprises the next tier of counties to the northwest, stretching from the Lehigh Valley to Lancaster County. Diner densities are thickest in the Allentown-Bethlehem-Easton area, somewhat less around Reading, and thin out toward Lebanon and Lancaster. Diners average fourteen per county.

The Anthracite Region and the Poconos, in northwestern Pennsylvania, has about five diners per county, though they are mostly concentrated in the seven southeasternmost counties. This region has two distinct diner personalities: those serving the depressed cities and towns of Pennsylvania's anthracite coal fields and those serving increasing numbers of tourists on the main roads to the Pocono Mountains.

Central Pennsylvania, with its lightly populated ridges and plateaus, is the diner dead zone, with an average of less than one diner per county.

Western Pennsylvania, despite its large population, has far fewer diners than are found east of the Susquehanna River. Most of the diners in the western third of the state are clustered around Pittsburgh or Erie, giving it an average of just over one per county.

DINER ARCHITECTURE

KEVIN PATRICK

West Shore Diner, a rare 1930s Silk City in Lemoyne.

KEVIN PATRICK

Park Dinor, a 1948 Silk City in Erie. The monitor roof was a distinguishing feature on diners by this company until the early 1950s.

Glider Diner, a 1951 Mountain View in Scranton. The cowcatcher corners are unique to this manufacturer's cars.

BRIAN BUTKO

KEVIN PATRICK

Prospect Diner, a 1955 Kullman on the Lincoln Highway, east of Columbia. The distinctive overhang was introduced by the manufacturer in that year.

BRIAN BUTKO

Blue Comet Diner, a remodeled 1957 Mountain View in Hazleton. Though the diner has been encased in environmental elements, a beautiful sign lives on.

BRIAN BUTKO

Norwin Diner, a 1976 Kullman on Route 30, east of Pittsburgh. Mediterranean motifs, such as arched windows, became popular on diners of the 1970s.

KEVIN PATRICK

Oak Lane Diner, a 1950 Paramount in Philadelphia. Patrons are greeted by a newly built postmodern vestibule.

DINER REMODELING

Zinn's Diner has seen many structural changes in the five decades of its existence. The Paramount opened in 1950 in Denver (see photos on page 115), and ten years later a giant Dutchman named Amos was erected in front to go along with the Pennsylvania Dutch home-cooking theme.

In 1969, Zinn's was expanded and environmentalized by Fodero. The stainless was covered with a stone facade, a shallow mansard roof with a cupola was added, and a new, sturdier, talking Amos was raised. See the photo on page 114 for later renovations.

DINER ART

Steve Boksenbaum. "Wolfe's Diner, Dillsburg (an O'Mahony)," 1997. Watercolor.

Chuck Biddle. "Twilight at the Summit" [Somerset], 1990. Color pencil.

Kevin Kutz. "Blue Diner" [Scotty's near Wilkinsburg], 1985. Oil on canvas.

DINER EPHEMERA

Through the years, entrepreneurs have proudly depicted the facades and interiors of their diners on postcards. The Willow Grove Diner, a 1948 Fodero, served the intersection of Routes 611 and 263, north of Philadelphia, for decades. Lesher's Diner, formerly on Routes 11 and 15 in Liverpool, north of Harrisburg, proclaimed on the verso of their postcard: "Have your car serviced at adjoining Amoco while dining in our delightful diner. 24 hour service."

Matchbooks were also a common way to advertise diners, but with the recent trend in smoke-free dining this form has tapered off. New College Diner is now Ye Olde College Diner in State College, famous for its grilled stickies. Effort Diner, still in business in Effort, is known for its Pennsylvania Dutch cooking. Birmingham Grille and its annex were divided: the main diner is now Andy's Truckee Diner in Truckee, California, and the annex is now attached to Ruthie and Moe's Diner in Cleveland, Ohio.

COLLECTION OF BRIAN BUTKO

METRO PHILADELPHIA

Flame-studded oil refineries, Independence Hall, a bustling Delaware River waterfront, a nonstop international airport, a vibrant city center, and the tranquility of Fairmount Park—this is Philadelphia as portrayed by six painted panels that have graced the inside of the Melrose Diner since 1961. Murals like these convey a diner's rootedness in its neighborhood and region. It's a trait typically expressed on the menu—and you can bet scrapple is on the menu at the Melrose—but occasionally expressed more vividly by murals, on signage, or in the diner's name.

Like most of the city's big diners, the Melrose is open twenty-four hours a day, and here time is measured by the sweep of a knife and fork across the dial of a large outside clock. The diner caters to everyone from the late-night reveler looking for breakfast to the down-and-outer shuffling in for a cup of coffee, to the proud mother from down the block picking up baked goods for a christening. It seems like if you stay at one of the big U-shaped counters long enough, you'll eventually meet the entire population of South

Philadelphia. As the old jingle, still emblazoned on the napkins, goes, "Everybody who knows goes to the Melrose."

And they've been going since 1935. The current diner, however, is a 1956 Paramount with rooftop corners resembling a silver wedding cake. As a modern stainless steel diner, the Melrose is like 40 percent of the seventy-four diners in Metro Philadelphia. Not that they are all alike—not by a long shot. The brilliant red and yellow trim on the Melrose is unlike that of any diner in the state. That's what makes diners so interesting: Recognizable patterns exist in their design, architecture, and neighborhood setting, but how these patterns play out at any given diner is always delightfully unique.

The Melrose sits on a wedge of land bounded by Passyunk Avenue, Snyder Avenue, and 15th Street. This is deep in the heart of South Philadelphia, surrounded by a sea of two-story row homes. Trolley buses glide down Snyder, and the Broad Street subway is a block away. Could the diner just as easily have been located at 21st and Snyder, say, or 15th and Porter? Probably not. Virtually every one of Pennsylvania's 260 diners operates in one of only six neighborhood settings. The Melrose, like thirteen other Metro Philadelphia diners, is at an edge-of-business-district location. The reference is not to downtown Philadelphia, some twenty blocks north, but to the smaller South Philadelphia shopping district that grew up around Broad Street, Passyunk Avenue, and Snyder Avenue, right above the subway terminal. This is a typical in-town diner location. Although there are a few rare diners that sit at the center of the business district, most do not. Like the Melrose, most lie within easy strolling distance from a shopping district, but on less expensive land toward the edge.

Neighborhood shopping districts were originally clustered around commuter rail stations, with businesses favoring row-building storefronts to catch

The Melrose Diner, a 1956 Paramount, is synonymous with South Philly.

commuters running to and from the trains. As Johnny-come-latelies to the scene, diners were placed at the end of the business district, but close enough to get in on the action. A common strategy was to set them sideways on narrow lots, with one of their short ends facing the street. The Melrose, though fronting on 15th Street, is shoehorned sideways to both its principal traffic streets. Like the Melrose, Anna's Pizza, at the edge of the old Overbrook shopping district, and the Wayne Junction Diner, within a block of a busy North Philadelphia train station, are both set perpendicular to the street in edge-of-business-district locations.

Some of the oldest diners in Philadelphia are found at edge-of-business-district locations in communities that predate the automobile. The Quaker Diner, now sheathed in brown pebble panels and topped with a mansard roof, a 1939 O'Mahony underneath it all, is set sideways to Rising Sun Avenue at the edge of the Five Points business district in the city's Burlholme section. Two other older O'Mahonys, though not set sideways, also operate at edge-of-business-district locations: Mil-Lees Luv Inn, an updated stainless steel diner on Rising Sun Avenue between the Lawndale business district and the now-

THE MELROSE DINER SUCCESS STORY

In 1929, Richard Kubach immigrated to the United States. By 1935, he had purchased a nineteen-stool diner that had been abandoned and vandalized. Kubach installed the most modern equipment, and within a year, it had the fastest turnover per stool of any diner in Philadelphia. This success encouraged him in 1940 to buy a state-of-the-art O'Mahony with air-conditioning, 10-foot glass block extensions to each end, and tile in twenty-one colors. In 1956, he upgraded to the 106-seater that still serves South Philadelphia.

The Melrose is considered to be one of the most successful diners in history. In Jim Quinn's *But Never Eat Out on a Saturday Night* (Dolphin, 1983), Kubach offered some insight into why:

On buying the best: "We never ask the price of anything."

On trusting employees: "I have never counted my money. I have good people and I don't need to count it."

On paying workers more: "A dishwasher has to pay the same as you do for a pair of shoes."

On the value of employees: "I tell all the people who work here, we need you more than you need us."

defunct Crescentville Station of the old Reading lines, and Bob's Diner, which is adjacent to the Leverington Cemetery on Ridge Avenue and has been serving up food at the southern end of Roxborough for half a century. Although the neighborhood has changed considerably, Bob's still has a stainless steel and red porcelain enamel facade, an outdoor clock with letters that spell out "Welcome Diner," and a hint of a monitor roof that was quickly going out of style when the diner opened.

Certainly one of the oldest unaltered diners in the city is the Wayne Junction, a 1940 Paramount that still sports rounded glass block corners and green porcelain enamel fluting. There is not much of a business district at Wayne Junction, but as the name implies, the neighborhood grew up around a major rail station. The diner was placed in a classic industrial-age neighborhood, where commuters grabbing breakfast before boarding their inbound trains mingled with workers headed for the day shift at one of the surrounding textile mills. For this neighborhood, however, the industrial age is over. The diner still sits across the tracks from an active train station, but like the mills looming nearby, it lies silent and empty.

It's likely that turn-of-the-century Philadelphia had numerous lunch wagons and dining cars, but it wasn't until 1930 that diners appeared in city directories. Instead, places like the Rite-Bite Lunch came and went without leaving any hint of their presence (although a photo survives of that 1920s

COLLECTION OF RICHARD J. S. GUTMAN

Bob's Diner in the Roxborough section of Philadelphia is surrounded by a cemetery, but until 1957, the Lyceum—which served as both town hall and boxing ring—loomed behind the 1947 O'Mahony. The dressing rooms are still downstairs below the diner.

RICHARD J. S. GUTMAN

The Wayne Junction, a 1940 Paramount, has fallen on hard times. It's been closed since 1992.

Tierney at the Atwater Kent Museum). In 1930, half a dozen diners showed up with such typical names as the Ideal Diner (3208 Lancaster Avenue), Superior Diner (502 Montgomery Avenue), Elite Dining Car (2215 Chestnut Street), and De Luxe Diner (4806 Chestnut Street). Although the spelling varied, by 1940, there were four "DeLuxe" diners operating in Philadelphia: the DeLux at 1411 Snyder; two DeLuxe diners, one at 5610 Chestnut Street and the other at 34th Street and Grays Ferry Avenue; and the original, which oddly was then called a dining car.

Two things happened after World War II that make the historical diner trail a little easier to track. Telephones became more widespread, and thus more diners were listed in directories, and the word *diner* was used more definitively to describe factory-built restaurants. As a result, by 1952, fifty-seven diners showed up in the Philadelphia Yellow Pages.

These were peak years for the diffusion of the diner, with many settling into business at another typical in-town diner location, the commercial arterial, whose constant traffic, streetcars, and storefronts made it a perfect place to open a diner. Of the thirty-two diners remaining in Philadelphia, twenty-one are located along the city's busy commercial arterials, all of which originated as the main wagon roads from town. To the northeast, Frankford Avenue led into Bristol Pike, which angled toward New York. Inbound traffic from the north and northwest converged onto Broad Street via Old York Road, Bethlehem Pike, and Germantown Pike. Access from the south was over the old Island Road, which crossed the Schuylkill River and continued to Broad Street over what are now Penrose Avenue and Passyunk Avenue. And Market Street and Chestnut Street were the main

ROBERT O. WILLIAMS

Bob Williams has been a photographer at the *Philadelphia Inquirer* for thirteen years, but his passion lies along roads less traveled—small towns, old movie theaters, and especially, diners.

"I like the architecture and the food," he says, "but it's the people and a diner's sense of community that draws me. The photographs I've collected on my journey are a tribute to an institution I feel I know intimately. I've met and photographed some of the warmest, most generous people in diners."

He put his photos and thoughts together in *Hometown Diners*, published by Abrams in the spring of 1999. You'll find a few more of Bob's photos throughout this book (see pages 40, 49, 56, 59, and 61).

Robert O. Williams captures the human side of diners in his photographs. Here, a waitress clowns with breakfast regulars at Crestmont II, a real gem and a family operation.

westbound arterials, leading into Lancaster Pike, West Chester Pike, and Baltimore Pike to the southwest.

By the turn of the century, these busy thoroughfares were laced with streetcar lines and flanked by storefronts, causing them to be the corridors of development for an expanding industrial city. As the flood of cars and trucks began to reshape the city, small barrel roof diners with little, paved parking lots began to pop up on the odd parcel or corner lot.

Over the past century, Philadelphia's commercial arterials have accumulated a thick and varied cultural landscape representing many style periods,

RICHARD J. S. GUTMAN

Above: The Penguin Diner, a 1942 Sterling, was made to look like a streamlined train emerging from a tunnel and has the design patent to prove it. The Penguin was on Bristol Pike (U.S. 13) next to Poquessing Creek on the fringe of Philadelphia. Below: The Vale-Rio Diner, opened in 1948, was a variation on the Valerio family name. The diner sported Paramount's distinctive new exterior of burnished circles, as shown in this ad, and is in fact the only such diner left in the state.

but noticeably absent are these cozy, prewar barrel and monitor roof diners. A diner operating along a major urban arterial was playing in the big leagues. Patronage was heavy, and the street was alive twenty-four hours a day. Successful owners traded up regularly and expanded their operations with each diner purchase. The quaint little lunch car was weeded out of this setting decades ago—places like the twenty-stool Mayfair Diner, a 1928 O'Mahony that served diner-goers on Frankford Avenue in the city's Mayfair section. It opened there in 1932 but was already too small six years later and so was replaced. Even many midcentury diners are gone,

COLLECTION OF RICHARD J. S. GUTMAN

"Custom-Built" gives you DINER PERSONALITY

When in the vicinity of Phoenixville, Pa., why not visit the Vale-Rio Diner and meet "Charley" Valerio. You'll find him a swell fellow who's always glad to talk "shop" with his fellow operators.

To us at Paramount Diners, the word "custom-built" means something . . . the construction of a diner to fit the requirements of its location and operating conditions. We have never believed that the policy "any diner for any location" was sound business for either the operator or the manufacturer.

And we have translated our belief into positive action. Now, through our patent,

#2,247,895, it is possible for the diner operator to purchase any unit from 106" x 36" to any desired length or width. Moreover, such Paramount innovations as the built-in, draft-free vestibule, the rounded booth and many other Paramount features are available.

These outstanding achievements in diner engineering are solely a product of Paramount Diners.

Let's all PATRONIZE DINERS

Diners are good places to eat in, better places to own. Let's be proud of our industry and let's patronize diners every chance we get.

PARAMOUNT DINERS, INC.

500 Belmont Avenue   Phone SHerwood 2-9025   Haledon 2, N. J.

AMERICAN DINER MUSEUM

Above: The original Oak Lane Diner, a mid-1930s model. Below: The new Oak Lane Diner was featured on the cover of the industry's journal in 1950. Paramount's innovations included electric eyes for the swinging kitchen doors and a customer waiting room.

The **DINER** *And* **Counter Restaurant**

JULY
1950

Vol. IX
No. 7

LAUREL PUBLICATIONS
247 W. FRONT ST.
PLAINFIELD, N. J.

IN THIS ISSUE

Controlling Portions Saves
Money 16

Operation Depression
Produces Profit 19

Sanitation Thru
Self-Inspection 21

You Can't Stop Learning! .. 24

POSTMASTER: If addressee has removed please notify us of new address on Form 3547, postage for which is guaranteed.

like the spectacular Penguin Diner farther north on Frankford. A rare 1942 Sterling-brand diner, the Penguin looked like a train emerging from a tunnel-shaped kitchen.

The Philadelphia area has, however, retained numerous postwar stainless steel diners. On the edge of the Phoenixville business district, the pink-topped Vale-Rio Diner was one of the first to satisfy postwar needs in suburban Philadelphia. Pat Valerio recalls its opening in 1948: "The area was really in need of a diner. We brought the diner in at 7 P.M. the night before Thanksgiving. Soon we had a line of customers waiting on the street, so we opened that night." The booths were redone a few years ago to match the gray and burgundy interior, and when the copper roof had to be covered, Pat asked the roofers to use pink rubber.

The northern gateway to the city, where Old York Road angles across Broad Street, is flanked by the Oak Lane Diner, a stainless steel sentinel whose wedding-cake corners are surmounted with Paramount's signature silver gazing balls, a rare find in Pennsylvania. To make the Oak Lane sit level to the slope of Broad Street, it was perched on a high foundation made of Wissahickon schist, a local rock flecked with silvery specks of mica. In a 1950 article in *Diner and Counter Restaurant,* Oak Lane owner Wray Wiley said that when he bought the old Oak Lane in 1944, people told him it was a poor location because it was way out on North Broad Street, about 4 miles from the center of Philadelphia. But six years later, he opened the larger present diner that cost more than $100,000 (the equivalent of $700,000 today). Old-time dinermen thought Wray was getting away from the original concept of the diner, but he believed that a "diner-restaurant" had become a necessity.

The postwar stainless steel diners being trucked into Philadelphia suburbs didn't need to be set to the sidewalk or squeezed onto a tight lot sideways. There was plenty of room and plenty of parking, and the diners came in sections. But as in the city, diner location was not random. Most were set up at the highway equivalent of in-town locations, diners sparkling on the brand new suburban commercial strips that were frequently suburban extensions of urban arterials.

No diner location in Metro Philadelphia better illustrates this postwar urban-suburban transition than Littleton's Diner on Cheltenham Avenue, a 1958 Paramount astride the line between Philadelphia and Montgomery County. On the city side of the diner is a small retail row set close to the sidewalk and street, surrounded by row homes regimented along a grid of avenues. On the suburban side of the diner across Cheltenham Avenue is the sprawling Cheltenham Shopping Center, set in the middle of a 4,500-car parking lot, beyond which are single-family housing developments and apartment complexes arranged along curving streets. The diner arrived soon after the Delaware Valley's largest Gimbel's department store opened across the street in 1955, and just before the Gimbel's was joined by an open air mall in 1960. The diner and the shopping center were also located just down the street from the newly opened Fort Washington Expressway, the four-lane, Route 309 replacement to Bethlehem Pike.

Littleton's Diner also exhibits another trait common to diners along commercial arterials and highways on the suburban edge of town—it's located one lot away from a busy intersection (Cheltenham Avenue and Ogontz Avenue), adjacent to a gas station on the corner. Of the seventeen diners in Metro

Philadelphia sited one lot away from an intersection, fourteen are adjacent to gas stations that sit at the intersection. Nearly half of the diners sit next to or across the street from gas stations, and a quarter have corner locations. This illustrates both the diner's symbiotic relationship with other roadside services and the desire for the diner to be seen by as many motorists as possible.

Some diners of the late fifties and early sixties were made with exaggerated modern characteristics. Eleven such diners can be found in the state, four of which are in Metro Philadelphia, and six in the adjacent Pennsylvania Dutch Country.

At the same time, diner manufacturers were fabricating similar-looking dining rooms to graft onto older diners. Only a handful of these diner grafts survive in a recognizable state, but two are in suburban Philadelphia. The Preston Diner (a 1958 Silk City) faces Governor Printz Boulevard, the busy commercial arterial that carries Route 291 through Essington. It originally operated as the Penrose Diner 5 miles north up 291 at the southern gateway to the city, on the corner of Penrose Avenue and 20th Street. In 1963, the Penrose owners traded up to a giant DeRaffele unsurpassed in exaggerated detailings, including a towering, steel A-frame entryway and crinkle-cut, folded-plate eaves. The old Silk City was shipped to the industrial suburb of Essington, where it was grafted onto an early 1960s factory-built dining room to increase its capacity.

On the far western fringe of Philadelphia, another diner graft sits at an edge-of-town location along Route 41 just north of Avondale. Long known

KEVIN PATRICK

The Preston Diner, a 1958 Silk City, has a circa 1960 Kullman dining room grafted onto the original car.

THE BIGGEST DINER?

The manufacturers were always competing to build the biggest diner. Kullman claimed to be leading in 1953 with the Mari-Nay on Lancaster Avenue (Route 30) in Rosemont. It was named for the armed services owners Bill Shannon and Jim Forsythe served in, the Marines and the Navy. Their first Mari-Nay was a sixteen-stool, second-hand Kullman with four employees; next was a 1948 Kullman, a sixty-three-seater with a red fluted porcelain exterior. When the 1953 model arrived, it opened when only 80 percent complete because of overwhelming demand.

In a period article, the dinermen explained, "Business in Lower Merion Township had been on the upgrade since the end of the war. Housing developments were springing up all around us. In addition, we are surrounded by four colleges—Villanova, Rosemont, Bryn Mawr, and Haverford. Tied in with the heavy traffic passing along the Lancaster Pike, the potential was here."

The result was a U-shaped diner of more than 6,000 square feet, with three entrances, that seated 213. A special college-students dining room featured kidney-shaped tables to simulate counters (to keep the kids from tying up valuable counter space) and a mural featuring the four college campuses. The diner employed sixty at peak hours; $300,000 gross was expected the first year, and a downstairs banquet room soon opened to serve another 130.

The diner industry finally got wise to the changing food service currents when O'Mahony introduced the diner-drive-in in 1954, but it was too late—O'Mahony was gone by 1956, and the Mari-Nay was bulldozed for McDonald's in the early 1990s.

as the Avon Grove Diner, but recently rechristened Eric's Diner, the 1952 Mountain View is joined to a 1961 Kullman-built dining room. From the north, the diner shows its more sedate modernist side; from the south, the big-windowed Jetsonian dining room dominates. A 1980s green mansard roof joins the two.

The sixties were a transitional period during which manufacturers experimented with nonstainless alternatives to diner design. The Continental Diner, a 1963 Fodero on East Market Street in Philadelphia is a big-windowed, low-base diner exhibiting the hallmark traits of exaggerated modernism from the fifties, but the boxy building has few canted elements, the stylistic details are restrained, and most significantly, the exterior window base is stone, not stainless. The building is topped with an eye-catching sign made of three stacked dice crowned with a metal-spiked sparkle.

Court Diner, in Media, a 1964 Kullman that still has a hint of stainless.

On U.S. Route 30 in Wayne, Minella's Main Line Diner exhibits a transitional style one step closer to colonial. This 1964 Fodero has a flat roof with broad eaves, but exterior stainless steel is used more as trim to the bricklike formstone facade accented with coach lamps and spread-eagle wall decorations. Even farther down the colonial path is the brick-faced Court Diner in Media and its twin, the family-operated Astor Diner, a 1970 Musi, operating one lot away from the intersection of Sumneytown Pike and Church Road at the edge of North Wales.

The environmental movement of the sixties through the eighties not only changed the look of new diners, but also set the standard for the remodeling of old ones. During this age of diner-restaurants, establishments reached humungous proportions, adding multiple dining and banquet rooms and full-size bakeries, while keeping the requisite counter area. More than 40 percent of the diners in Metro Philadelphia exhibit the environmental style. They are commonly found along the commercial arterials of Philadelphia but are especially numerous on the main highways leading into suburban towns.

The Mediterranean variant of the environmental style, commonly associated with an increase of Greek diner owners in the sixties and seventies, is more closely linked to New Jersey than to Greece. Stone facades, arched windows, and mansard roofs are its hallmarks. But as common as the style was in the Garden State, its spillover into adjacent Pennsylvania was surprisingly limited. Only sixteen of Pennsylvania's 260 diners exhibit this style, ten of those along the commercial arterials and suburban strips of Metro Philadelphia. One of the largest is the Country Club Restaurant, a 1968 Fodero on Cottman Avenue, northeast Philadelphia's busy crosstown arterial. The 250-seat, twenty-section diner replaced a 1956 Kullman, itself a stunning mix of aqua and coral Formica walls and ceiling, pink terrazzo floor, walnut Formica counter and tabletops, copper appointments, bamboo curtains, and tropical plants. The 1968 Country Club, which owners Noel and Simone Perloff call a Jewish-American diner, has made it a two-story Arabian fantasy of beige stucco and arches. There is still counter and booth service, but most of the action is in the spacious dining room.

In the 1970s, Fodero produced a stock model diner with stylized Mediterranean features—a pebble-paneled facade with angular arches and large windows, having just a hint of leftover exaggerated modernity. One such diner is the Golden Sword on Philadelphia's Whitaker Avenue. A carbon copy ended up on the other side of the state as Ritter's Diner in Pittsburgh, and Lancer's Diner-Restaurant on Easton Road in Horsham is stylistically a close relative.

The Broadway Diner, a 1985 Kullman on Roosevelt Boulevard, exemplifies the late-modern style of the eighties. Covered in black reflective glass, this diner perfectly captures the decade's high-tech influences.

In contrast a new postmodern diner on Frankford Avenue projects a view of the future that looks a lot like our past. The Dining Car, a 1981 Swingle, features a monitor roof, black porcelain enamel facade with white

KEVIN PATRICK

The Perloff family's first Country Club Diner was a huge 1956 model. They've had this even longer Fodero since 1968.

ROBERT O. WILLIAMS

Yvelissa Munoz visits the Silk City Diner with Angelo and Lou Zaccardo. A number of clubs— including one attached to the diner—now dot the area, bringing out lots of late-night eaters.

Broadway lettering, and numerous other dining car details on a new retro diner with an oversized dining room.

In the nineties, older diners are increasingly getting a postmodern facelift. The easiest, lowest-cost option is the addition of rounded eave awnings, typically backlit, like those of the Broad Street Diner. Chrome, neon-trimmed eave lines are also becoming popular. Such a piece now accentuates the mansard roof on the Mediterranean-style Aramingo Diner in Philadelphia's Kensington neighborhood.

Another diner detail frequently updated is the vestibule. Designed to mitigate the draft caused by opening the door, the vestibule has become a prominent postmodern style statement. A number of Philadelphia diners have added retro-diner vestibules that use an overabundance of old-style materials assembled in ways that bear little resemblance to vintage diner vestibules but still project plenty of atmosphere.

The real vestibule to the Silk City Diner, a 1959 Silk City, at 435 Spring Garden Street, has been closed in favor of a red-and-white-checkered entryway that towers over the diner and allows access to either the restaurant or an adjoining nightclub. Inside, the Silk City is a mélange of retro diner details: vintage jukebox, pink boomerang-pattern countertop, blue boomerang-pattern tabletops, all tied together by the old pink and gray interior color scheme.

Andy's Diner at Bustleton Avenue and Red Lion Road in the northeast, the Suburban Diner farther out at Bustleton Avenue and Street Road in

KEVIN PATRICK

Above: The Penrose Diner, a 1963 DeRaffele, as it looked in 1990. Below: The Penrose today, after a postmodern remodeling.

KEVIN PATRICK

Feasterville, the Club House Diner east on Street Road, and the Oregon Diner on South Philadelphia's crosstown arterial, Oregon Avenue, all have been outfitted with spacious postmodern vestibules. The most amazing is the silver-ball-topped, wedding-cake-cornered, glass block and stainless entrance now fronting the Oak Lane Diner. Even Swingle's postmodern Dining Car, needing a larger waiting area and a place to showcase its baked goods, added a huge vestibule with brilliant stainless steel, rounded windows, and glass block.

Above: This late-1940s Paramount, shown here in 1971, was traded in at Swingle and was remodeled. Below: Swingle remade the diner a second time, but with the original circle-embossed facade already scrapped, the resulting American Diner got a new exterior.

Some diners have undergone a full postmodern facelift including an entirely new facade, vestibule, and eave trim, possibly with the addition of a bronze-glass atrium for expanded seating. To the consternation of diner lovers, the Penrose Diner was recently changed from a pristine example of exaggerated modernity to the height of postmodern remodeling using stylized architectural forms from antiquity. The stainless is buried beneath white stucco, and the soaring A-frame entry is now a peak-and-circle pediment supported by classical columns. A contrasting postmodern interpretation is the American Diner at Chestnut Street and 42nd Street, a late-1940s Paramount that had been covered over, then was reconditioned by Swingle back into a red-trimmed stainless steel diner. The rounded glass block corners and roof profile definitely say Paramount, but the circle-embossed stainless steel facade was lost in the earlier conversion, necessitating a new stainless facade and vestibule.

DINER DRIVES

The first glance at a diner-finder map of Metro Philadelphia may give the impression that the region's diners are scattered helter-skelter. Upon closer inspection, however, this proves not to be the case. Diners favor the main roads, whether in town or on the highway. Some of these main roads pass through multiple types of diner-friendly landscapes and are virtual outdoor museums showcasing numerous diner styles of varying ages. More than forty of the region's diners line seven historic highways radiating out from Philadelphia, with diner frequency averaging about one for every four miles.

FRANKFORD AVENUE–BRISTOL PIKE (U.S. ROUTE 13)
Nearly as old as the city itself, Frankford Avenue–Bristol Pike was established as the King's Highway to New York in the 1690s. The road's first bridge across Poquessing Creek, a heavy masonry arch span, was constructed in 1697 and still carries traffic today. Beginning in the Northeast section of Philadelphia, the first diner outbound is the Red Robin Diner, a formstone-facade colonial. Originally the site of the Devon Diner, it sits on a triangular lot at a bend in Frankford Avenue, which carries not only a lot of cars at this location, but also four lanes of trolley buses. Much of the surrounding brick row housing was built immediately after World War II, including the Devon Theater across the avenue from the diner.

Outbound from Tacony, Frankford Avenue passes the Mayfair Diner and The Dining Car before crossing into Bucks County and turning into Bristol Pike. The four suburban diners on Bristol Pike are all mansarded. The Croydon Family Diner and Restaurant, at the edge of Croydon's small, depot-oriented business district, is a recent Mediterranean remodel. On the U.S. Route 13 bypass around Bristol, the colonial-style Golden Eagle Diner has also undergone a recent remodel to include a dining room atrium and some new neon.

PHILADELPHIA DINERS

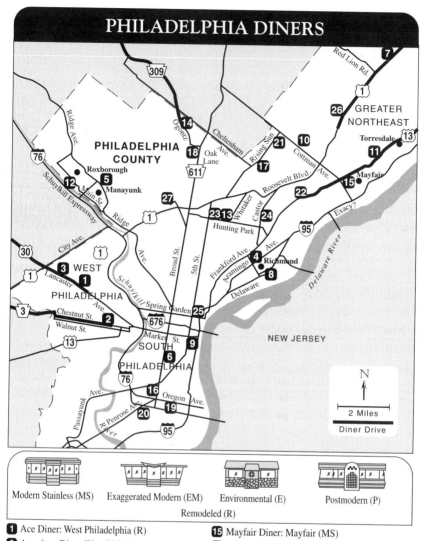

Modern Stainless (MS)   Exaggerated Modern (EM)   Environmental (E)   Postmodern (P)

Remodeled (R)

1 Ace Diner: West Philadelphia (R)

2 American Diner: West Philadelphia (MS)

3 Anna's Pizza: Overbrook (MS)

4 Aramingo Diner: Richmond (E)

5 Bob's Diner: Roxborough (MS)

6 Broad Street Diner: South Philadelphia (E)

7 Broadway Diner: Greater Northeast (P)

8 Chio's Diner: Richmond (R)

9 Continental Diner: Olde City (EM)

10 Country Club Restaurant: Greater Northeast (E)

11 The Dining Car: Torresdale (P)

12 Domino Diner: Manayunk (MS)

13 Golden Sword Diner: Feltonville (E)

14 Littleton's Diner-Restaurant: Cedarbrook (MS)

15 Mayfair Diner: Mayfair (MS)

16 Melrose Diner: South Philadelphia (MS)

17 Mil-Lee's Luv-Inn Diner: Lawndale (MS)

18 Oak Lane Diner: Oak Lane (MS)

19 Oregon Diner: South Philadelphia (R)

20 Penrose Diner: South Philadelphia (R)

21 Quaker Diner: Burholme (R)

22 Red Robin Diner: Wissinoming (E)

23 Restaurante Ecuanondureno: Hunting Park (MS)

24 Sand Trap Café: Juniata (MS)

25 Silk City Diner: Northern Liberties (MS)

26 Tiffany Diner: Greater Northeast (E)

27 Wayne Junction Diner: Wayne Juntion (MS)

Farther north, the DeGrand Diner and Dallas Diner show Mediterranean influence.

ROOSEVELT BOULEVARD–LINCOLN HIGHWAY (U.S. ROUTE 1)

With the dawning of the auto age, the Lincoln Highway replaced Bristol Pike as the main road out of Philadelphia toward New York. The Lincoln was marked over existing roads in 1913 as the nation's first transcontinental automobile road. The Lincoln Highway Association ran the route along the best, most direct roads available; in Philadelphia, that meant the newly constructed and actively expanding Roosevelt Boulevard through the

Above: Master Diners built the huge William Penn Grill, featured in this ad, in 1948. An L-shaped dining room was added by Kullman in 1953. Below: The Skyline Diner, on the old Lincoln Highway (U.S. Route 1) in Penndel, has been remodeled, but this shot from the 1970s shows that it's really a 1956 Paramount.

RICHARD J. S. GUTMAN

KEVIN PATRICK

The Transit Diner once found a hungry market along the Lincoln Highway in Morrisville, but the road and town are now bypassed by U.S. Route 1. The reconditioned 1941 Silk City car is now a bait and tackle shop.

Greater Northeast and Lancaster Pike to the west. Before the days of limited-access highways, this was the most heavily traveled road in the country, causing it to be a principal spine through Dinerland.

Many diners have been lost along this route, like Frank's Diner at Oxford Circle, the Golden Arrow (a 1949 Comac and another diner before that) near Langhorne, the Trailblazer (a 1950s Paramount) in Bensalem, and the Yankee Clipper (a 1940 O'Mahony) at Lincoln Point. A number, though, are still out there. North from Broadway is the Skyline Diner, on the old U.S. Route 1 bypass around Langhorne. Not far beyond it is the commodious Blue Fountain Diner, environmentalized in the early nineties, although the diner's towering, twin-pointed sign retains the vitality of the exaggerated modern period. The diner is operated by only its second set of owners, these since 1975.

A small taste of what the old Lincoln Highway diner days were like can be had on Bridge Street at the edge of the Morrisville business district. Here, set up against the sidewalk, is the 1941 Transit Diner, one of only three unaltered monitor roof diners in the five-county region. But you can no longer get a meal here, unless you're a fish—it's now HL's Live Bait and Tackle Shop.

LANCASTER AVENUE–LINCOLN HIGHWAY (U.S. ROUTE 30)

The approximate route of Lancaster Avenue has been the main road west from Philadelphia since it led into the Great Conestoga Road in the early eighteenth century. The route was rebuilt in 1795 with crushed rock as the

Above: The Ace Diner, a reconditioned 1940s Silk City on the Lincoln Highway, west of Philadelphia, in 1991. Below: The Ace was remodeled in the mid-1990s.

Philadelphia and Lancaster Turnpike, one of the first toll roads in the nation. Then, about the same time that early auto and truck traffic initiated its re-marking as the Lincoln Highway, diners started arriving to feed the motorized masses. Some have disappeared, such as John's Diner at 3210 Lancaster Avenue, the 1947 Overbrook Diner, the Mari-Nay (a 1953 Kullman) in Rosemont, the Exton Diner (a 1950s Paramount), and a 1955 Mountain View also in Exton.

Today, the first diner west on Lancaster Avenue is the Ace Diner, a reconditioned 1940s Silk City that has been remodeled, in West Philadelphia. The

Ace operates on a heavy truck route through an industrial neighborhood adjacent to the Pennsylvania Railroad's Main Line tracks, classic urban diner country. Hard times have come to this urban-industrial area, yet the diner manages to stay in business.

The next diner out is now Anna's Pizza, a 1954 Fodero, in Overbrook, then a string of classic diners scattered along the Lincoln Highway throughout the Main Line suburbs. The next two, though both from the fifties, represent a period in the 1970s and '80s when Asian entrepreneurs recycled old diners into Chinese restaurants. The Chung Sing Chinese Restaurant is at the edge of Ardmore, and other than its pagodalike mansard roof, little has been altered. The China Buddha Restaurant sits on the sidewalk at the edge of the Wayne business district. At the edge of town, set back from the highway, is Minella's colonial-style diner.

Just west of Malvern is the Frazer Diner, the state's only unaltered example of a mid-1930s, streamline moderne O'Mahony. The monitor roof, wood interior trim, and tile floor were diner standards when O'Mahony unveiled this model, but the porcelain enameled base, rounded corners, and half-moon end windows were state-of the-art. The diner was split lengthwise and originally shipped to the Lincoln Highway as the Paoli Diner before being moved farther west to Frazer. Now ensconced in the western Main Line suburbs, the Frazer Diner, set in isolated splendor behind a large gravel lot, retains some of the aura of the preinterstate roadside, when the suburban edge of Philadelphia was still far to the east.

BRIAN BUTKO

The Frazer Diner, originally in Paoli, is one of the rare monitor roof survivors in the region.

COLLECTION OF BERNIE HEISEY

You've seen this diner before if you watched Steve McQueen battle the Blob. The Silk City diner made famous by the 1958 movie escaped the Blob but not the bulldozer. It was replaced in the 1960s by the current Downingtown Diner—a.k.a. Cadillac Diner.

There are two famous movie diners: the Fells Point Diner, set up in Baltimore for the movie *Diner,* and the diner that was munched in *The Blob.* That diner was the old Downingtown Diner. Locals still talk about it, at least those who've lived there long enough to remember 1957, like the gas station owner across the street. "Steve McQueen stood right over there. He was lean-

ROBERT O. WILLIAMS

Dave Nelson ran Downingtown's Cadillac Diner with help from his two daughters. The diner closed in 1999 and a new owner is restoring it.

ing on a car taking a break and talking to the crowd. Nobody knew who he was. I mean, we all knew he was the star and everything, but nobody knew his name, he was just a kid then. I remember he bummed a cigarette from a girl in the crowd." A nearby movie memorabilia collector owns the original Blob (really red-drenched silicone), which he keeps in a 5-gallon bucket, but the diner didn't fare as well. The old Silk City was bulldozed in the 1960s to make way for a newer Silk City, there today as the Cadillac Diner, which just closed in 1999 but is scheduled to reopen in the fall.

West of Downingtown is the exaggerated modern Ingleside, and at the edge of Coatesville, the Crestmont II. This 1950s Paramount was to be destroyed in 1978 when Donald Michnuk drove by and saw the wrecking ball. His family reopened it as the Crestmont II that October.

ROUTE 309–BETHLEHEM PIKE
The Diner Drive straight north from Philadelphia is Route 309, which splits from North Broad Street at Ogontz Avenue, extends past Littleton's Diner, and becomes the Fort Washington Expressway to Bethlehem Pike. Way up 309 where the restaurants serve oyster pie, few diners have not been heavily remodeled. Assumedly there is a large, stainless steel diner beneath the post-modern pastiche of the R&S Keystone Restaurant just south of Sellersville. Nearby, it's hard to see any diner in the environmental-style restaurant known as Angelo's, but it's in there somewhere. The same holds true for the Coopersburg Diner, on the 309 bypass just south of that town (putting it in our Dutch Country region). However, within its stone-faced, barnlike exterior, and buried behind a dining room and front booth row addition, is a diner interior right out of a 1940s Paramount advertisement, complete with the tubular chrome-framed fascia and center clock above the counter.

On the bypass at the edge of Quakertown, the Plain and Fancy Restaurant is like no other diner in the state. The 1960 Fodero appears to be a transitional style employing stainless door and window frames, with large plate glass and a fair amount of stone facing. The whole thing hunkers down beneath a large, red, overhanging, gable-end roof. On the inside, there is a double row of booths lined up before a half-length counter, all to one side of an expansive dining room.

RIDGE PIKE (OLD U.S. ROUTE 422)
Ridge Pike has long offered an alternative path west through Reading, rather than the Lincoln Highway through Lancaster. The route angles northwest out of Philadelphia following the drainage divide between the Schuylkill River and Wissahickon Creek and Germantown Pike being located farther northeast. Early westbound motorists, especially truckers, took this route to

BUCKS & MONTGOMERY DINERS

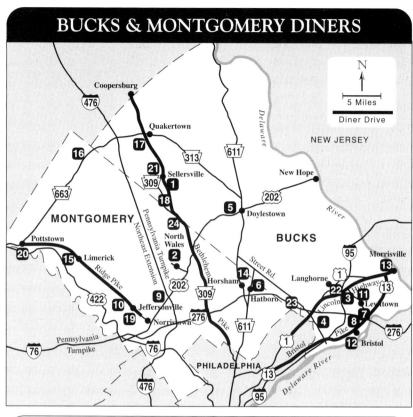

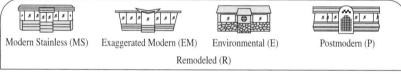

Modern Stainless (MS)   Exaggerated Modern (EM)   Environmental (E)   Postmodern (P)

Remodeled (R)

1 Angelo's Family Restaurant: Sellersville (R)
2 Astor Diner: Lansdale (E)
3 Blue Fountain Diner: Langhorne (R)
4 Club House Diner: Bensalem (P)
5 Country Food Market: Doylestown (MS)
6 Daddypop's Diner: Hatboro (MS)
7 Dallas Diner: Levittown (R)
8 DeGrand Diner: Bristol (R)
9 Double Tt's Diner: Blue Bell (R)
10 Gateway Diner: Jeffersonville (MS)
11 Golden Dawn IV Diner: Levittown (E)
12 Golden Eagle Diner: Bristol (R)
13 HL's Live Bait and Tackle Shop: Morrisville (MS)

14 Lancer's Diner-Restaurant: Horsham (E)
15 Limerick Diner: Limerick (E)
16 Pennsburg Diner: Pennsburg (R)
17 Plain & Fancy Restaurant: Quakertown (E)
18 R&S Keystone Restaurant: Telford (P)
19 Ray's Dining Car: Jeffersonville (MS)
20 Royal Diner Family Restaurant: Pottstown (EM)
21 Royann Diner: Sellersville (R)
22 Skyline Diner: Penndel (R)
23 Suburban Diner: Feasterville (R)
24 Zoto's Diner: Line Lexington (E)

BRIAN BUTKO

One of two Ray's Dining Cars outside Philadelphia. This one is an early 1960s Silk City on Ridge Pike in Jeffersonville.

get to the William Penn Highway, less steep than the Lincoln Highway across the Allegheny Mountains. In the mid-1920s, when the William Penn Highway adopted route number U.S. 22, this became U.S. 422 (meaning a spur of U.S. 22). The entire route was bypassed when U.S. 422 was relocated onto a limited-access expressway in the mid-1980s. As on all the other Philadelphia radials, diners abounded, and a few still remain.

Ray's Dining Car, owned by Ray Carroll, is at the edge of Jeffersonville. Set atop a stunning black-and-white-checked foundation, this big-windowed wonder is a twin to the Downingtown Diner, both early 1960s Silk Citys. Its light blue and white, gold-flecked interior and brown terrazzo floor are original, as is the recessed ceiling with angled risers inset with lights, a feature unique to Silk Citys of this age. Another Ray's Dining Car, on Germantown Pike in East Norristown, is a remodeled Big Boy restaurant.

Just west from the Ray's on Ridge Pike is the Gateway Diner, a modern blue and stainless 1950 Fodero that was operating at this highway location long before the arrival of the suburban fast-food franchises and split-level houses around it. Even farther out on the rural-suburban fringe is the Limerick Diner, owned by Edward and Kathryn Moore since it opened in 1969. A mere crossroads hamlet widely known for the nearby nuclear power plant, Limerick would pass by a speeding car window unnoticed if not for this spacious diner, which has kept its environmental style through a recent remodel. Anchoring the western end of this Diner Drive is the Royal Diner Family Restaurant, with exaggerated modern detailings, just west on High Street from the Pottstown business district. This twenty-four-hour diner has the distinction of having been the first Dempsey's Diner, a Pennsylvania Dutch Country diner chain headquartered in suburban Reading. Route 422 was also home to the Rosedale Diner, a 1951 Fodero. Less than two decades after opening, it was moved to a field and left to rot, forgotten until it appeared on the cover of the 1973 Hall and Oates album, *Abandoned Luncheonette.*

CHESTNUT STREET–WEST CHESTER PIKE (ROUTE 3)

From the city's inception in 1682, westbound and southbound traffic from Philadelphia struck west on Market Street until crossing the Schuylkill River, whereupon the road forked into three branches, all of them destined to become Diner Drives. Angling northwest was Lancaster Pike, straight west was West Chester Pike, and turning southwest was Baltimore Pike. As industrial-age Philadelphia added thirty-three blocks from the Schuylkill River to the western city limits, Market Street was bound in streetcar lines and buried beneath the Market-Frankford elevated rail line. Navigating this all-important thoroughfare by car was a nightmare, resulting in a pair of parallel streets—Chestnut and Walnut—being made one-way in opposite directions. The traffic was sought out by diners, including some of the earliest to show up in the Philadelphia business directories, like the Elite Dining Car at 2215 Chestnut Street and the De Luxe farther west at 4806 Chestnut.

There is only one diner on Chestnut Street now, and that one, although looking well aged in its corner lot surrounded by row homes, is relatively new to the neighborhood. This is the stainless steel American Diner, reconditioned by Swingle and brought to West Philadelphia in 1988. Out in the suburbs along West Chester Pike, however, are a number of noteworthy diners that have been around for years.

The first diner outbound is actually located on Township Line Road, one lot away and separated from West Chester Pike by a rehabbed gas station in the typical fashion of inner suburban diner location. This is the Llanerch Diner, a one-of-a-kind "picture frame" diner design presented as an alternative to the then-fading stainless steel styles. The 1968 Swingle is an amalgam of stone-faced and windowed rectangles framed in heavy white borders. Although it was an innovative, modern design that did not rely on Colonial or classical inferences, not another one was built for Pennsylvania.

A little more expected in Philadelphia's suburbs is the huge Mediterranean-style Country Squire Restaurant, set next to a corner gas station in Broomall. Beyond are two stainless Mountain View diners from 1953: Mountain View #352, in Newtown Square, now operating as Hill's Seafood

Llanerch owner William R. Gustafson bought a diner at this Upper Darby site in 1964—an O'Mahony that had been reconditioned in 1952. The neon sign was the only part to survive a 1968 fire, which led to the installation of this Swingle "picture frame" model. Joe Jones, who started at the diner in 1947, is still the chef.

Market, and the D-K Diner (#361) standing slanted to the road at the edge of West Chester. Although the D-K's serial number shows that it was ordered at a later date than Hill's, it was constructed in an earlier style.

BALTIMORE PIKE–U.S. ROUTE 1
U.S. Route 1, which followed the three-hundred-year-old route of the Post Road, was the preinterstate highway backbone of the East Coast megalopolis. U.S. Route 1 South followed Baltimore Avenue toward Baltimore and Washington, passing through the streetcar suburbs of East Lansdowne, Lansdowne, Clifton Heights, and Media—prime diner country. Interurban and streetcar lines once brought the high-density residential patterns of the city into what is now the inner suburbs. Springfield and the lower-density outer suburbs beyond Media were a later product of the automobile.

The Olympic Diner, a 1953 Mountain View (#372) on the narrow, two-lane part of Baltimore Avenue, is set to the sidewalk perpendicular to a street crowded with row buildings. The relatively small diner has been covered with a 1970s-style mansard roof and homemade, pseudo-Tudor facade. Beyond Clifton Heights, Baltimore Pike opens up into a suburban commercial strip, where Springfield's R-Way Diner sits behind a parking lot facing a five-lane highway, with a drive-through bank, car dealership, and sprawling shopping center as neighbors. R-Way is a unique entity: Set on a brick foun-

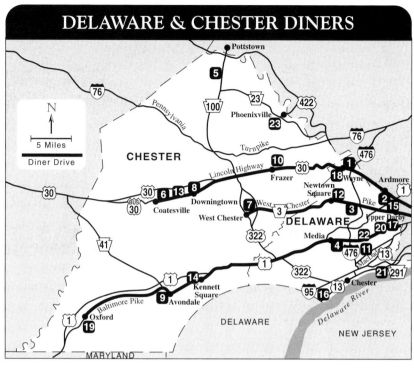

DELAWARE & CHESTER DINERS

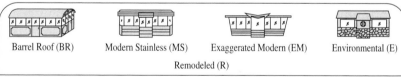

Barrel Roof (BR) Modern Stainless (MS) Exaggerated Modern (EM) Environmental (E)

Remodeled (R)

1 China Buddha Restaurant: Wayne (MS)
2 Chung Sing Restaurant: Ardmore (MS)
3 Country Squire Restaurant: Broomall (E)
4 Court Diner: Media (E)
5 Coventry Diner: Pottstown (R)
6 Crestmont II Diner: Coatesville (MS)
7 D-K Diner: West Chester (MS)
8 Downingtown/Cadillac Diner: Downingtown (MS)
9 Eric's Diner: Avondale (MS)
10 Frazer Diner: Frazer (MS)
11 Gateway Diner: Holmes (E)
12 Hill's Seafood Market: Newton Square (MS)

13 Ingleside Restaurant: Thorndale (EM)
14 Kennett Diner: Kennett Square (BR)
15 Llanerch Diner: Upper Darby (E)
16 Marcus Hook Diner: Marcus Hook (E)
17 Marlene Diner: Upper Darby (R)
18 Minella's Main Line Diner: Wayne (E)
19 Miss Oxford Diner: Oxford (MS)
20 Olympic Diner: Clifton Heights (R)
21 Preston Diner: Essington (EM)
22 R-Way Diner: Springfield (MS)
23 Vale-Rio Diner: Phoenixville (MS)

KEVIN PATRICK

Above: Kennett Diner, a 1920s O'Mahony in Kennett Square. Below: Karan Masha takes orders and light-hearted abuse from the breakfast club of regulars at the Kennett Diner.

ROBERT O. WILLIAMS

dation, fronted by a round-cornered glass block vestibule, and topped with a broad expanse of corrugated steel, the restaurant employs the classic diner materials, but not in the fashion of any major manufacturer. More than likely, this was a local contractor-built restaurant whose style was inspired by the diners around it.

Located at the end of the interurban line, the Delaware County seat of Media shares a lot of the same characteristics as other inner suburbs. But its Court Diner, a large, early colonial-style diner at the edge of town, is undoubtedly a product of the auto age. Beyond Media, the three remaining Baltimore Pike diners are located at the edges of three of the largest towns, all of them bypassed by the U.S. Route 1 expressway built between 1965 and 1970.

The Kennett Diner on State Street at the edge of Kennett Square is the oldest diner in the five-county metro Philadelphia region, a 1920s O'Mahony. It once sat on the banks of the Delaware River by the Chester Ferry and was nearly lost before finding a new home here. It's now covered with aluminum siding and attached to a 1950s stuccoed dining-room addition, but it retains its barrel roof, pink marble counter, and original wooden cabinets.

Tiled into the green and white floor of Eric's Diner is its old name, "Diner at Avon Grove." Located outside Avondale, this 1952 Mountain View had the advantage of operating along a stretch of old U.S. 1 that was concurrent with Route 41, the main road between Wilmington, Delaware, and the Pennsylvania Dutch Country. The double-duty traffic flow must have influenced the need to attach a Kullman dining room in 1961. Although eventually bypassed by U.S. 1, the diner is not far from an expressway interchange. It's also next to a Mexican grocery, there to serve the many workers in the local mushroom industry. Eric's new owners, Luigi Toto and Maria Drumheller, make everything from scratch—all sauces, soups, even pasta. Inside walls have nostalgic paintings and a map showing Chester County's remaining diners.

At the end of this drive is the Miss Oxford Diner, a 1954 Silk City that replaced a 1940s Mountain View. The diner was restored in recent years and has the distinction of being the southernmost diner in the state, yet the only one with the New England-type "Miss" appellation.

MAYFAIR DINER
1954 O'MAHONY
7373 Frankford Ave. (Cottman exit of I-95), Philadelphia

KEVIN PATRICK

For many, the diner business is a lifelong vocation, and as a family becomes wedded to the business, the diner becomes an integral part of the neighborhood. Business links are also established, especially between diner owners and manufacturers, which often encourage owners to trade up. This is well illustrated at the Mayfair Diner, which represents three generations of Mulhollands and O'Mahony diners.

This story begins at a South Broad Street hot dog stand operated by Henry Struhm and Ed Mulholland during Philadelphia's 1926 Sesquicentennial. Their success paved the way for the 1928 purchase of a twenty-stool O'Mahony set up at 41st Street and Chestnut Street. With local politician Tom Morrison as part owner, the operation was called the Morrison and Struhm Diner. They soon added a secondhand O'Mahony at 31st and Spring Garden. Meanwhile, Henry married Ed's sister Loretta.

In 1932, as West Philadelphia's fortunes sank during the Depression, the diner at 41st and Chestnut was repainted and moved to the northwest corner of the semirural intersection of Frankford Avenue, Cottman Avenue, and Ryan Avenue. The diner was renamed the Mayfair after that part of the city.

Frankford Avenue was the Northeast's main axis of development. Area produce farms were rapidly being replaced by middle-class neighborhoods of two-story row homes, and the Mayfair Diner was ready to cash in on the growing numbers of hungry patrons. Soon after the move, Tom Morrison's share was bought out by Henry Struhm, who became responsible for half of the twenty-four-hour working day, while Ed Mulholland took over the other half.

COLLECTION OF RICHARD J. S. GUTMAN

The Morrison & Struhm Diner in Philadelphia was remodeled into the first Mayfair Diner.

In 1938, the old Mayfair was sold to a South Jersey owner to make way for a new O'Mahony. With no room on the corner lot to expand, Henry Struhm built a dining room two blocks north on Frankford and moved the diner there in 1941.

Before the decade was over, Henry Struhm was back at the O'Mahony plant for a new diner. It was years in the making, as Struhm worked out the design he wanted to the minutest detail. A diner was built, rejected, and sold to someone else before the new Mayfair met with Struhm's satisfaction. Finally, a stainless steel and green flexglas structure was shipped in 1954 and attached to the dining room. It took until 1956 to refurbish the dining room inside and out to match the diner. During the renovation, business continued in the old diner, which was repositioned on the lot to face Bleigh Street. The old diner was eventually sold into service in Vincentown, New Jersey. The connected diner and annex stretched 130 feet, balanced by O'Mahony's signature clock-topped vestibule.

ROBERT O. WILLIAMS

At most diners, you'll find one or two waitresses; at the Mayfair, you may see as many as ten or twelve at any time of day. Debbie Mulholland, granddaughter of one of the founders, says that the goal of the diner is to treat people as if they were guests at home.

The Struhm and Mulholland families celebrated by having Thanksgiving dinner there before its December opening.

Henry Struhm died later in the 1950s, and Ed Mulholland joined his sister Loretta as a full partner. By Loretta's death in 1965, Ed's three children had grown up inside the Mayfair Diner, which incorporated in that year with Ed and his two sons, Jack and Ed, Jr., as partners. The Mayfair has operated as the neighborhood kitchen and community center ever since.

Having recently turned ninety, Ed Mulholland, Sr., has relinquished control of the diner to his sons, and a new generation of Mulhollands is learning the trade.

The Mayfair serves breakfast around the clock and offers different menus daily for lunch and dinner. Crab cakes and deviled crab are popular, as are German foods, such as pork and sauerkraut and Dutch meatballs. Desserts change daily and include layer cakes, whipped cream cakes, fruit pies, and rice pudding.

DADDYPOP'S DINER
1953 MOUNTAIN VIEW #356
232 N. York Rd., Hatboro

FEATURED DINER

KEVIN PATRICK

Owner Ken Smith has high praise for old diners: "The original diner builders were geniuses. Mine was built with enough intelligence to tile almost everything and stainless steel the rest. The health department can't argue with it."

Ken worked at an A&W drive-in as a kid, and did an eight-month stint at McDonald's while in the Army. He trained to be an engineer but bought

ROBERT O. WILLIAMS

A baby gets an early start on diner culture from his mom at Daddypop's.

the diner in 1987. "I've made safety equipment and put helmets in outer space but I got tired of politics in corporate life," Ken says. "I do all the repair work, but my main function is public relations, plus I'm a safety valve when we get lots of orders. Business is great, crazy. It's mostly locals during the week—they're here when we open—but it's reversed on weekends. We have a wall with coffee cups for regulars to keep them involved."

The diner, originally named the Hatboro Diner, came in two pieces totaling 40 by 31 feet. It's been remodeled through the years, but Ken says he can only restore it so much. "Cooking behind the counter just wouldn't be viable now. The counter's been moved a foot closer to the wall to give the customers more room." To fit in with the Hatboro streetscapes, decorated in Victorian style, Ken has landscaped his eatery with brick sidewalks, gas lamps, a 14-foot clock, a wishing well, and old farm equipment.

Like more and more diner owners, Ken serves only breakfast and lunch: "We have fewer than sixty seats, so turnover at night won't pay the labor and refrigerator bills. But we have a lot of characters—we get magicians and clowns in full regalia. Even our dishwasher—he's a pro wrestler, 6 foot, 8 inches, and 315 pounds."

As in most diners in this part of the country, scrapple is on the menu; other specialties are home fries and sausage with gravy over biscuits. Ken, from New England, also makes a popular clam chowder. A couple of years ago, he bought the Tumble Inn Diner in Claremont, New Hampshire, a 1938 Worcester run by his daughter.

The Daddypop's name is a combination of the two names Ken's family called his grandfather, for whom Ken's wife, Beth, suggested naming the diner. Beth died a few years ago at thirty-five, making it tough sometimes for Ken, but he says: "The diner has filled a hole in my life. Customers can always go there and find someone to talk to, kill the boredom. That's why the counter is an essential requirement. We're hanging on with white knuckles to a lifestyle we're comfortable with."

THE DINING CAR
1981 SWINGLE #881DKV
8826 Frankford Ave., Philadelphia

KEVIN PATRICK

When Joe and Joyce Morozin decided they wanted a new diner, they came up with a radical idea—a modern, efficiently designed restaurant with the look and feel of a 1930s diner. Retro diners are all the rage now, but not in 1981, when Swingle delivered The Dining Car to Torresdale. It was the first in a wave of postmodern diners that looked to the past for inspiration, and the Morozins' success has directly influenced the trend. Robert Giaimo spent a week at The Dining Car before launching his Silver Diner, a retro chain that has grown to twelve units.

The Morozins bought their first Swingle in 1962 and operated it as the Torresdale Diner (#862DKV) on Frankford Avenue just south of Academy Road. Joe sold that diner to a Greek family, who moved it to East Greenbush, New York, when the retro Swingle arrived. By that time, Joe's son, Joe, Jr., and his daughter, Nancy, were stepping in to run The Dining Car.

Joe Swingle, who had begun his career at O'Mahony, designed The Dining Car after O'Mahony's 1930s Monarch diner. The past provided the inspiration, but present economics generally meant that everything had to be bigger. Whereas the old Torresdale Diner had arrived in three pieces, The Dining Car came in six. A new prep kitchen–dining room section was added in 1986, bringing the seating to 258, and an expanded vestibule–bakery showroom arrived two years later. Joe, Jr., feels the size is perfect: "The old diners were too small. You would never be able to run them with a high enough profit margin. The big, new diners, like those 400- and 500-seaters over in Jersey, are too big. The overhead costs with the heating and air-conditioning, staffing, and electricity are too high."

The diner features a monitor roof above a large-windowed facade with a black base. Inside, the right half of the restaurant is set up as a diner with a tile floor, an eleven-stool counter, a double row of booths in the center, and a row of booths along the windows. Three of the diner's four corners have a large, round bench booth and table. The carpeted left side is the restaurant dining room, with a service bar, booths along the windows, and tables in the center. A stylized art deco theme is carried throughout the gray-and-white interior, highlighted with burgundy, chrome, and quilted mirrors.

In addition to three sisters who help Joe, Jr., run the diner, there's a full-time staff of two chefs, two kitchen managers, and seventeen short-order cooks. The chef and assistant chef have been there twenty-four years.

"We specialize in trying to give good quality at good prices," Joe, Jr., says. "We don't buy anything premade. Sauces, soups, gravies—we make it all." The variety ranges from chicken croquettes and baby-beef liver to roast turkey and lobster. Several kinds of meatloaf are served, including lamb, turkey, and veal. Seafood is a favorite, especially crab imperial, deviled crab, and broiled seafood sampler. The diner also employs four full-time bakers who whip up everything from dinner rolls to apple walnut pie.

Like the Torresdale before it, The Dining Car is open twenty-four hours, even though Joe, Jr., admits that the business warrants a late shift only on the weekend. "Monday and Tuesday nights, it's dead in here. But it doesn't matter. My dad said that truckers out on I-95 know that they can take the Academy Road exit day or night and find us open, and they've been doing that for more than thirty years. And the people in the neighborhood know that no matter what time it is, regardless of the weather, they can come here and get a bite to eat. The diner will be open."

INGLESIDE RESTAURANT

1956 FODERO

Lincoln Highway, Thorndale

FEATURED DINER

BRIAN BUTKO

The most impressive feature about the Ingleside Restaurant is its architectural integrity. After more than forty years, this diner still has its showroom shine, inside and out. But what strikes you most is all the pink: The exterior porcelain strips, the window awnings, the outside neon, the stools and booths, the tile floor in the vestibule, and the main aisle between the counter and booths are all pink or mostly pink, and it's all reflected in the mirrored backwall and center strip on the diner's recessed ceiling. The Ingleside is undoubtedly the pinkest diner in the state.

This L-shaped Fodero with corner vestibule is an unmistakable presence on the old Lincoln Highway (Business Route 30) between Downingtown and Coatesville. Day and night, two oversize, pink neon rooftop signs proclaim "Ingleside Restaurant." The 115-seat Ingleside is modest by today's Jersey diner-restaurant standards, but in the 1950s, a seven-section diner like this was flagship class. The shape allowed for more booths, which is what most of the short end of the L is devoted to.

This was the third diner operated by Pennsylvania diner legend Christian G. Zinn. The first was the Town Diner at the eastern edge of Coatesville (also on the Lincoln Highway), and the second was Zinn's Diner, opened in 1950 at U.S. 222 (now 272) and the Pennsylvania Turnpike. On Christmas Eve 1956, this diner was opened as Zinn's on the family's Ingleside Farm in Thorndale. In 1966, the U.S. 30 Downingtown-Coatesville Bypass opened and took away 70 percent of the diner's business; a year later, the diner was

This black and white photograph conceals the very pink interior of the Ingleside.

sold and renamed the Ingleside. The concurrent suburbanization of the western Main Line brought back the business lost to the bypass.

The Ingleside serves breakfast all day and has a bakery on the premises. Meatloaf and chicken croquettes are their specialties.

FEATURED DINER

COVENTRY DINER
CIRCA 1962 SILK CITY #2471, REMODELED
1435 S. Hanover St. (Route 100 S.), Pottstown

Routes 611, 309, and 100 are the north-south workhorse roads of southeastern Pennsylvania. Unlike the traffic on the parallel Northeast Extension of the turnpike, traffic on these roads is predominantly local, made up of delivery trucks, commuters, and the occasional dirt-clodded tractor. Road-

RICK GRESH

The Coventry vestibule being installed in 1967.

side businesses are a mix of convenience stores, farm and garden centers, and diners. One such place is the Coventry Diner, operating in a semirural setting adjacent to the Modern Motel on Route 100 just south of Pottstown.

The Coventry, typical of diners, has seen multiple owners and multiple remodelings. The diner is an early 1960s Silk City (like the nearby Ray's Dining Car and Downingtown Diner) that originally saw service near Allentown. It was moved to this location by George Morgan in 1967. From 1977 to 1984, the diner was owned by Daniel and Eleanor Gresh. Rick Gresh, a distant relative, has owned it since. Rick started out as a short-order diner cook in 1970, learning from cooks who had been "front men" in the old diner days before the arrival of a back kitchen. He served as head chef at a number of area restaurants, and eventually sought a diner of his own. About that time, the Conventry was put up for sale, and Rick bought it from Daniel and Eleanor, who, he was surprised to find out, were his father's cousins.

Aside from the typical booth-and-counter arrangement, the original diner is most apparent in the windows, vestibule, and ceiling of lighted, angled risers typical of these Silk Citys. Morgan built a sixty-seat dining room addition on the north side, and the entire diner was remodeled by the Greshes in the late 1970s. Following the well-established fashion, they covered the diner with stucco and brick, erected a green mansard roof parapet, and added a few exterior coach lamps. Rick Gresh remodeled the diner again in the 1980s, adding a larger kitchen and another dining room to boost seating capacity to 175. The new dining room was built onto the end of the older one, and the semicolonial exterior was extended to envelop the enlarged building. The Early American theme was not carried to the interior, however, which projects a more updated, plush appearance and has a self-serve salad bar. Rick says he's considered restoring the diner to its original form, though he realizes that much work is involved in undoing the past remodelings.

The Coventry offers a diverse menu, including a wide variety of seafood specials, such as homemade crab cakes, broiled deviled clams, and lobster tail. More than forty sandwiches (some available on a croissant), and hoagies are offered plus nearly twenty pies, including peanut butter, shoofly, and strawberry rhubarb. In addition, the diner offers daily specials, such as oyster stew, pig sandwich (barbecued roast pork and sautéed onion on a kaiser roll), vegetable fettucini alfredo, and sweet potato fries, plus Pennsylvania Dutch side dishes, such as potato filling, cottage cheese with apple butter, chowchow, and buttered noodles.

DINER DIRECTORY

ARDMORE

Chung Sing Restaurant
210 E. Lancaster Ave. (Rt. 30)
(610) 649-8115
1952 Fodero, remodeled. Originally
Dean's.
Chinese food.
Open daily, 11 A.M.–10 P.M.

AVONDALE

Eric's Diner
641 Gap-Newport Pike (Rt. 41 N.)
(610) 268-3661
Reconditioned 1952 Mountain View
#454 and remodeled 1961 Kullman
annex. Formerly Avon Grove Diner.
*American and Italian food made fresh
daily; mushroom soup.*
Open daily, 6 A.M.–10 P.M.

BENSALEM

Club House Diner
2495 Street Rd.
(215) 639-4287
Postmodern.
*American food; largest salad bar in the
area (fifty items); homemade pastries.*
Open 24 hours.

BLUE BELL

Double Tt Diner
1765 DeKalb Pike
(610) 279-4600
Circa 1960 Kullman. Formerly
Whitpain Diner.
*Homemade food and pastries; 200 items
on menu.*
Open 24 hours.

BRISTOL

DeGrand Diner
5627 U.S. Rt. 13
(215) 788-6060
1970. Possible remodel of a 1952
L-shaped Kullman on this site.
*American and Italian food; bakery;
catering.*
Open daily, 6 A.M.–10 P.M.

Golden Eagle Diner
300 Bath St. (at U.S. 13 N.)
(215) 785-6926
1974 DeRaffele, remodeled in 1993.
*American food; steaks, chops, seafood;
bakery, cheesecake.*
Open 24 hours.

BROOMALL

Country Squire Restaurant
2560 West Chester Pike (at Sproul Rd.)
(610) 353-0550
1963 Musi.
American food; bakery; banquets.
Open 24 hours.

CLIFTON HEIGHTS

Olympic Diner
142 E. Baltimore Pike
(610) 259-9123
1953 Mountain View #372. Originally
Clifton Diner.
American food; hot cakes, chipped beef.
Open Sun.–Thurs., 6 A.M.–10 P.M.;
Fri.–Sat., 24 hours.

COATESVILLE

Crestmont II Diner
1323 E. Lincoln Highway
(Business Rt. 30)
(610) 384-5326
Circa 1950 Paramount. Originally the
Madison, then Anthony's Diner.
*American food; steaks, seafood, hot roast
beef and turkey sandwiches.*
Open daily, 6:30 A.M.–9 P.M.

DOWNINGTOWN

Downingtown/Cadillac Diner
81 W. Lancaster Ave. (Bus. Rt. 30)
Circa 1962 Silk City #6671. Moved from
Bethlehem to replace old Silk City.
Closed.

DOYLESTOWN

Country Food Market
224 W. State St. (U.S. 202)
Circa 1950 O'Mahony, remodeled.
Formerly Ed's Diner.
No meals served.

ESSINGTON

Preston Diner
118 Powhattan Ave.
(610) 521-3888
1958 Silk City #5802 and a circa 1960
Kullman addition. Formerly Penrose
Diner.
*Homemade American food; real potatoes;
rice pudding; banquets.*
Open Sun.–Thurs., 6 A.M.–9:30 P.M.;
Fri.–Sat., 24 hours;

FEASTERVILLE

Suburban Diner
14 W. Street Rd.
(215) 355-0155
1940s postmodern remodel. Moved
from Florida in the 1940s.
*American food; steaks, chops, seafood,
pasta, sautéed dishes, salad bar; bakery.*
Open 24 hours.

FRAZER

Frazer Diner
189 W. Lancaster Ave. (Rt. 30)
(610) 251-9878
Mid-1930s O'Mahony.
American food.
Open Mon.–Fri., 6 A.M.–2 P.M.;
Sat.–Sun., 7 A.M.–2 P.M.

HATBORO

Daddypop's Diner
232 N. York Rd.
(215) 675-9717
1953 Mountain View #356. Originally
Hatboro Diner.
Open daily, 6 A.M.–2 P.M.
For more information, see page 60.

HOLMES

Gateway Diner
2215 Macdade Blvd. (at Cedar)
(610) 532-2825
1970s Mediterranean modern.
American food.
Open daily, 6 A.M.–10 P.M.

HORSHAM

Lancer's Diner-Restaurant
858 Easton Rd.
(215) 674-5088
1970s. Former Horsham Towne Diner
Restaurant.
Greek and American food.
Open Mon., 7 A.M.–11 P.M.; Tues.–Sat.,
24 hours; Sun., closes at 11 P.M.

JEFFERSONVILLE

Gateway Diner
2540 Ridge Pike
(610) 539-9855
1950 Fodero.
American food; daily specials.
Open daily, 6 A.M.–10 P.M.

Ray's Dining Car
1968 W. Main St.
(610) 630-0450
Circa 1962 Silk City #5471. Former site
of BrenVale Diner.

KENNETT SQUARE

Kennett Diner
719 Old Baltimore Pike
(610) 444-9970
1920s O'Mahony. Former Marley's
Breakfast House. Formerly at Eric's
Diner site in Avondale.
Open Tues.–Sun., 6 A.M.–2 P.M.

LANGHORNE

Blue Fountain Diner
2029 E. Lincoln Highway (Rt. 1)
(215) 949-3533
1963 Fodero.
Greek food; baked goods; daily specials.
Open 24 hours.

LANSDALE

Astor Diner
609 Sumneytown Pike (at Church Rd.)
(215) 699-5637
1970 Musi.
American food; steaks, seafood, chicken;
homemade pies; cocktails.
Open Mon.–Sat., 6 A.M.–11 P.M.;
Sun., 6 A.M.–10 P.M.

LEVITTOWN

Dallas Diner
7025 Rt. 13
(215) 547-0990
1970s. Mediterranean modern with
mansard.
American food; steaks, chops; bakery.
Open 24 hours.

Golden Dawn IV
7115 New Falls Rd.
(215) 945-4554
1985 Kullman.
Petite meals.
Open Mon.–Thurs., 6 A.M.–2 A.M.;
Fri.–Sat. 24 hours; Sun., 6 A.M.–midnight.

LIMERICK

Limerick Diner
411 W. Ridge Pike
(610) 489-3500
1969 Swingle #869D.
Pennsylvania Dutch food.
Open 24 hours.

LINE LEXINGTON

Zoto's Diner
Rt. 309 and Hilltown Pike
(215) 822-1948
1973 Fodero.
American food.
Open Mon.–Thurs., 7 A.M.–10 P.M.;
Fri.–Sat., 7 A.M.–11 P.M.

MARCUS HOOK

Marcus Hook Diner
10th St. and Green St. (U.S. Rt. 13)
(610) 497-5441
1950s. Originally the Rainbow Diner at
4th and Morton in Chester.
American food.
Open Mon.–Tue. and Sat., 6 A.M.–7 P.M.;
Wed.–Fri., 6 A.M.–8 P.M.;
Sun., 6 A.M.–2 P.M.

MEDIA

Court Diner
140 E. Baltimore Pike
(610) 566-4403
1964 Kullman, remodeled in
colonial style.
American and Italian food; breakfast all
day; stews and goulash, quiche, prime rib.
Open 6 A.M.–midnight.

MORRISVILLE

HL's Live Bait and Tackle Shop
78 E. Bridge St. (Rt. 32 S.)
(215) 295-1400
1941 reconditioned Silk City, remodeled. Former Transit Diner.
No food served.

NEWTOWN SQUARE

Hill's Seafood Market
3605 W. Chester Pike (Rts. 3 & 52)
(610) 359-1888
1953 Mountain View #352. Originally
Green Hill Diner.
No meals served.

OXFORD

Miss Oxford Diner
233 S. Third St. (Rt. 10)
(610) 932-2653
1954 Silk City #5465.
American food; pork barbeque;
milkshakes; car cruises.
Open Mon.–Fri., 7 A.M.–8 P.M.;
Sat.–Sun. 7 A.M.–2 P.M.

PENNDEL

Skyline Diner
200 W. Lincoln Highway (Rts. 1 & 413)
(215) 757-7940
1956 Paramount, remodeled.
American food; breakfast and lunch only.
Open 6 A.M.–2 P.M.

PENNSBURG

Pennsburg Diner
321 Pottstown Ave. (at Washington St.)
(215) 679-2190
1968 Swingle #568DVU (former 1959
Silk City #5906).
American food.

PHILADELPHIA

Ace Diner
5517 Lancaster Ave.
(215) 877-7157
1940s Silk City, remodeled.
American food; breakfast and lunch only.
Open Mon.–Fri., 6 A.M.–3 P.M.

American Diner
4201 Chestnut St.
Circa 1949 Paramount, redone by
Swingle in 1988 as #888DVU.
Closed.

Anna's Pizza
6211 Lancaster Ave.
(215) 878-9797
1954 Fodero, remodeled. Originally
Overbrook Diner.
Hoagies, grinders, seafood; delivery.
Open daily, 9 A.M.–7 P.M.

Aramingo Diner
3356 Aramingo Ave.
(215) 291-2903
1970 Musi/1976 DeRaffele. On site of
1957 Mountain View/1963 Fodero.
American food; blue plate specials;
cheesecake.
Open 24 hours.

Bob's Diner
6053 Ridge Ave. (at Lyceum)
(215) 483-9002
1947 O'Mahony. Formerly 20th Century
Diner, Kohler's Diner, and Paul's Diner.
Home-cooked fast food; fluffy omelets.
Open Mon.–Thurs. and Sat.,
7 A.M.–9 P.M.; Fri., 7 A.M.–10 P.M.;
Sun., 7 A.M.–8 P.M.

Broad Street Diner
1135 S. Broad St. (at Ellsworth St.)
(215) 334-1611
1960s early environmental.
American food; breakfast all day;
ribs; cocktails.
Open 24 hours.

Broadway Diner
11650 Roosevelt Blvd. (at Bennett Rd.)
(215) 676-1331
1985 Kullman. Former Ritz of
Philadelphia.
American food.
Open 24 hours.

Chio's Diner
3447 Richmond St.
(215) 739-7528
Remodeled. Formerly Jersey Queen
Diner.
American food; breakfast and lunch only.
Open Mon.–Sat., 2 A.M.–2 P.M.

Continental Diner
183 Market St.
(215) 922-2344
1963 Fodero.

Country Club Restaurant
1717 Cottman Ave.
(215) 722-0500
1968 Fodero.
Chicken noodle matzo ball soup; brisket
with kasha varnishkas; cheesecake; blintzes.
Open Sun.–Thurs., 7 A.M.–11 P.M.;
Fri.–Sat., 7 A.M.–1 A.M.

The Dining Car
8826 Frankford Ave.
(215) 338-5113
1981 Swingle #881DKV.
Open 24 hours.
For more information, see page 62.

Domino Diner
5110 Umbria St.
(215) 483-7734
1948 O'Mahony. Former Carroll's Diner
from Medford, Massachusetts, rehabbed
by Swingle in 1963 as #763DR. Remodeled 1995.
American food; country-style breakfast;
homemade soups and sauces.
Open Mon.–Sat., 6 A.M.–10 P.M.;
Sun., 6 A.M.–9 P.M.

Golden Sword Diner
4210 Whitaker Ave. (at E. Hunting
Park Ave.)
(215) 739-1476
1970s Fodero.
American food; breakfast all day;
cocktails; bakery; banquets.
Open 24 hours.

Littleton's Diner-Restaurant
8001 Ogontz Ave. (at Chelteham Ave.)
(215) 424-4034
Circa 1958 Paramount, remodeled. First
Littleton's here was a 1941 Silk City.
American food; breakfast all day.
Open 24 hours.

Mayfair Diner
7373 Frankford Ave.
(215) 624-8886
1954 O'Mahony, remodeled.
Open 24 hours.
For more information, see page 58.

Melrose Diner
1501 Snyder Ave.
(215) 467-6644
1956 Paramount. 1961 city murals
above back counter.
American food; large menu; bakery,
cheesecake.
Open 24 hours.

Mil-Lee's Luv-Inn Diner
5717 Rising Sun Ave.
(215) 722-1400
1930s O'Mahony.
Open 24 hours.

Oak Lane Diner
6528 N. Broad St. (at York Rd.)
(215) 424-1026
1950 Paramount "Zenith" model.
American food; breakfast all day.
Open Mon.–Sat., 7 A.M.–midnight;
Sun., 7 A.M.–10 P.M.

Oregon Diner
302 Oregon Ave.
(215) 462-5566
Circa 1960, remodeled.
American food; lunch and dinner specials;
cocktails; bakery.

Penrose Diner
Penrose Ave. (at 20th St.)
(215) 465-1097
1963 DeRaffele, remodeled. Third
on site.
American food; cocktails.
Open Sun.–Thurs., 6 A.M.–midnight;
Fri.–Sat., 24 hours.

Quaker Diner
7241 Rising Sun Ave. (near
Cottman Ave.)
(215) 745-5055
1939 O'Mahony, remodeled. Old
sign rehabbed.
American food; barbecue ribs, crab cakes,
stuffed flounder with crabmeat, sautéed
dishes.
Open Sun.–Thurs., 5:30 A.M.–11 P.M.;
Fri.–Sat., 24 hours.

Red Robin Diner
6330 Frankford Ave. (at Levick St.)
(215) 338-8643
Late 1960s Fodero. Original site of
Devon, a 1948 Fodero, later Frankford
Diner, then Carillon Diner.
Greek food; pastitsio, veal parmesan.
Open 24 hours.

Restaurante Ecuanondureno
N. 5th & W. Bristol Sts.
1953 Mountain View #362, remodeled.
Originally Lionel Diner, then Bristol
Diner.

Sand Trap Café
4417 Castor Ave.
(215) 743-0319
1950s remodeled.
American food; chicken wings, cheeseburgers.
Open Mon.–Sat., 9 A.M.–2 P.M.;
Sun., 11 A.M.–2 P.M.

Silk City Diner
435 Spring Garden St.
(215) 592-8838
1959 Silk City #5907. Formerly American Diner, Dee Dee's Diner. Postmodern entrance.
American food; chocolate bread pudding; lounge adjacent.
Open Mon.–Thurs., 7 A.M.–midnight;
Fri.–Sun., 24 hours.

Tiffany Diner
9010 Roosevelt Blvd.
(215) 677-3916
1970s.
Greek and Italian food; breakfast all day; gourmet salads; bakery.
Open 24 hours.

Wayne Junction Diner
Wayne Ave. & W. Berkley St.
1940 Paramount.
Closed.

PHOENIXVILLE

Vale-Rio Diner
114 Nutt Rd. (at Bridge St., Rt. 23)
(610) 933-3988
1948 Paramount.
Seafood, veal.
Open Mon.–Wed. 5 A.M.–11 P.M.;
Thurs.–Sat. 24 hours; Sun. until 11 P.M.

POTTSTOWN

Coventry Diner
1435 Hanover St. (Rt. 100 S.)
(610) 323-9712
Circa 1962 Silk City #2471, remodeled.
Open daily, 5:30 A.M.–10:30 P.M.
For more information, see page 65.

Royal Diner Family Restaurant
80 High St. (at York St.)
(610) 323-7295
1950 DeRaffele. Former Dempsey's Diner.
American and Italian food; repeat winner for best food in local newspaper.
Open 24 hours.

QUAKERTOWN

Plain & Fancy Restaurant
Rt. 309
(215) 536-3290
1960 Fodero, remodeled.
American food; breakfast all day; bakery.
Open 24 hours.

SELLERSVILLE

Royann Diner
1318 Rt. 309
(215) 257-4089
Remodeled.
Homemade American food; breakfast all day; mashed potatoes; grilled cinnamon buns, apple dumplings.
Open daily, 6 A.M.–10 P.M.

Angelo's Family Restaurant
321 S. Main St.
(215) 257-0491
1960s, remodeled. Formerly Sellersville Restaurant.
American food; breakfast all day; oyster pie, broiled crabcakes.
Open 24 hours.

SPRINGFIELD

R-Way Diner
880 Baltimore Pike
(610) 543-9779
1955 homemade in diner style.
American food; breakfast all day.
Open Mon.–Sat., 6 A.M.–4 P.M.;
Sun., 7:30 A.M.–2 P.M.

TELFORD

R&S Keystone Restaurant
4714 Bethlehem Pike
(215) 257-3330
Circa 1950.
American and Pennsylvania Dutch food;
broiled and fried seafood, veal cutlet, home-
made cole slaw, oyster pie; rice pudding.
Open Mon.–Thurs., 5:30 A.M.–8 P.M.;
Fri.–Sat. 5:30 A.M.–9 P.M.;
Sun. 7 A.M.–8 P.M.

THORNDALE

Ingleside Restaurant
3025 E. Lincoln Highway
(610) 384-7833
1956 Fodero. Originally Zinn's.
Open Mon.–Sat., 6:30 A.M.–8 P.M.;
Sun., 7:30 A.M.–8 P.M.
For more information, see page 64.

UPPER DARBY

Llanerch Diner
Township Line Rd. & West Chester Pike
(610) 789-9964
1968 Swingle #968DV.
American food; snapper soup, chipped beef,
big burgers.
Open 24 hours.

Marlene Diner
7260 Marshall Rd.
(610) 623-4117
1949 O'Mahony, remodeled.
Mediterranean modern rubble stone
with black arches.
American food; breakfast all day;
homemade hot turkey and roast beef
platters; pies; cocktails.
Open 24 hours.

WAYNE

China Buddha Restaurant
175 E. Lancaster Ave.
(610) 688-8433
1955 Mountain View #446, remodeled.
Chinese food.
Open Tues.–Fri., 11:30 A.M.–3 P.M. and
5 P.M.–9:30 P.M.; Sat.–Sun.,
4:30 P.M.–10:30 P.M.

Minella's Main Line Diner
320 Lancaster Ave. (Rt. 30)
(610) 687-1575
1964 Fodero. Originally the
Colonial Diner.
American food; breakfast all day.
Open 24 hours.

WEST CHESTER

D-K Diner
609 E. Gay St. (Rt. 3)
(610) 692-2946
1953 Mountain View #361; 1955 addition to rear. Replaced Modern Diner.
Voted best breakfast and best lunch in town.
Open Mon.–Sat., 6 A.M.–3 P.M.;
Sun., 7 A.M.–3 P.M.

PENNSYLVANIA
DUTCH COUNTRY

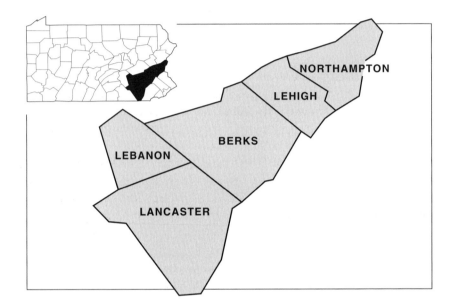

On the U.S. 422 bypass around Myerstown, the Kumm Esse Diner calls out to townies, tourists, and truckers with a name that means "come eat." The next diner down the road to the west is Lebanon's Eat Well. Diners telling travelers to eat and eat well, with part of the message in German, can only mean one thing—you're deep in Pennsylvania Dutch Country. If there's any region in the state famous for food, it's this one: chicken and waffles, pot pie, schnitz und knepp (ham and apples with dumplings), corn pie with milk, and plenty of buttered noodles.

Bud and Joyce Mitstifer have been tantalizing patrons with beef heart over filling, pepper cabbage, and corn and apple fritters since they bought the Kumm Esse Diner, also famous for strawberry pie, in 1994.

At Ephrata's Cloister Diner, Elva Stauffer's pig stomach dinner, stuffed with sausage, bread cubes, and potatoes, is a favorite.

At Risser's Diner in Stouchsburg, deep-fried corn nuggets is a popular Dutch side dish, along with chowchow (a sweet-and-sour vegetable relish) and bread with apple butter.

The food is just a single patch in an extensive cultural quilt woven into southeastern Pennsylvania since the early eighteenth century. Few are the diners in this five-county area that don't advertise Pennsylvania Dutch cooking, and while architectural styles reflect national trends, many diners are still dusted with Dutch regionalism, exemplified by the hex signs that decorate the Coopersburg Diner, the Gap Diner's country-style exterior, and Amos, the giant Amishman outside Zinn's Diner. Some incorporate the word *Dutch* in their name, such as Frackville's Dutch Kitchen, the Dutch Valley Diner in Shoemakersville, or the long-gone Dutch Diners in Shartlesville and Palmyra.

The word *Dutch* here actually means German. Most of the original German-speaking settlers who peopled William Penn's colonial frontier were from a region known as the Palatinate. Pennsylvania Dutch foodways came largely from Palatine Lutherans and Calvinists who were attracted by the availability of fertile farmland. Those foodways were also brought by minority sects—Mennonites, Amish, and Moravians—who came seeking land and religious freedom. To complement the agricultural economy of the region, the Penn family encouraged the creation of market towns approximately 60 miles from Philadelphia and 20 to 30 miles from each other: Lancaster (1730), Reading (1748), Easton (1752), and Northampton, now Allentown (1762). These formed an arc of towns at the opposite ends of radial roads emanating from Philadelphia, laying the urban foundation for the Pennsylvania Dutch Country and the future foci for the region's diners.

KEVIN PATRICK

The Kumm Esse in Myerstown invites patrons to "come eat" in Pennsylvania Dutch.

As in other areas of the Northeast, the first diners in Dutch Country cities came in the wake of industrialization. The small cities of the region are similar to Worcester, Massachusetts; Waterbury, Connecticut; and Paterson, New Jersey: gritty factory towns of densely built houses and mills that flourished between 1860 and 1920. In Reading, the diner was introduced in lunch wagon form by Mrs. Anne Blome in 1897. According to a February 4, 1940, article in the *Reading Eagle,* her Old Bean Wagon was a "high-bodied, rambling restaurant on wheels" that was pulled to Penn Street near 5th Street by a team of horses to take advantage of the heavy evening downtown trade. The horses were stabled until closing time, then rehitched to pull the wagon away. Beans were dished out for a nickel a plate. Mrs. Blome eventually found a stationary, twenty-four-hour location at 3 North 3rd Street before finally opening a traditional restaurant a few doors away. Although the *Reading Eagle* article claimed that this was *the* first diner, other lunch wagons have been documented a few decades earlier.

In the 1930s and '40s, Walter J. "Bill" Moore operated Moore's Restaurant chain in Reading, consisting of a restaurant at 4th Street and Penn Street and four diners, each of which was a pair of Ward & Dickinson dining cars linked together. The diners were on South 6th Street (called Moore's #2), in West Reading (#3), on 9th Street and Penn Street (#4), and next to the Colonial Hotel on North 5th Street, between Washington Street and Court Street. When a new post office was opened, this last diner supposedly moved to 421 Penn Street until the seventies.

Similar to later fast-food chains, independent diner chains like Moore's lowered the cost of expanding by using efficiently designed, standardized

RICHARD J. S. GUTMAN

Bill Moore had a number of restaurants in Reading, including this Ward & Dickinson diner graft on South 6th Street.

units. Only it wasn't a corporate design department creating the units, but outside firms specializing in prefabricated restaurants—diner manufacturers. If a larger restaurant was needed, multiple diners were bought and attached at the site.

A native of upstate New York, Bill Moore was familiar with Ward & Dickinson (W&D), out of Silver Creek, New York, and bought his first one to operate in Williamsport, Pennsylvania, in the mid-1930s. Actually, he only bought half a diner; Lee Dickinson retained a half interest in the business as an investment. W&D regularly used this as a means of spreading their diners throughout Pennsylvania, providing the capital to facilitate the creation of small diner chains, while simultaneously creating a market for manufactured diners. When Bill Moore established his Reading chain a few years later, the business relationship continued, with Lee Dickinson a silent partner in each diner. Moore also helped other owners by brokering diner purchases.

PENNSYLVANIA DUTCH COOKING

Pennsylvania Dutch cooking encompasses a wide variety of food. Schnitz und knepp is ham with apples and dumplings. Chicken pot pie is not actually a pie but chicken and noodles in a stew. Scrapple, usually served for breakfast, is a loaf made from a seasoned mixture of meat and cornmeal that's sliced and fried. Chowchow is a sweet-and-sour relish of corn, onions, beans, and other vegetables. Corn is a popular ingredient and is used in many recipes, such as fritters, deep-fried corn nuggets, and corn pie with milk. But probably the best known Dutch food is shoofly pie, basically a crumb cake with a molasses bottom.

In 1947, Florida native Philip Rowe graduated from Cornell University's restaurant and hotel management program. As a graduation gift, he was given a diner by his grandfather, Lee Dickinson. Ward & Dickinson was out of business by then, but there were still plenty of W&Ds around. Philip's diner was a "Wardy" from Wilkinsburg, Pennsylvania (the former Feiler's or Scotty's), that was moved to 325 Buttonwood Street in Reading. Rowe's partner there and at the nearby Topps Diner was Edward Shain, Moore's brother-in-law.

"Reading was a good diner town," recalled Rowe, "and my grandfather had a partnership with Bill Moore, who owned some diners there." Reading in the 1940s and '50s was the quintessential diner town, densely packed with working-class neighborhoods, textile mills, steel plants, and the sprawling shops of the Reading Railroad, which bisected the city north-south.

Rowe gradually took over his grandfather's interest in the Moore chain, then bought out Bill Moore, who was twenty years his senior. Rowe thus set out on a lifelong career of owning, operating, and brokering diners throughout southeastern Pennsylvania. "I've probably owned forty or fifty different diners and restaurants over the course of my life," says Rowe. When he acquired Pottstown's Dempsey Diner in 1968, he bought not only the diner, but also the rights to the name, simply because he liked it. He started using the Dempsey name on his other diners, like the former Bellevue Diner in Laureldale. Under the Dempsey's Diner banner, Philip Rowe created a single identity for his diners, resurrecting the idea of the small diner chain so common before World War II.

Into the eighties, each restaurant was graced with a chubby, fiberglass Dutch Boy mascot, Dempsey's Dutch Country equivalent of the Big Boy, a few restaurants of which Rowe also owned. Dempsey's currently has six outlets: four diners and two former Big Boy's. The oldest diner is a 1950s Kullman that originally operated as the Wheatland Diner on Columbia Avenue at the west edge of Lancaster near Wheatland, home of President James Buchanan. When Rowe purchased it in the late seventies, he added a dining room, stone-faced vestibule, and orange mansard roof to the diner. The chain also includes the old Dutch Diner of New Castle, Delaware, and two environmental-style diners: a circa 1980 DeRaffele in Harrisburg and a Swingle in Hummelstown (a 1966 Swingle that was traded in and rehabbed in 1978). The chain has lately been eliminating its Dutch Boy mascots and renaming its outlets Dempsey's American Kitchens.

Business links in the diner world are much less visible than in corporate chains, but they are similarly pervasive. Because the diner industry is so concentrated in the Northeast, strong ties and interrelationships among operators, owners, brokers, and manufacturers are forged over the years.

No Ward & Dickinsons are known to have survived in the five-county Dutch Country region, but the past can still turn up in unexpected places, like behind the stone facade of Paul's Gyro Restaurant in Allentown. From North 8th Street, nothing about the building reveals its true identity, but the barrel ceiling inside belies its origins as a diner from the twenties or thirties. An expanded dining area and kitchen have been added onto the original structure, which was set sideways on the lot and up against the sidewalk in the common fashion of an old in-town diner located only half a block from the city's downtown diamond. Locals remember it as the Supreme Diner.

A more stunning surprise is the Cloister Diner on U.S. Route 322 at the west edge of Ephrata. Cloaked within a brick facade and cedar shake mansard roof is a 1950 Silk City with a barreled, yellow porcelain-enameled ceiling and a brilliant blue tile wall and counter base set off with a diamond-pattern strip.

BRIAN BUTKO

Though Ephrata's Cloister Diner has been remodeled outside, the 1950 Silk City interior is mostly intact.

Most Dutch Country diners date to the postwar diner boom or later, and their locations were largely dictated by the automobile as influenced by long-distance travel or suburbanization. The region became the western gateway to an emerging megalopolis. The Lincoln Highway through Lancaster was a conduit for cars and trucks in and out of Philadelphia, and the William Penn Highway, which originally followed an alignment from Easton through Allentown to Reading, Lebanon, and Harrisburg, became the main road between New York City and points west.

By the 1930s, the William Penn Highway, as U.S. Route 22, had been realigned along a more direct route between Allentown and Harrisburg, while the old route was marked as parts of U.S. Routes 222 and 422. Roadside diners abounded, favoring edge-of-town locations to catch the incoming travelers while also being convenient for the local trade. In addition, edge-of-town sites provided access to utilities and municipal services not otherwise found at more isolated locations. Currently, half of all the diners in this region have an edge-of-town location in thirty different Dutch Country communities. Lebanon, for example, has three diners—the Eat Well, Mel's, and D'Alexander's—guarding the gates of town, and it's virtually impossible to enter Allentown over any main road without passing a diner.

The highways also made it easy to deliver diners by truck from North Jersey manufacturers. This is probably why Pennsylvania Dutch Country has

RICHARD J. S. GUTMAN

Barney's Diner, at left, a circa 1950 Silk City, once graced 606 State Street in Emmaus. The 1955 Silk City (#5563), at right, was grafted on in 1961, and the whole thing was bricked over in 1975.

such a high concentration of the Paterson Vehicle Company's Silk City diners. Although this is decidedly the most popular diner make in the state, accounting for 16 percent of all diners whose manufacturers are known, Silk Citys make up 28 percent of known Dutch Country diners, more than twice the number of the next most popular brand.

Today, as jobs are decentralized to the western suburbs of New York and Philadelphia, commuters and urban residents want to live farther out in Pennsylvania where the perceived quality of life is better and less expensive. Pennsylvania Dutch farms are now sprouting housing developments for transplanted suburbanites. Originally the gateway to megalopolis, Pennsylvania Dutch Country is becoming the western extension of megalopolis, and this has influenced the distribution and architectural style of diners in the region.

In general, diner numbers increase with population density and proximity to New Jersey manufacturers. At the same time, successful metropolitan diners are more likely to remodel sooner. New Jersey has the greatest concentration of diners, but most of them have been remodeled to project the last dominant style trend—the environmental. These same characteristics spill into the adjacent Pennsylvania Dutch Country, where a recognizable pattern exists among diner densities, styles, and locations.

Mirroring population density, diner density is greatest in the Allentown-Bethlehem-Easton metropolitan area and decreases to the west. At least 46 percent of all Dutch Country diners are in the region's two easternmost counties—those closest to New Jersey—and 75 percent of all Dutch Country diners were either built in the environmental style or remodeled along those lines, having been bricked up, stoned over, or stuccoed, and perhaps given a mansard roof. The percentage of environmentally remodeled diners, however, like diner and population densities, decreases toward the more rural west.

It's not surprising that Easton, near the New Jersey border, has welcomed a steady stream of diners. The Palace Lunch and Club Diner are seen in 1920s O'Mahony ads. The 1930 city directory lists Nick's Lunch Wagon at 306 South Main Street. The 1941 directory lists Walt's Diner, a newly refurbished Silk City, and the Wilson Diner. The Wilson, on Route 22, was a 1941 National run by Al Hook, who later opened Hook's Diner in Allentown. Seven diners were listed by 1957.

> ## DINERS ONLINE
>
> The Internet is full of diner-themed sites of varying degrees of quality and accuracy. Far above the rest is Roadside Online, at <www.roadsidemagazine.com>, a companion to Randy Garbin's *Roadside Magazine*, with news updates every couple of days.
>
> Tops for diner locations and identification is Ron Saari's Diner City, at <www.dinercity.com>. This site offers photos grouped by state and identified by type and address.
>
> The most entertaining is The Diner Page, run by Dave Goldberg, at <www.astro.princeton.edu/~goldberg/diner.html>, where surfers will find colorful descriptions of several dozen Pennsylvania diners.

Lehigh and Northampton Counties have twenty-two restaurants known to have been classic stainless steel diners from the forties to sixties. Only six of these are pristine or lightly remodeled. (A light environmental remodel might include a mansard roof or a new vestibule, but all or nearly all of the exterior stainless facade would have to be visible.) The rest have been heavily remodeled or environmentalized beyond recognition. Immediately to the west, Berks County has fourteen such diners, with only two in near-pristine condition. But in Lancaster County, five of the nine classic diners are in near-original shape. The most rural and remote western county, Lebanon, has only five classic diners but every one is near pristine.

Ironically, Dutch Country's oldest near-pristine diner is also one of its newest. Espresso Café, a 1939 monitor roof Kullman, was recently brought from Florida to serve Adams Antique Mall just south of Adamstown. North on Route 272, the Adamstown Diner retains a hint of streamline moderne in its vertical, red porcelain panels and half-moon end windows. It was Mom's Diner until 1997; the interior has since been redone with new booths, stools, counter, ceiling, and mirrors in place of the menu boards, all topped by a neon strip.

KYLE WEAVER

Jennie's Diner, a 1959 Silk City in Ronks, is usually packed with a mix of tourists, truckers, and locals.

In Allentown, a 1947 Paramount, which was originally Hook's Diner, survives as a dining room in Saylor's Restaurant at 19th Street and Tilghman Street. The only other minimally altered Dutch diner of this age is Heisey's, located north of Lebanon on Route 72. Except for the brick vestibule and red-trimmed white awning, this red and stainless, late-forties O'Mahony with muted monitor roof is a dead ringer for Bob's Diner in Philadelphia.

The region's best examples of modern stainless steel diners from the fifties are in Lancaster and Lebanon Counties. The Neptune Diner, at the northern edge of Lancaster at North Prince Street and 9th Street, is a resurrection of the old Deluxe Diner, which sat idle for a number of years. The stainless steel and red-trimmed Neptune could have come right from the pages of a midcentury issue of *Diner* magazine: With its squared-off eaves and cowcatcher corners, it's a textbook example of a Mountain View diner during that company's most distinctive years. Inside are a beige, octagonal-pattern tile floor and a cream-colored tile wall and counter base highlighted with a strip of maroon. The simplistic interior is centered on the symmetrically split counter, and booths wrap around the windowed periphery. Also on North Prince Street, Clark's Diner served the 100 block from 1955 until closing in 1979; three years later, the Silk City was hauled to U.S. Wrecking, where it still rests.

Some 10 miles east, Jennie's Diner is every bit as much a pristine example of a 1950s Silk City as the Neptune, set back from busy Route 30 behind an ancient vertical neon. The scene is made complete by the trucks inevitably lined up behind the classic red-trimmed diner. The ensemble is that much more amazing, considering that it sits at the eastern edge of Lancaster's famed Lincoln Highway East. This tourist strip, one of the state's premier vacation destinations, is dotted with Pennsylvania Dutch–themed attractions, though in recent years these have been dwindling, giving way to outlet shopping centers. Jennie McElrath, who's owned the diner since 1981, features a lot of Dutch cooking. Almost right across the road for years was Hart's U.S. 30 Diner. A slightly smaller 1954 Silk City, the now-closed Lehigh Pizza, sits in blue-trimmed splendor at the edge of the South Bethlehem business district.

Other noteworthy Dutch delights from the fifties include the Clearview and Mel's. The Clearview Diner, on Route 230 between Mount Joy and Elizabethtown, was bought and lightly restored by Adam Kontis in late 1998. Originally a 1948 Paramount, the diner was enlarged and updated in 1954. Mel's Diner on U.S. Route 422 at the eastern edge of Lebanon has been expanded and remodeled, but it retains much of its integrity as a finely crafted O'Mahony, with a quilted stainless exterior and rare X panels above

WINTERS HERITAGE HOUSE MUSEUM

Elizabethtown's 1945 flood relocated Baker's Diner, floating it across Market Street. This was originally the first Kuppy's Diner, from Middletown, which was later moved to Elizabethtown. The 1933 Ward & Dickinson, with matching kitchen behind, crashed into a garage, dangerously close to the bank of Conoy Creek.

the side doors. Along with the Adamstown Diner, Mel's has the distinction of being one of two Dutch diners with vertically fluted porcelain-enameled panels on the facade (in this case, tan). Mel's is still heralded by a neon wrap-around arrow sign, a one-time staple of the American roadside that is rapidly disappearing.

Nearly half of the state's minimally altered exaggerated modern diners are in the Dutch Country region, with most others in Metro Philadelphia. This style was defined by two manufacturers: Kullman in the late fifties, and DeRaffele in the early sixties.

Although capped by a dowdy mansard from the 1970s, the Eat Well Diner in Lebanon is a good example of a stock model Kullman of the period. The exterior stainless has lengthwise strips of blue porcelain enamel, and rounded corners are accentuated by vertical stainless and enamel strips. The canted plate-glass front wraps around the corner in an exaggerated example of a detail pioneered by modern architects of the Bauhaus in the early twentieth century. The Starlite Restaurant in Fogelsville and the Tic Toc on the western edge of Easton are two more environmentally suppressed Kullmans of this type.

DeRaffele advanced the style another notch with a stunning design that was almost entirely window. Few diners express this better than the Tom Sawyer, on U.S. Route 222 in the Allentown suburb of Wescoesville. Its broad, flared-eave roof appears to float over the low stainless steel and two-strip porcelain base, especially at night, when the restaurant is brilliantly lit from within and by recessed lights in the eaves. Abandoning the last remnant of streamline modernity, DeRaffele corner windows of the early sixties were not rounded, but met at right angles. The Kumm Esse Diner, with the exception of its newer brick vestibule, oddly set toward the corner, is a twin to the Tom Sawyer.

DeRaffele's way of adapting this type of diner to the confines of an urban neighborhood is found in downtown Allentown. Here, the Silver Star Diner was shoehorned between a church and the corner of 9th Street and Linden Street by relocating the vestibule to the short end of the building. The L-shaped interior is long on the 9th Street side.

Although less flamboyant than the DeRaffeles, Fodero also produced exaggerated modern diners in the late fifties and early sixties. A characteristic example is the Hamilton Family Restaurant at Hamilton Street and St. Elmo Street in Allentown. Trimmed in gold enamel, the diner has a huge visual front and squat stainless base, but more sedate lines and few canted elements. The windows are larger and the eave line thinner than the 1956 Fodero operating in Thorndale as the Ingleside, but the L-shaped floorplan is the same: corner entrance, long side to the left ending in a small dining room, short side to the right, mostly triple rows of booths.

Out on the west edge of Lebanon, D'Alexander's Diner is another 1960 Fodero, this one still with its original corner vestibule and a lighted sputnik sign. The diner was established by Ed Pushnik, whose name still appears in the terrazzo floor. The back wall is made of small ceramic tiles, representing a search for new materials, and the associated shift away from stainless that was just beginning at this time. The transition is that much more apparent in the West Reading Diner from the mid-1960s where the exterior stainless is reduced to trim highlighting a facade of small gray and white tiles. By the time Allentown's Queen City Diner was built at the end of the decade, the large windows and small base were still evident, but the stainless was gone. Gone too was the modern architect's fascination with corner windows.

BRIAN BUTKO

D'Alexander's Diner, a 1960 Fodero, formerly called Pushnik's, is an institution in Lebanon.

The most unique transition diner in the state is Allentown's Golden Gate. This rare Manno, one of two in the state, is a wild blend of virtually every material used in the sixties. The base and corner posts are covered with gray formstone, the large windows are separated by stainless vertical supports, and the windowsills, brows, and roof line are enamel panels in orange and turquoise. Borrowing from its competitors, the color scheme is that of an early 1960s burger chain, and the zigzag, folded-plate roof—apparent in the undulations of the ceiling—mimics contemporary coffee shops. Rimming the top of the diner is a white, fencelike balustrade that adds a touch of quaintness while partially obscuring rooftop utilities—the precursor to the mansard.

The Dutch Country has dozens of environmental-style diners, but only a few Mediterranean modern diners. The Trivet Diner on Tilghman Street at the west edge of Allentown is a 1980s DeRaffele version of the Mediterranean theme. By the mid-1970s, the diner-hiding environmental style had been perfected to the point that it was hard to tell factory-made diners from on-site restaurants, and with the many establishments that continue in this style, it's still hard.

KEVIN PATRICK

Golden Gate Diner, a 1964 Manno in Allentown.

Although wall-mounted coach lamps abound, the Dutch Country has few colonial diners. The best examples are probably Schmeck's Family Restaurant on Route 61 south of Hamburg and a 1981 Swingle operating as the Deluxe Restaurant in Shillington.

What is peculiar to Dutch Country, however, is the inordinate number of red mansard diners. These have either brick or stucco facades and are capped with low mansard roofs colored red to reddish brown. Largely nonexistent in other parts of the state, there are eight of them around Allentown and Reading. All of these diners are 1970s and 1980s remodelings that cloak the original structures. Some are clearly disguised diners, like Miller's Diner in Northampton, Berk's Family Restaurant at the edge of Leesport, and the Stadium Restaurant in Reading, all of which are mid-fifties Silk Cities. Others are not diners in the factory-built sense of the word. The Pantry Diner in Allentown is a converted hot-dog stand, and the Bear Swamp Diner in Macungie was a gas station a decade ago. Apparently the selling feature of such a remodeling is that it can make any building— diner or otherwise—look like a typical Dutch Country restaurant. With such a large number of red mansard diners out there, they have defined the look for restaurants of this type in the eastern Dutch Country.

Today, stainless, neon, and tile are back, but not in the way they were used in the past, regardless of how much fifties bric-a-brac has been stuffed into the place to give it ambience. Allentown's Poodle Skirt Diner, a 1956

Silk City stuccoed over in the 1970s, now has a black, white, and gray facade with an inverted, reflective-black mansard and the obligatory black-and-white checkered stripe. The design, however, has more in common with 1990s late modernism than with 1950s modernism.

Allentown's Sunrise Diner underwent renovation in fall 1998. Yet another early 1960s DeRaffele, the Sunrise had a stone-faced vestibule and red mansard added in the 1970s. It's now a postmodern retro diner with a heavy, stainless-trimmed red roof, and a black and white vestibule with glass-block lights. The original stainless and porcelain enamel base was covered in the remodeling. It's ironic that a retro-diner look based on mythologized fifties architecture would replace the Sunrise's *real* vintage diner appearance. Such is the nature of postmodern remodelings, further emphasizing that these are not diner re-creations, and definitely not restorations, but a completely new style.

Similar materials were used in the 1991 remodeling of Allentown's New City View Diner, which combined architectural elements from a number of different diners. This huge, exaggerated modern 1960 DeRaffele, once part of the Dempsey's Diner chain, now resembles a *Star Wars* spaceport, with its stainless trim and black reflective panels. The diner has a titanic, atriumlike vestibule flanked by monumental piers decorated with glass block, arranged as stylized art deco pylons suggestive of two rocket ships. Its bowed-out design, formed by an outward-canted base and inward-slanting windows, was actually borrowed from a newer DeRaffele operating as the Thruway Diner in New York.

In 1990, DeRaffele replaced Manheim's Lyndon Diner, an early 1960s Silk City, with a late-modern diner of mixed materials and abstract design. Seven years later, DeRaffele was back in Dutch Country to convert an old

COLLECTION OF BRIAN BUTKO

Gelbach's Diner (1954 Silk City #5432) as it looked before it was remodeled into the Stadium Restaurant in Reading.

RICHARD J. S. GUTMAN

KEVIN PATRICK

KEVIN PATRICK

Top: A study in renovation: The original B&G Diner, a 1956 Silk City in Allentown. Middle: The diner, shown here in 1989, was environmentalized and renamed the Master Chef. Bottom: The diner today as the Poodle Skirt, a postmodern nod to its fifties roots.

KEVIN PATRICK

Above: Dempsey's Diner was a pristine 1960 DeRaffele on MacArthur Road in Whitehall Township, north of Allentown. Below: The same diner was recently redone as the New City View Diner.

KEVIN PATRICK

Elby's Big Boy Restaurant off the Lancaster bypass into a chrome-covered retro diner, the Lyndon City Line Diner. There's no question that DeRaffele has positioned itself on the cutting edge of diner styles, turning out flamboyant diners for the 1990s with the same passion for flair as in the early 1960s.

The Silk City Diner in Stevens, just south of turnpike exit 21, has been remodeled so that the original car, the former Dutchman's Diner, is now a dining room, with booths and counter in a new annex. Although the 9th

The 9th and Marion Diner, a 1958 Silk City in Reading, was once covered over with environmental materials but has been lovingly restored.

and Marion Diner in Reading, originally the Evergreen Diner, retained its beautiful green and yellow arched Formica ceiling, the outside was covered over for years. Now, however, it has been restored to its original appearance.

DINER DRIVES

D utch Country Diner Drives follow the old main roads that led westward from New York City and Philadelphia long before the interstates. The William Penn and Lincoln Highways not only were Pennsylvania's most important cross-state links, they also were the gateway highways tying the country's East Coast port cities to the rest of the nation. Only the Cherry Turnpike across upstate New York and the National Road west from Baltimore carried comparable amounts of prewar transAppalachian traffic.

The diner route lies well off today's main lines of travel—I-78 and the Pennsylvania Turnpike—but it is remarkably close to the through lines of the railroad era. Diners were first brought to Dutch Country cities by railroad, carried on the Lehigh Valley Railroad to Allentown; the Reading Railroad through the Lehigh, Schuylkill, and Lebanon Valleys; and the Pennsylvania

LEHIGH & NORTHAMPTON DINERS

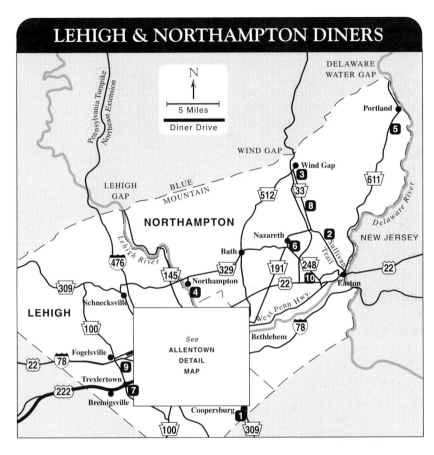

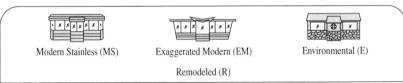

Modern Stainless (MS)   Exaggerated Modern (EM)   Environmental (E)

Remodeled (R)

1 Coopersburg Diner: Coopersburg (R)   6 Nazareth Diner: Nazareth (E)
2 Forks Diner: Easton (R)   7 New Pied Piper Diner-Restaurant: Trexlertown (E)
3 Gap Diner: Wind Gap (R)   8 Sullivan Trail Diner: Nazareth (R)
4 Miller's Diner: Northampton (R)   9 Starlite Restaurant: Fogelsville (R)
5 Mount Bethel Diner: Mount Bethel (E)   10 Tic Toc Restaurant: Easton (R)

Railroad across Lancaster County from Philadelphia. Automobile highways originally served the same cities built by the railroads, and early motorists—and the roadside diners being set in place to serve them—were rarely out of earshot of the railroad whistle.

Now the railroads are virtually ignored by the traveling public, and the main roads have been renumbered and relocated. The distribution of diners, however, still conforms to the nearly forgotten original alignments of the William Penn and Lincoln Highways, along which nearly one-third of the region's diners still operate. Federal trunk highways 22 and 30 superseded the Penn and Lincoln Highways in the 1920s. By 1940, a network of branch highways, marked with three-digit route numbers ending in 22 or 30, such as U.S. Routes 122 (now State Route 61/10), 222, 322, 422, and 230, crisscrossed the Dutch Country. Within a day's delivery of New York–area manufacturers, diners were rolled out along these expanding rivers of asphalt and concrete. These first diners established a pattern carried on by successive generations, so that now 60 percent of all Dutch Country diners are operating along roads that have, or once had, numbers ending in 22 or 30.

TILGHMAN STREET–UNION BOULEVARD (OLD U.S. ROUTE 22)

Allentown is the first place of any consequence west of New York that lies beyond the industrial satellite cities of North Jersey. In many ways, the city has acted as a western outpost of a New York–centered megalopolis—from the silk industry that decentralized to Allentown in the nineteenth century, to the current in-migration of New York–area businesses and suburbanites, to the Dutch Country–bound buses that leave the Port Authority each day. The connection undoubtedly applies to diners as well.

There are fourteen diners within the Allentown city limits and eight more in the immediate suburbs. No other Pennsylvania city outside Philadelphia has more. Expectedly, the state's most diner-filled Diner Drive is here. Eight diners—nearly one per mile—line Tilghman Street–Union Boulevard, a commercial arterial that cuts across the north side of Allentown from Bethlehem to Kuhnsville. This was a result of a unique alignment of diner history and geography.

Following an established practice for early automobile roads, the original William Penn Highway was routed through the downtowns of Easton, Bethlehem, and Allentown. It then angled along the southern margin of the Lehigh and Lebanon Valleys, through downtown Reading and Lebanon to Harrisburg, an alignment eventually marked as parts of U.S. Routes 222 and 422. As traffic increased during the 1920s, this route through the cities of the Pennsylvania Dutch Country became a traffic nightmare, hardly appropriate for a major trunk route serving the nation's largest city. Access to New York was improved during the early 1930s, when the Penn Highway (U.S. Route 22) was rebuilt along the north side of the valley between Harrisburg and Allentown, passing through little more than rural farmland and cross-

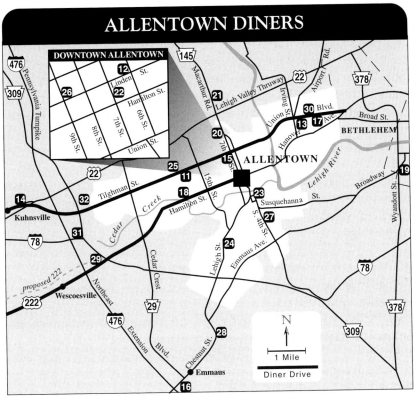

ALLENTOWN DINERS

11 Charcoal Restaurant: Allentown (R)

12 City Center Diner: Allentown (MS)

13 Chris's Family Restaurant (Union Blvd.): Allentown (R)

14 Chris's Family Restaurant (Tilghman St.): Allentown (E)

15 Dina's Diner: Allentown (R)

16 Emmaus Diner: Emmaus (R)

17 Golden Gate Diner: Allentown (EM)

18 Hamilton Family Restaurant: Allentown (EM)

19 Lehigh Pizza: Bethlehem (MS)

20 Lehigh Valley Diner: Whitehall (R)

21 New City View Diner: Whitehall (R)

22 Paul's Gyro Restaurant: Allentown (R)

23 Poodle Skirt Diner: Allentown (R)

24 Queen City Diner: Allentown (E)

25 Saylor's Restaurant: Allentown (MS)

26 Silver Star Diner: Allentown (EM)

27 Sunrise Diner: Allentown (R)

28 Superior Diner: Emmaus (R)

29 Tom Sawyer Diner: Allentown (EM)

30 Top Diner: Allentown (R)

31 Trivet Diner: Allentown (E)

32 Trivet Family Restaurant: Breinigsville (E)

road hamlets. In Allentown, the realignment took through traffic off busy downtown Hamilton Street and put it four blocks to the north on Tilghman Street—called Union Boulevard east of the Lehigh River—effectively creating an early bypass.

From the 1930s to the 1950s, Tilghman-Union developed into Allentown's premier automobile row, serving long-distance travelers and locals alike in an environment as much shaped by vehicular traffic as the older downtown was shaped by pedestrian and rail-based traffic. This period of development coincided not only with the diner's golden age, but also with the New York–area diner manufacturers' expansion into the Pennsylvania market. What better place to sell diners than on a vibrantly expanding commercial strip in an industrial city within a day's delivery of the factory gate?

In the 1950s, U.S. Route 22 was relocated yet again, this time to the limited-access Lehigh Valley Thruway built around the city to the north. Within a few years of the thruway's completion, the City View Diner opened just north of the MacArthur Road interchange on Allentown's main north-south arterial. Tilghman-Union's halcyon days had passed, but not before the route was established as the city's main Diner Drive, a tradition that continues today. The Tilghman-Union diner lineup includes three Silk Citys, a DeRaffele, a Swingle, an O'Mahony-Fodero graft, a Manno, and a Paramount. Owing to the prosperity of the strip—and possibly the proximity of New Jersey—all but one have styles established after 1965.

The Top Diner is three blocks west on Union Boulevard from the Golden Gate's Manno-made zigzag roof. The Top has been environmentalized, with the obligatory mansard roof and a stone facade that covers a side door still partially visible in the window frame above the masonry. Inside, the Top reveals its true identity as a rare double-wide 1953 Silk City.

A block west, Chris's Family Restaurant is also covered by stone, but through the remodeling, it's possible to detect a 1955 O'Mahony with a more recent Fodero dining room grafted onto its eastern end. Long known as Anderson's, the diner was bought by Chris Kirkopoulos and updated with neon trim and a black-and-white-checked backwall. Chris's is a familiar story: He once owned the Peter Pan Diner in Kuhnsville on the suburban western end of Tilghman Street. In 1989, he sold that 1958 Mountain View to an operator who moved it to Falmouth, Massachusetts, and he traded up to a used but larger, stone-faced Swingle, the former Pot O Gold from Hamburg. He named the new place Chris's Family Restaurant, adding a second Chris's to his two-unit Tilghman-Union chain when he bought Anderson's.

The busy Union and Irving Street intersection was once graced by one of Pennsylvania's most noteworthy diners, the Penn State Flyer, a yellow, double-ended Sterling Streamliner built by the J. B. Judkins Company in 1941. Many Streamliners were designed with a rounded bullet-shaped profile on one end, but the Penn State Flyer was streamlined on both ends. It operated during Tilghman-Union's diner heyday but was moved to Scranton in 1956 soon after the opening of the Lehigh Valley Thruway.

KEVIN PATRICK

The former Anderson's Diner, Chris's Family Restaurant in Allentown has had its exterior stainless partially covered.

Two more environmentalized Silk Cities operate on the Tilghman Street end of the city. The formstone and stucco Dina's Diner functions in the row home–crowded 700 block, and the stone-faced and mansard roofed Charcoal Restaurant operates at 18th Street. The Charcoal's large, neon boomerang sign provides a hint of what Tilghman Street looked like in the old days. Just a block away, at 19th and Tilghman, is the oldest extant diner on the strip, a 1948 Paramount absorbed into Saylor's Restaurant.

The two newest Tilghman-Union diners operate beyond the city limits to the west, both near the tangle of on- and off-ramps from I-78, I-476 (the Pennsylvania Turnpike's Northeast Extension), U.S. Route 22, and Route 309. Besides Chris's, there is the Mediterranean modern Trivet Diner, a 1980s DeRaffele operating as one of yet another two-unit diner chain, the second of which is in Breinigsville.

As America started replacing its aging federal highway system with limited-access interstates, the golden age of the diner gradually faded into the diner dark ages. The opportunity to spread diners to the new roadside service nodes clustering around interstate interchanges was lost to the fast-food franchises. Because of the early construction date of the Lehigh Valley Thruway, however, the Allentown area holds the distinction of being one of the few places where diners did diffuse to expressway exit ramps. Hungry motorists battling traffic-choked U.S. Route 22 can exit for diners at five different locations: Northampton Road in Easton for the Tic Toc Restaurant, Airport Road for the on-site-built Bethlehem Diner, MacArthur Road for the New City View and Lehigh Valley, Kuhnsville for Chris's, and Fogelsville for the Starlite Diner. Farther west, at Hamburg, the rusting tower sign of the old Pot O Gold Diner still looms over the Route 61 interchange where the diner sat until it was moved to Allentown. And halfway to Harrisburg, Trainer's long-established Midway Diner still beckons U.S. Route 22/I-78 travelers at the Bethel exit with its original neon sign, but the building now bears more resemblance to a house than to a diner.

U.S. ROUTE 222

U.S. Route 222 strikes right through the heart of Pennsylvania Dutch Country, stretching from Allentown through Reading to Lancaster. The road provides a veritable cross section of the region, bounded by office parks and new suburban subdivisions in the Lehigh Valley, operating as an unplanned commercial strip on the fringes of Reading, slowing to the trot of a horse-drawn Amish buggy in the farmlands of Lancaster County, and functioning as a spine for the region's tourist attractions and antiques malls. It also strings together a reasonable cross section of Dutch Country diners.

With fifteen diners scattered along 75 miles of highway, the diner density averages one for every 5 miles. As in the region as a whole, about half of these have an environmental style. Six are heavily environmentalized, and two are modern stainless diners capped with mansard roofs but with facades less severely remodeled. Three other modern stainless diners are in near-pristine condition, as are three exaggerated modern diners. One diner was recently remodeled in late-modern or postmodern style. Even the diner manufacturers represented on U.S. Route 222 reflect the general pattern found in the Dutch Country as a whole, with four DeRaffeles and three Silk Cities, followed by two Kullmans, two Foderos, a Mountain View, and a Swingle.

The northern end of U.S. Route 222 is right in downtown Allentown, where southbound motorists first drive west on Linden Street, then bounce over to Hamilton Street, passing three diners before crossing the city limits. The first is an idle 1953 Kullman at 6th Street and Linden Street that was capped with a mansard roof in the 1970s and last saw action as the Center City Diner. Right around the corner, on 7th Street, is a barrel roof diner disguised as Paul's Gyro Restaurant. Farther west on Linden, at 8th Street, is the Silver Star, a 1960 DeRaffele with broad, flared eaves and a four-petal floral pattern in its terrazzo floor. This is the first of three exceptional exaggerated modern diners from the early sixties that line U.S. Route 222 one after the other. The Hamilton Family Restaurant is next at Hamilton Street and St. Elmo Street. This corner-entrance, gold and stainless 1959 Fodero recently added on a giant postmodern vestibule across which "Ham-Fam" is written in neon cursive. Beyond Dorney Park, in suburban Wescosville, is the Tom Sawyer, a stunning 1962 DeRaffele in mint condition, with a colorful, metal box sign depicting a neon-trimmed Tom toting a fishing pole in the wake of a giant flashing arrow. Now that's exaggerated modern, probably the best example in the state. Unfortunately, the ensemble is threatened by possible destruction due to the proposed construction of a U.S. Route 222 bypass from I-78 to the west side of Trexlertown.

The whole west end of Allentown Dinerdom is filled with DeRaffeles, including the 1987 New Pied Piper Diner-Restaurant in Trexlertown and the Breinigsville Trivet. The muted environmental exterior of these two diners contrasts with the exuberantly flashy DeRaffeles of a few decades ago and a few miles back down the highway. Nonetheless, they are representative of what DeRaffele was building toward the end of the environmental period. It is immediately apparent that, unlike environmental remodels, these diners were designed and built as complete packages to look and function as modern restaurants defined by the prevailing standards of the 1970s and 1980s. If the buildings are left unaltered, diner fans of the future will be clamoring to preserve them as those today struggle to save a 1950s stainless steel Silk City or Kullman.

Breinigsville's large, L-shaped Trivet sits on a patch of land between two generations of U.S. Route 222. The old road goes through the hamlet, and the new road curves around it. The Trivet is part of a small chain that began in 1967 in an old restaurant on Chestnut Street in Emmaus. About ten years later, the restaurant was bought by three Greek partners, who, through hard work and perseverance, came to own two additional Trivets, contracting with DeRaffele to build both. The Breinigsville restaurant was built in the environmental style, and the newer place on Tilghman Street was built with a Mediterranean influence.

Beyond the suburbs of Allentown, the DeRaffele is replaced by the Silk City. There are at least four Silk Citys on or just off U.S. Route 222 between Breinigsville and Reading. Kutztown's Airport Diner has operated adjacent to a small airfield on the west edge of town since 1960. Although recently remodeled with an enlarged dining room, a stone vestibule, and a mansard roof trimmed in pink neon, still visible is the zigzag exterior stainless, a 1960s Silk City feature. Inside, the decor is largely original, including a bluish terrazzo floor with large white diamonds; light blue, gold-veined counter and tabletops; and a stainless backwall machined with the same zigzag pattern as on the exterior.

Temple's 5th Street Diner, like the diners on adjacent Pottsville Pike (Route 61), was environmentalized years ago. This late 1950s Silk City is similar in age and model to the nearby 9th & Marion Diner, which had its 1970s remodeling stripped away to reveal the original stainless exterior. With the 1950s retro look superseding the earth tones of environmentalism, many diner owners can bring their diners up-to-date simply by removing the remodeling to expose their diners' original facades. Unfortunately the 5th Street Diner's stainless steel was destroyed during the remodeling. The current owner, however, plans to refashion it in retro style.

On the other side of Reading, U.S. Route 222 passes the Deluxe Restaurant that Swingle built adjacent to the Shillington Days Inn. A few miles farther down the road is the diminutive Two Guys Diner, a 1930s Silk City encased in yellow siding and heavy mansard roof.

Upon entering Lancaster County, U.S. Route 222 broadens into a limited-access expressway. The old road, renumbered Route 272, passes through a fifty-year-old commercial landscape initiated by the opening of the Pennsylvania Turnpike's Reading-Lancaster Interchange (#21) in 1950. The turnpike is the original American superhighway, the granddaddy of them all. When its Philadelphia Extension sliced through the farmland of southeastern Pennsylvania, the region was in the midst of a diner boom. Naturally, a few gravitated toward the promise of profits at the end of the new road's exit ramps. Four diners are still operating along Route 272 within five miles of the interchange, each a time capsule of diner activity tied to the turnpike.

Before the turnpike arrived, there was the Adamstown Diner. This modern dining car represents a time when the only road through the dairy farms was a two-lane Route 222, when motorist services clung to the edge of the occasional town, and when diners were synonymous with stainless. Closer to the interchange, Zinn's Diner was one of the first establishments in a turnpike town of gas stations, motels, and restaurants that sprouted up around the interchange in the 1950s. Standing at the threshold of the Dutch Country tourist landscape, Zinn's prospered, and it expanded its operation in the 1970s with Fodero dining-room sections and an environmental facade.

The turnpike brings tourists, and the tourists bring money that supports roadside businesses, which attempt to attract the tourists by maintaining updated styles. This is particularly true at such competitive interchanges as this one, where the Silk City Diner envelops a reworked 1957 Silk City within a larger postmodern shell, complete with new neon sign and black-and-white-checkered tile floor. The newest interchange diner is the 1939 Kullman brought to the Adams Antique Mall, embodying the characteristics of our burgeoning postmodern economy of nostalgia and heritage preservation.

At the end of the U.S. Route 222 Diner Drive is the Neptune Diner, on the north end of Lancaster's Prince Street. This recently reopened and little-changed Mountain View was laid on its foundation in 1951 at a site that took advantage of Lancaster traffic coming in on four different radial roads from the north, as well as foot traffic from the nearby railroad station.

U.S. ROUTE 422

U.S. Route 422 evolved as the alternate route to Harrisburg. From Philadelphia, most travelers historically went by way of Lancaster, and now they use the turnpike. You can still take U.S. Route 422, but no one does. West of Reading, it was the original alignment of the William Penn Highway, abandoned in the early 1930s for a shorter

Pennsylvania Dutchmen are common motifs for diners and other establishments in and around Lancaster County. This is the original Amos at Zinn's Diner in Denver.

route to the north. It was later christened the Benjamin Franklin Highway, though few call it that. It's just 422. Although weak as a long-distance link, it is hardly devoid of traffic. Quite the opposite. It is the regional main street carrying virtually all the local cars and delivery trucks that ply the road from Pottstown to Reading, from Reading to Lebanon, and from Lebanon to Harrisburg. As such, there are plenty of motorists out there to pull off the road for breakfast and lunch, but only the larger communities can support a twenty-four-hour operation. Owing to this type of roadside geography, six out of seven diners are located at the edges of towns.

In 40 miles of highway, there are nine diners, putting the diners at about one for every four miles. Nearly every one reflects an exaggerated modern style in some way, as if the diner wave didn't get to Route 422 until about 1960 and then never came back. Some have been remodeled, but in most cases, their original form shows through.

Just over the Berks County line from Pottstown is Michael's Restaurant. For westbound traffic, it sits at the end of a four-lane expressway at the first traffic light in 25 miles. That's not bad for business, and possibly it has influenced its three-generation appearance. The core of Michael's is an early 1960s

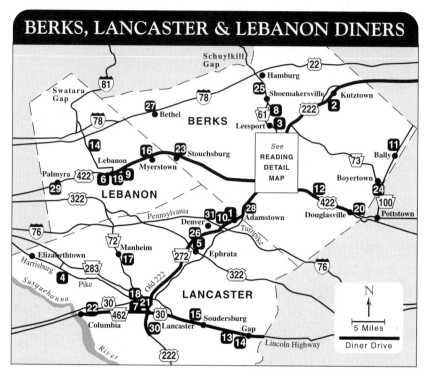

BERKS, LANCASTER & LEBANON DINERS

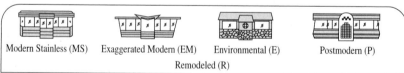

Modern Stainless (MS)   Exaggerated Modern (EM)   Environmental (E)   Postmodern (P)

Remodeled (R)

1 Adamstown Diner: Adamstown (MS)

2 Airport Diner: Kutztown (R)

3 Berk's Family Restaurant: Leesport (R)

4 Clearview Diner: Elizabethtown (MS)

5 Cloister Diner: Ephrata (R)

6 D'Alexander's Diner: Lebanon (EM)

7 Dempsey's American Kitchen: Lancaster (R)

8 Dutch Valley Diner: Shoemakersville (R)

9 Eat Well Diner: Lebanon (EM)

10 Espresso Café at Adams Antiques:
   Denver (MS)

11 Family Restaurant and Diner: Bally (R)

12 Fegely's Restaurant: Birdsboro (R)

13 Gap Diner: Gap (R)

14 Heisey's Diner: Lebanon (MS)

15 Jennie's Diner: Ronks (MS)

16 Kumm Esse Diner: Myerstown (EM)

17 Lyndon Diner: Manheim (R)

18 Lyndon City Line Diner: Lancaster (P)

19 Mel's Diner: Lebanon (MS)

20 Michael's Restaurant: Douglassville (R)

21 Neptune Diner: Lancaster (MS)

22 Prospect Diner: Columbia (EM)

23 Risser's Diner: Stouchsburg (R)

24 Saville's Diner: Boyertown (R)

25 Schmeck's Family Restaurant: Hamburg (E)

26 Silk City Diner: Stevens (R)

27 Trainer's Midway Diner: Bethel (R)

28 Two Guys Diner: Adamstown (R)

29 Weiland's Flowers: Palmyra (R)

30 Willow Street Restaurant: Willow Street (R)

31 Zinn's Diner: Denver (E)

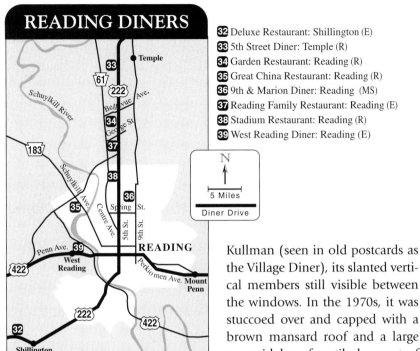

READING DINERS

32 Deluxe Restaurant: Shillington (E)
33 5th Street Diner: Temple (R)
34 Garden Restaurant: Reading (R)
35 Great China Restaurant: Reading (R)
36 9th & Marion Diner: Reading (MS)
37 Reading Family Restaurant: Reading (E)
38 Stadium Restaurant: Reading (R)
39 West Reading Diner: Reading (E)

Kullman (seen in old postcards as the Village Diner), its slanted vertical members still visible between the windows. In the 1970s, it was stuccoed over and capped with a brown mansard roof and a large pyramidal roof vestibule, most of which is still visible behind a new postmodern fascia trimmed by a rounded, underlit awning. Most architects would probably say that these superficial details hardly constitute postmodern architecture, but remember that this is the commercial roadside, where the point is not architectural purity, but rather to project a sense of being up-to-date to speeding motorists. Just east of Reading, near Birdsboro, is the remodeled Fegely's Restaurant. Inside is a classic 1930s dining car.

The next stop is the West Reading Diner, an edge-of-business-district diner. It's located one lot from a gas station–cornered intersection in the inner suburban borough of West Reading, just over the Schuylkill River from the city of Reading. The diner's setup is reminiscent of those in Philadelphia, and the nature of the diner conforms perfectly, right down to sitting sideways on the lot flush against the sidewalk. This twenty-four-hour diner is thought to be a transitional DeRaffele from the mid-1960s, although some have suggested that it may have been built by Superior, a short-lived company. It has flared eaves, recessed lighting, a large visual front, copious amounts of chrome—the whole bit. But about a third of the exterior surface area is covered with white and gray ceramic tile panels. Nailed to the facade is an array of coach lamps, a hallmark of the trend toward environmentalism.

KEVIN PATRICK

You can tell from this sign—shown here in 1989, but now gone—that Risser's Diner on Route 422, Stouchsburg, was originally the Blue Star Diner.

On the western edge of Berks County, most Route 422 travelers barely notice the string of buildings off to the south side of the road that marks the village of Stouchsburg, or that the road is actually a bypass deliberately constructed to steer traffic around that village and nearby Womelsdorf. The early 1950s rerouting spelled opportunity for Howard Mogel and Gerald Werner. In 1954, they opened a new forty-eight-seat Fodero called the Blue Star Diner. Typical for the bypass roadside of the day, a giant star-shaped arrow sign was erected to catch the eye of speeding motorists soon enough to give them a chance to slow down and pull in. Alas, the star was pulled down in the 1990s, and the base of the diner, now called Risser's, was bricked in to match an expanded dining room, but enough of it is still visible to show the distinctive lines of a mid-1950s Fodero. The roadscape story is repeated a few miles down the highway at Myerstown, which was bypassed in the 1940s, creating a new roadside service strip lined with gas stations, motels, and the Kumm Esse Diner.

As the largest Route 422 town between Reading and Harrisburg, Lebanon has hosted at least four highway diners over the years. Eat Well Diner and Mel's Diner anchor Lebanon's east end, Pushnik's 1960 Fodero operates on the west end as D'Alexander's, and Heisey's is a few miles north on Route 72. Heisey's, from 1951, and Mel's, from the mid-1950s, are both modern stainless O'Mahonys, the firm that still dominated the industry during that period. By the time Kullman and Fodero made Lebanon's other two diners, however, O'Mahony was out of business, and diner styles had become decidedly more exaggerated.

LINCOLN HIGHWAY (U.S. ROUTE 30)

As a Diner Drive, the Lincoln Highway across Lancaster County is almost as famous for the diners it once held as for the diners that are still there. This route was one of the nation's earliest turnpikes, originating in 1792; carried the nation's first transcontinental highway, dating from 1913; and remains infamous as a traffic-choked despoiler of Lancaster County's bucolic farmland. The nature of the Lincoln Highway's roadside development has caused it to lose at least as many diners as it has gained. A mixed bag of four diners now operate along the route, an average of one every 6 miles, and four others are known to have been removed from the highway. This isn't unusual, as diners are shuffled about all the time, but once pulled from Pennsylvania's Lincoln Highway, they haven't come back.

The first diner approached when coming into Lancaster County from the east is the Gap Diner, located at the busy intersection of U.S. Route 30 and Route 41 just down the hill from the village of Gap. The Gap Diner's coach-lamped and cupola-topped environmental exterior belies the fact that beneath its wood-paneled skin is an exaggerated modern diner trucked to the site in 1959. Aside from the diner's vertical stacked diamond sign, the only other visible sample of its pre-seventies self is a large canted window (part of the original vestibule) to the left of the main entrance. Its appear-

COLLECTION OF RICHARD J. S. GUTMAN

This small 1959 Kullman forms the basis of the current Gap Diner.

ance is a sign of its success: The colonial makeover came in the 1970s, when the William Penn Room was added to the left side of the diner, and was reaffirmed in the 1980s, when the Old Gap Room was added to the right.

The eastern portal to the tourist strip of Dutch distractions and outlet malls was once flanked by two stainless steel diners on opposite sides of the street, just a quarter mile apart. On the north side, the little-changed Jennie's (originally Gehman's) operates as if it were 1959, as if the air-conditioning advertised in neon above its door were still a new thing. It's a small detail that makes a good diner even better. On the south side, however, there is a sprawling service station where Hart's U.S. 30 Diner used to be. This ninety-nine-seat, red and stainless 1957 Kullman was bought in the late 1980s by actor Ken Kercheval for his new Kentucky wife, Ava Fox, who wanted to set up a diner in Southern California. Upon entering the U.S. 30 Diner, Ken reportedly said to the waitress, "I'll have a sandwich, she'll take the diner." And she did. Unfortunately, neither the plans nor the marriage worked out. Ava nonetheless received the diner in the divorce settlement and shipped it to her uncle's farm in Kentucky, where it now awaits a buyer.

R. Arnold Savage's Hyway Diner and Mobil station combination operated from 1937 to 1956 in what is now the loop of the westbound ramp where the Lancaster bypass joins the old road. The venerable, old O'Mahony closed down soon after the death of its owner and the opening of the bypass. Farther west, the long-lost Mari-Bob Diner once operated at the junction of the Lincoln Highway and the Old Philadelphia Pike.

With its stone face and orange mansard roof, Dempsey's American Kitchen on Columbia Avenue (Route 462) west of Lancaster may look like a Howard Johnson's wannabe, but it's an old Kullman that started life as the Wheatland Diner, named after the nearby home of President James Buchanan. It was briefly called the Tip Top in the seventies before joining the Dempsey's chain.

There is no better example of early exaggerated modern than Columbia's Prospect Diner. Sitting just east of town on a triangle of land formed by old and new routings of the Lincoln Highway, this 1955 Kullman expressed the manufacturer's desire to accentuate certain architectural design elements. This not only made the modern, functional lines of the diner more stylish, but also increased the building's visibility from the highway. Although the rounded corners are not flared, as was the case in later Kullmans, the alternating strips of stainless and porcelain are vertically arranged, in contrast to the horizontal lines of the front and sides. This visual exclamation point would become the signature element of a classic Kullman. The Prospect's windows are larger than those of older diners, but not nearly as large as later Kullman canted visual fronts. Its most prominent feature is its massive, flared-eave roof, which sits incongruously on the diner like an oversize bonnet. The broad, up-turned eave line, along with the canted visual front, eventually came to define the exaggerated modern style, but it took a few more years for Kullman, DeRaffele, and other manufacturers to refine the design into an integral extension of the rest of the building.

For forty-four years, Bob's Diner in Columbia anchored the western end of the Lincoln Highway Dutch Diner Drive. Bob Weisser's experience is a classic tale of the returning World War II veteran opening a diner on the burgeoning roadside. After diner shopping, Bob selected a 1947 Mountain View and set it up next to his father's garage, now the Napa Auto Parts store. Bob's had the signature cowcatcher corner plates of modern Mountain Views but a facade of navy blue, porcelain panels, and rounded, glass-block corner windows left over from prewar streamline designs.

The retirement of Bob Weisser's generation in the 1980s loosened many diners from their moorings. Bob's finally pulled out in 1990, originally bound for England and the Fat Boys chain, but instead exchanged hands a number of times stateside. In 1995, new owner Dan O'Brien tried to set up shop in St. Charles, Maryland, as the Flashback Diner, but the diner was rejected by the local planning board. It now sits empty, restored, and for sale for $85,000.

SAVILLE'S DINER
1968 SWINGLE, REMODELED
830 E. Philadelphia Ave., Boyertown

KEVIN AND LORI BUTKO

The mobility of diners is well illustrated by the story of Saville's Diner, which begins in February 1960 when Kane's Diner (1959 Silk City #5906) was delivered to Boyertown. Joseph Saville bought the diner two years later. When he wanted a larger place in 1968, a three-way swap was made by Swingle: Saville's Silk City was reconditioned and sent to Pennsburg as the Thomas (now Pennsburg) Diner. (Its serial number, #568DVU, indicates that Swingle delivered the used diner and vestibule in May 1968.) Meanwhile, Joe Saville bought the used Colonial Diner (1961 Swingle #361DV) from East Brunswick, New Jersey, and had it reconditioned as Saville's (#468DVU). Finally, Swingle replaced the Colonial with a new Colonial Diner (#468DV).

A dining room was added to Saville's in 1977 by PMC (Paramount), and the exterior was refaced. Today the diner is owned by Joe's daughter, Rita Chavka. An enclosed handicapped ramp was recently added, and the dining room remodeled, but the 1968 counter area retains its terrazzo floors, wagon wheel lights, and copper hood. Saville's serves home-cooked American-style food, including homemade soups and sweet potato fries. The diner is known for its desserts, especially eclairs.

LYNDON DINER
1990 DERAFFELE
Route 72 (Lancaster Turnpike), Manheim

LYNDON CITY LINE DINER
1997 DERAFFELE CONVERSION
1370 Manheim Pike, Lancaster

When it comes to diner styles, few dinermen are as prepared for the new millennium as Lyndon Quinn. His two Lancaster County diners, both DeRaffele creations from the last decade of the twentieth century, are on the cutting edge of diner design. Lyndon was born into the diner business. His father owned Bill's Diner, a 1961 Silk City on Lancaster's Dillersville Avenue. Lyndon took over in 1978, moving it to Route 72 on the southern edge of Manheim and renaming it the Lyndon Diner. The popular stainless steel diner, set slanted to the road, was a prominent landmark for northbound traffic coming into town. It became well known for its crab cake dinners and freshly made desserts, and by 1990, Lyndon was looking to expand.

Wholeheartedly embracing the most recent diner styles, Lyndon contracted with DeRaffele to build a five-section diner. This new 140-seater is a

LYNDON QUINN

Lyndon City Line Diner.

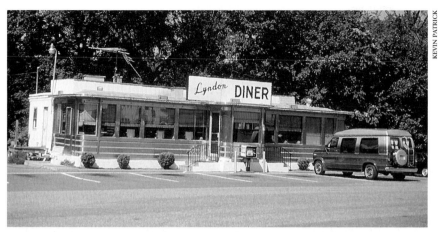

KEVIN PATRICK

The original Lyndon Diner in 1988. The 1960 Silk City was replaced in 1990.

sleek, late-modern diner with large windows and conspicuously applied reflective materials, including stainless steel trim. There is a hint of environmentalism in the mansardlike roof and the white stone foundation and corners, but the overall appearance is a clear departure from that style.

Lyndon returned to Lancaster to build an even bigger diner in 1997. This time Lyndon had DeRaffele gut and remodel an old Elby's restaurant that had been operating as the Park City Diner. By the end of the nineties, the style trend was toward postmodern reinterpretations of the past. Lyndon City Line Diner opened on Manheim Pike as a large, metropolitan retro diner with a brilliant reflective exterior created by a mirror-finish stainless steel facade. The large, boxy eave fascia is trimmed in red neon, and a glass-block cupola rises above the commodious vestibule as a salute to art deco. A black-and-white-checked border runs below the windows.

Inside, the City Line is a 195-seater with a gray marble tiled floor inlaid with dark green diamonds. Green marble covers the backwall, and the vestibule interior is a pinkish gray. The tile-floored right half is dinerlike, with a double row of half booths in the center and a relatively short, nine-stool, black-topped counter. The carpeted left half is restaurantlike, with booths and tables.

Lyndon has not lost sight of his origins (his menus say, "Remembering you always, Dad"), nor the recipe for his success. Both diners have huge menus with affordable prices. The City Line menu, for example, has appetizers such as fried calamari and crab imperial stuffed mushrooms. Entrees range from baked beans with hot dogs casserole to broiled lobster tail. There's also a wide selection of pasta, seafood, steaks, and all the regular diner foods you'd expect.

FEATURED DINER

ESPRESSO CAFÉ AT ADAMS ANTIQUES
1939 KULLMAN
2400 N. Reading Rd. (Route 272), Denver

BRIAN BUTKO

The state's oldest Kullman greets visitors to Adams Antiques mall in Denver, just north of Zinn's Diner and turnpike exit 21 on Route 272. Owners Bryan Sweigart and wife, Rosemary Vigilante, decided to buy the diner after Bryan saw pictures of it being restored in Florida. They were intrigued by its style and liked the idea of incorporating it into their antiques mall. The diner sits in a small patio between the original mall and a newer structure. The lower half of the diner has pale yellow, fluted, porcelain-enameled panels; the clerestory on top has four little stained-glass windows. The inside has been updated a bit, with a mirrored menu board and a blue-and-white-tiled floor, but a black marble counter remains, as does the stainless backbar and abundant wood trim.

The backyard restorer in St. Augustine, Florida, said that the diner was originally Eulla Mae's, in a small town fifty miles inland, and became Cecil's when it was moved to St. Augustine. Bryan and Rosemary moved it north in 1995. "It's like a magnet," says Rosemary. "Even when it's closed, people ask about it and want to see inside it."

BRIAN BUTKO

It's only open on Sundays, when antiques shoppers are most numerous. Customers usually only want a snack while shopping at the many nearby antiques stores, and the diner serves light fare such as soup, sandwiches, pastries, and bagels.

Espresso Café at Adams Antiques was brought from Florida by Bryan Sweigart and his wife, Rosemary Vigilante, shown at the counter.

TOM SAWYER DINER

1962 DERAFFELE

4441 Hamilton Blvd., Allentown

FEATURED DINER

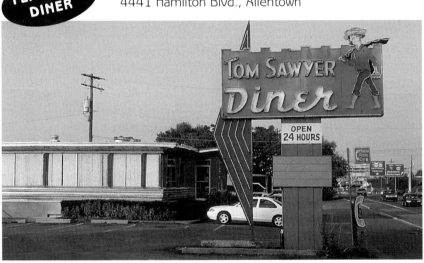

KEVIN PATRICK

Few diners express the exaggerated modern style as well as the Tom Sawyer, which sits just outside Allentown in the U.S. Route 222 commercial strip suburb of Wescosville, a location that has brought the diner plenty of business over the years. Development along Allentown's Hamilton Boulevard began in 1884 with the opening of Dorney Park in nearby Dorneyville.

With the coming of the automobile, gas, food, and lodging services opened up along the entire strip from Dorneyville through Wescosville to Trexlertown. After World War II, suburban subdivisions and industrial parks filled the farmland beyond U.S. 222, and Wescosville was central to the action, easily accessible to a legion of suburbanites, summer day-trippers to Dorney Park, and long-distance commuters who boarded buses across the street bound for New York City.

The Tom Sawyer arrived from the DeRaffele factory in 1962 with an angular, futuristic style. The broad eaves angle upward and point out like jet wings. The entire roof seems to be impossibly perched on walls of glass, looking especially ethereal at night when the well-lit interior turns the diner into a boxy fishbowl of dining efficiency. The sharp lines and hard edges of its stainless steel base are highlighted with two bands of pink porcelain enamel. The absolute beauty of the Tom Sawyer stems from its pristine condition. It's been well maintained and has gone unremodeled for nearly forty years. Even the neon of its elaborate roadside sign still glows.

The interior is bathed in natural light from the expansive visual front. A sharp-tipped chevron pattern in the terrazzo floor points to the right and left from the vestibule door, directing patrons between the front row of booths and the scalloped counter. The left side is devoted to a dining room whose small dimensions (by today's standards) are visually doubled by a full-size mirror covering the ceramic tile backwall, which, along with the false timber ceiling beams, brown booths and countertop, and wood railing dividers, were on the leading edge of the emerging environmental style.

The Tom Sawyer was opened by Dale Feight, who later owned the Effort Diner. The current owner, Mike Petropoulos, emigrated from the Isle of Lésvos, following friends and relatives who had settled in the Allentown area. Mike worked as a baker, supplying cakes and pies to area restaurants—working, like many of his compatriots, toward securing his own business. He took stewardship of the Tom Sawyer in 1987 and has maintained this classic since, offering a full menu of American, Pennsylvania Dutch, and Greek foods.

Unfortunately, the fabulous Tom Sawyer is now threatened by the same locational factors that made it successful. Traffic passing the diner has continued to rise, especially after the opening of the I-78 Wescosville interchange in the early 1990s. This stimulated plans for a limited-access 222 bypass, which will run right through the Tom Sawyer property en route from I-78 to Route 100 south of Trexlertown. It's not known whether the Tom Sawyer will be moved or destroyed.

ZINN'S DINER

1949 PARAMOUNT, REMODELED BY FODERO

2270 N. Reading Rd. (Route 272), Denver

There is perhaps no diner that better embodies the image of a Pennsylvania diner than Zinn's, with its Pennsylvania Dutch recipes, unchanged for half a century, and its giant talking Dutchman, Amos. It's not just some recent place cashing in on the Dutch theme; underneath its modern skin lies a stainless steel diner, cared for by three generations of Zinns.

Christian Lee Zinn II (known as Chris) now runs the diner, whose history he can recount to just after World War II. His grandfather, Christian Givler Zinn, or Christ, owned a greenhouse that raised, among other things, mushrooms and rubber plants. He argued with the proprietor of the Town Diner in Coatesville that running a restaurant was easy money compared with raising plants. As Chris relates, "The owner said, 'If you think it's so easy, why don't you try it?' He didn't know my granddad had left eighth grade to hitchhike across the country and had earned his keep as a short-order cook."

Christ liked the Town Diner so much that he bought it, but he was soon intrigued by a competitor to the north, the Island Diner (so named for the "island" it sat on between old Route 222 and its realignment). The location was about to get hot, with a Pennsylvania Turnpike exit opening a block away. Christ sold the Town in 1948 and bought the Island from Bill Sebastian, Sr., a local operator who always bought Silk City diners.

Business was so good at the Island that Christ ordered a new Paramount in 1949, a larger, innovative, all-stainless Zenith model. A newspa-

ZINN'S DINER

Above: The original diner that would become Zinn's sits at the Paramount factory in New Jersey in 1949. Below: Zinn's shortly after it opened.

ZINN'S DINER

per contest gave it its new name, Zinn's Modern Diner. The old Island was trucked off to a nearby town, and Zinn's opened in March 1950 with ninety seats, double the capacity of the Island.

Christ was helped by his wife, Margaret, and daughters, Shirley and Ann Marie. Son Lee joined the business a month later when he was discharged from the service. A 1954 trade article by Lee said the diner had already expanded, with an 18-foot section to the rear and a banquet room downstairs. Lee was proud of the operation, especially the 2 acres of paved parking, Pennsylvania Dutch cooks, and spotless kitchen always open to customers. Zinn's had served more than a half million customers the year before. "We were fortunate," Lee wrote, "in getting two modern gas service stations to open on either side of our diner, and a motel across the road is in the construction stage. The service stations attract passing motorists who, after having their cars serviced, usually eat at our diner. The stations on either side of our diner also help to keep open grounds so that our diner can be seen. . . . We don't feature curb service, but many times customers will tell us that they have left a disabled person in the car or that children are there. In such cases, customers can order what they wish and it is placed on a tray and taken out to the car."

In 1954, Christ bought a 300-acre farm along Route 30 near Coatesville and moved his family to the farm, where they lived in the old summer home of President James Buchanan. The roadside property soon sported a golf course, bowling alley, shopping center, and in 1956, another Zinn's Diner. That's when Lee took over the Zinn's in Denver.

Amos, the giant mascot, was erected at the Denver diner's entrance in 1960; Chris says Amos was named for his babysitter's dad. A sturdier Amos debuted in 1969, when Fodero expanded the diner and covered the stainless.

Fodero returned for two more additions, and in 1975, the 32-acre Zinn's Recreational Park opened behind the diner, with miniature golf, batting cages, and a pinball and video game arcade, among other attractions. Zinn's also has car cruise nights in the spring and summer. One of the biggest challenges the family faced was the 1977 opening of the Route 222 bypass, when their road was renamed Route 272 and they lost fifty thousand customers the first year.

Zinn's hasn't swayed from tradition; everything that was on the menu in 1950 is still available. The menu is huge, with many Pennsylvania Dutch specialties, such as scrapple, chicken corn soup, chicken or turkey and waffles, Wiener schnitzel, hot German potato salad, pickled beets, baked beef heart, and shoofly pie.

DINER DIRECTORY

ADAMSTOWN

Adamstown Diner
Willow St. and Lancaster Pike (Rt. 272)
(717) 484-2423
1941 Silk City.
*Homemade American food; meatloaf, beef
liver, pork and sauerkraut, chicken pot pie.
Open Sun.–Thurs., 5 A.M.–10 P.M.;
Fri.–Sat., 5 A.M.–11 P.M.*

Two Guys Diner
Rt. 222 N.
Circa 1930 Silk City.

ALLENTOWN

Charcoal Restaurant
1804 W. Tilghman St.
(610) 770-8900
1957 Silk City. Originally the Thomas
Diner, later Blue Moon Diner, then
West End Diner.
*Charcoal-grilled food; breakfast all day;
hamburgers, steaks.
Open daily, 6 A.M.–9 P.M.*

City Center Diner
601 W. Linden St.
1953 Kullman. Formerly Elliott's Diner
and Spiro's Linden Street Diner.
Closed.

Chris's Family Restaurant
922 Union Blvd.
(610) 437-9644
1955 O'Mahony with 1960s Fodero
dining room, remodeled. Formerly
Anderson's Diner, which replaced a circa
1940 O'Mahony.
*American food; breakfast all day;
baked goods.
Open 24 hours.*

Chris's Family Restaurant
5635 W. Tilghman St.
(610) 395-9252
1983 Swingle #383DK. Originally
McPeake's Country Diner at Route 61 exit
of I-78/U.S. 22, Hamburg, renamed Pot
O Gold a year later, then moved here.
*American food; breakfast all day;
baked goods.
Open 24 hours.*

Dina's Diner
736 W. Tilghman St.
(610) 434-2872
1940s Silk City. Originally Thomas's
Diner, then Leo Martin's North End
Diner, and then Kap's Diner.
*American food; pan-fried eggs; some Penn-
sylvania Dutch cooking.
Open 24 hours.*

Golden Gate Diner
1318 Union Blvd.
(610) 435-9111
Circa 1964 Manno.
*American food; breakfast all day.
Open 24 hours.*

Hamilton Family Restaurant
2027 Hamilton St. (at 20th St.)
(610) 433-6452
1959 Fodero, remodeled. Originally
Plain & Fancy Diner, then Dempsey's
Diner.
American food; breakfast all day;
baked goods.
Open 24 hours.

Paul's Gyro Restaurant
37 N. 7th. St.
(610) 434-9499
1930s, remodeled. Formerly Supreme
Diner.
Greek food.
Open daily, 7 A.M.–5 P.M.

Poodle Skirt Diner
911 S. 5th St.
1956 Silk City #5608, extensively
remodeled. Formerly B&G, Master Chef,
and Eagle Diner.
Closed.

Queen City Diner
1801 Lehigh St.
(610) 791-0240
Circa 1970 Kullman. Formerly
Sunnybrook Diner, Parkway Diner, and
Cascade Restaurant.
American food; daily specials; salad bar;
bakery.
Open 24 hours.

Saylor's Restaurant
701 N. 9th St. (at Tilghman St.)
(610) 432-5900
1948 Paramount. Originally Hook's
Diner.
Home-style American food; breakfast all
day; daily specials; bakery.
Open daily, 6:30 A.M.–9 P.M.

Silver Star Diner
845 Linden St. (at 9th St.)
(610) 821-9337
1960 DeRaffele. Formerly All
American Diner.
American food; breakfast all day;
baked goods.
Open 24 hours.

Sunrise Diner
1401 S. 4th St.
(610) 797-2233
1960 DeRaffele.
American food; baked goods.
Open 24 hours.

Tom Sawyer Diner
4441 Hamilton Blv. (Rt. 309. exit 16)
(610) 395-3261
1962 DeRaffele.
Open 24 hours.
For more information, see page 112.

Top Diner
1019 Union Blvd.
(610) 432-9821
1953 Silk City #5312.
American food; fresh seafood; baked goods;
live entertainment on weekends.
Open 24 hours.

Trivet Diner
4549 W. Tilghman St.
(610) 398-3886
1980s DeRaffele.
American food; baked goods.
Open 24 hours.

BALLY

Family Restaurant and Diner
Rt. 100
1950s.
Closed.

BETHEL

Trainer's Midway Diner
41 Diner Dr. (at I-78/U.S. Rt. 22, exit 5)
(717) 933-4402
1951 Silk City, remodeled beyond
recognition.
*American and Pennsylvania Dutch food;
breakfast all day; corn fritters, pepper cabbage; homemade pies, including shoofly.
Open 24 hours.*

BETHLEHEM

Lehigh Pizza
306 Broadway
1954 Silk City #5413. Formerly
Community Diner.
Closed.

BIRDSBORO

Fegely's Restaurant
4680 Perkiomen Ave. (Route 422)
(610) 779-9921
1930s O'Mahony, remodeled.
Interior intact.
*American food; breakfast all day
(except Sun.); homemade soups,
roast turkey, beef.
Open Mon.–Fri., 6 A.M.–8 P.M.;
Sat., 7 A.M.–8 P.M.; Sun., 11 A.M.–7 P.M.*

BOYERTOWN

Saville's Diner
830 E. Philadelphia Ave.
(610) 369-1433
1961 Swingle #361DV, reconditioned as
#468DVU; PMC dining room remodeled.
*Open daily, 5 A.M.–10 P.M.
For more information, see page 108.*

BREINIGSVILLE

Trivet Family Restaurant
Rt. 222
(610) 395-7316
1970s DeRaffele.
*Pennsylvania Dutch food; breakfast
all day; baked goods.
Open 24 hours.*

COLUMBIA

Prospect Diner
Columbia Ave. (Rt. 462)
(717) 684-7141
1955 Kullman.
*American food; baked goods.
Open Mon.–Sat., 5 A.M.–2 P.M.;
Sun., 7 A.M.–11 P.M. (closed Sun.,
July–Sept.)*

COOPERSBURG

Coopersburg Diner
Rt. 309
(610) 282-1853
1942 Paramount, remodeled.
Formerly Topp's Diner.
*American food; breakfast all day;
baked goods.
Open 24 hours.*

DENVER

Espresso Café at Adams Antiques
2400 N. Reading Rd. (Rt. 272)
(717) 733-6109
1939 Kullman. Formerly Eullah
Mae's and then Cecil's Diner of
St. Augustine, FL.
*Open Sundays only.
For more information, see page 111.*

Zinn's Diner
2270 N. Reading Rd. (Rt. 272, exit 21
of turnpike)
(717) 336-2210
1949 Paramount, remodeled by Fodero
in 1969, 1973, and 1976.
Open daily, 6 A.M.–11 P.M.
For more information, see page 114.

DOUGLASSVILLE

Michael's Restaurant
Rt. 422 W.
(610) 385-3017
Early 1960s Kullman, remodeled.
Formerly Village Diner.
American food; bakery; banquets.
Open 24 hours.

EASTON

Forks Diner
3315 Sullivan Trail (Rt. 115)
(610) 252-1028
1970s Mediterranean modern.
Remodeled.
American food; breakfast all day;
daily specials.
Open daily, 6 A.M.–10 P.M.

Tic Toc Restaurant
2510 Northampton St.
(610) 252-6466
1957 Kullman. Formerly Dempsey's
Diner.
American food; breakfast all day;
seafood, steaks.
Open 24 hours.

ELIZABETHTOWN

Clearview Diner
Rt. 230
(717) 367-4525
1948/1954 Paramount, remodeled.
Pennsylvania Dutch food; banquets.
Open Mon.–Thurs., 6 A.M.–8 P.M.;
Sat., 6 A.M.–9 P.M.

EMMAUS

Emmaus Diner
1418 Chestnut St.
(610) 967-5877
1957 Paramount, remodeled in 1964.
Homemade American food; breakfast all
day; bakery.
Open daily, 6 A.M.–10 P.M.

Superior Diner
State St. & Emmaus St.
(610) 965-5750
Remodeled.
American food; breakfast all day;
daily specials; bakery; banquets.
Open 24 hours.

EPHRATA

Cloister Diner
607 W. Main St. (Rt. 322)
(717) 733-2361
1950 Silk City, remodeled.
Pennsylvania Dutch food;
pig stomach, schnitz und knepp,
corn and waffles, corn pie.
Open Mon.–Wed., 6 A.M.–7 P.M.;
Thurs.–Sat., 6 A.M.–8 P.M.;
Sun., 7 A.M.–2 P.M.

FOGELSVILLE

Starlite Restaurant
U.S. Rt. 22 & Rt. 100
(610) 395-4031
1957 Kullman, remodeled with addition in 1970s.
American food; steaks, seafood, sautéed dishes, omelettes; baked goods.
Open 24 hours.

GAP

Gap Diner
Rt. 30 & Rt. 41
(717) 442-4260
1959 Kullman, remodeled.
American food; breakfast all day; daily specials; baked goods.
Open daily, 6 A.M.–10 P.M.

HAMBURG

Schmeck's Family Restaurant
16515 Pottsville Pike (Rt. 61)
(610) 562-3251
1950s Wingard Dining Car, remodeled.
Pennsylvania Dutch food; pot pie, pork and sauerkraut; baked goods, apple dumplings.
Open daily, 6 A.M.–10 P.M.

KUTZTOWN

Airport Diner
15110 Kutztown Rd.
(610) 683-5450
1960 Silk City #6027, remodeled.
Pennsylvania Dutch food; breakfast all day; pot pie, pork and sauerkraut, lettuce with bacon dressing.
Open 24 hours.

LANCASTER

Dempsey's American Kitchen
1725 Lancaster Ave.
(717) 392-2232
1950s Kullman, remodeled. Originally Wheatland Diner.
Pennsylvania Dutch food.
Open 24 hours.

Lyndon City Line Diner
1370 Manheim Pike
(717) 398-4878
1997 DeRaffele conversion.
Open 24 hours.
For more information, see page 109.

Neptune Diner
924 N. Prince St.
(717) 399-8358
1951 Mountain View #296. Formerly Deluxe Diner.
American food; crab cakes, meatloaf, steaks, burgers, milkshakes.
Open Mon.–Thurs., 5:30 A.M.–10 P.M.; Fri.–Sat., 24 hours; Sun. until 3:30 P.M.

LEBANON

D'Alexander's Diner
1352 Cumberland St.
(717) 279-8373
1960 Fodero. Formerly Garrett's Connoisseur's Connection, and Pushnik's.
American food; breakfast all day; baked goods; lounge.
Open Mon.–Tues., 5:30 A.M.–9 P.M.; Wed.–Sat., 24 hours; Sun., 5:30 A.M.–2 P.M.

Eat Well Diner
1539 E. Cumberland St. (Rt. 422)
(717) 273-3849
1956 Kullman.
Pennsylvania Dutch and Greek food; breakfast all day.
Open daily, 6 A.M.–10 P.M.

Heisey's Diner
1740 State Rt. 72 N. (3 miles
north of town)
(717) 272-0891
1951 O'Mahony. Originally
Sprechner's Diner.
Pennsylvania Dutch home-cooked meals;
dining room and bar.
Open daily, 6 A.M.–10 P.M.

Mel's Diner
8 E. Cumberland St. (at Front St.,
Rt. 422)
(717) 273-1511
1955 O'Mahony. Formerly Lincoln
Diner.
American food; homemade doughnuts and
bread daily; creamed chipped beef.
Open Mon.–Sat., 6 A.M.–8 P.M.;
Sun., 6 A.M.–2 P.M.

LEESPORT

Berk's Family Restaurant
Rt. 61 and Rt. 73
(610) 926-0352
1955 Silk City, remodeled.
Formerly Hess's.
Open 24 hours.

MANHEIM

Lyndon Diner
665 Lancaster Rd.
(717) 664-4898
1990 DeRaffele.
Open 24 hours.
For more information, see page 109.

MOUNT BETHEL

Mount Bethel Diner
Rt. 611 N.
(717) 897-6409
Environmental.

MYERSTOWN

Kumm Esse Diner
101 W. Lincoln Ave. (Rt. 422 at Rt. 501)
(717) 866-4000
1960 DeRaffele. Originally Furman's.
Pennsylvania Dutch food; beef heart over
filling, pepper cabbage, corn and apple frit-
ters; strawberry pie, banana bread.
Open daily, 6 A.M.–11 P.M.

NAZARETH

Nazareth Diner
Rt. 248 and S. Broad St.
(610) 759-8555
1950s, remodeled.
American food; breakfast all day;
salad bar; baked goods.
Open 24 hours.

Sullivan Trail Diner
6221 Sullivan Trail
(610) 746-9490
1960s, remodeled.
American food; breakfast all day;
baked goods.
Open Mon.–Tues., 6:30 A.M.–2 P.M.;
Wed.–Sun., 6:30 A.M.–9 P.M.

NORTHHAMPTON

Miller's Diner
1205 Main St.
(610) 262-6321
1950s Silk City.
American food; breakfast all day;
baked goods.
Open 24 hours.

PALMYRA

Weiland's Flowers
501 E. Main St.
Circa 1956 Silk City, extensively remodeled. Formerly Dutch Diner.
No food served.

READING

Garden Restaurant
3455 Centre Ave. (Rt. 61 at Bellevue St.)
(610) 921-2130
1950s with 1956 Fodero annex, all
remodeled. Formerly Bellevue Diner,
and Trojan Diner.
American food; breakfast all day;
seafood, steaks, pasta, scrapple; pies.
Open 24 hours.

Great China Restaurant
1126 Schuykill Ave.
Circa 1960, remodeled. Formerly
Dragon Inn.
Chinese food.
Open Sun.–Thurs., 11 A.M.–10:30 P.M.;
Fri.–Sat., 11 A.M.–11:30 P.M.

9th & Marion Diner
1200 N. 9th St.
(610) 372-9933
1958 Silk City. Formerly Evergreen
Diner, Pennsylvania House, and
Hollywood Diner.
American food; breakfast and lunch only.
Open Mon.–Sat., 5 A.M.–2 P.M.;
Sun., 6 A.M.–2 P.M.

Reading Family Restaurant
2725 Centre Ave. (Rt. 61, at George St.)
(610) 929-3244
1950s, remodeled in 1970s. Formerly
Schwambach's Diner.
American food; breakfast all day;
baked goods.
Open daily, 5 A.M.–10 P.M.

Stadium Restaurant
1925 Centre Ave.
(610) 372-4212
1954 Silk City #5432, remodeled.
Formerly Gelbach's Diner.
Greek and Italian food; breakfast all day.
Open 24 hours.

West Reading Diner
411 Penn Ave. (Bus. Rt. 422)
(610) 376-5565
Mid-1960s Superior or DeRaffele.
Flared eaves, stainless trim, small
gray and white tile base.
American food; breakfast all day.
Open 24 hours.

RONKS

Jennie's Diner
2575 Lincoln Hwy. E.
(717) 397-2507
1959 Silk City #5904. Formerly
Gehman's Diner.
Pennsylvania Dutch food; breakfast all day.
Open 24 hours.

SHILLINGTON

Deluxe Restaurant
2295 W. Lancaster Pike
(610) 775-2577
1960 and 1981 Swingle, rehabbed
(formerly Peterpank Diner, Sayerville,
NJ, #360DV) now #1181DUKV. Former
Frangakis Diner at this site.
American food; beef stews, goulash,
casseroles, steaks, seafood.
Open daily, 5 A.M.–10 P.M.

SHOEMAKERSVILLE

Dutch Valley Diner
554 Shoemakersville Ave.
1956 Fodero, remodeled. Originally
Clark's Diner.

STEVENS

Silk City Diner
1640 N. Reading Rd.
(717) 335-3833
1957 Silk City #5709, remodeled.
Formerly Dutchman's Diner.
American food; chicken; baked goods.
Open Mon.–Thurs., 6 A.M.–9 P.M.;
Fri.–Sat., 6 A.M.–10 P.M.;
Sun., 7 A.M.–9 P.M.

STOUCHSBURG

Risser's Diner
Rt. 422
(610) 589-4570
1954 Fodero. Originally Blue Star Diner.
Pennsylvania Dutch food.
Open Mon.–Sat., 6 A.M.–8 P.M.;
Sun. 6 A.M.–3 P.M.

TEMPLE

5th Street Diner
5336 N. 5th St. Hwy.
(610) 929-0543
1959 Silk City, remodeled.
Homestyle American food;
breakfast all day; baked goods.
Open 24 hours.

TREXLERTOWN

New Pied Piper Diner-Restaurant
Hamilton Blvd. and Lower Macungie
Rd. (Rt. 222)
(610) 398-2000
1987 DeRaffele.
American food; breakfast all day;
steaks, seafood; baked goods.
Open 24 hours.

WHITEHALL

New City View Diner
1831 MacArthur Rd. (at Grape St.)
(610) 434-4366
1960 DeRaffele, remodeled. Originally
City View Diner, then Dempsey's Diner.
Pennsylvania Dutch food; stuffed cabbage,
chicken pot pie.
Open 24 hours.

Lehigh Valley Diner
1162 MacArthur Rd. (N. 7th St.
Extension)
(610) 434-8886
1956 Silk City. Formerly Neff's Diner
and Steckline's Diner.
American food; breakfast all day;
baked goods.
Open 24 hours.

WILLOW STREET

Willow Street Restaurant
Rt. 272 and 222 (5 mi. S. of Lancaster)
(717) 464-4428
Early 1960s Kullman, remodeled.
Formerly Willow Street Diner.
American food.
Open Mon.–Sat., 6 A.M.–9 P.M.;
Sun., 7 A.M.–9 P.M.

WIND GAP

Gap Diner
1041 S. Broadway (Rts. 115 and 512)
(610) 863-4342
1950s. Formerly Broadway Diner.
Homemade American food; breakfast
all day; steaks, roasts, haddock, shrimp;
homemade pies and cakes.
Open Sun.–Thurs., 6 A.M.–10 P.M.;
Fri.–Sat., 6 A.M.–11 P.M.

ANTHRACITE REGION
AND THE POCONOS

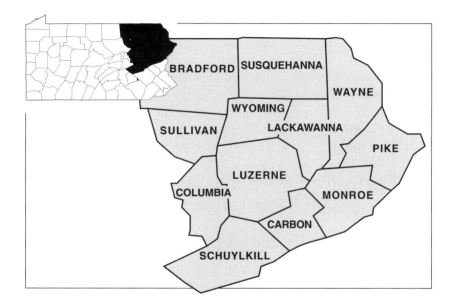

Mountains shield the Anthracite Region and the Poconos from the diner world of the megalopolis stretching from Boston to Washington, D.C. To the east, toward New York, the region is bordered by the high mountains that mark the edge of the Pocono Plateau. To the south, toward Philadelphia, Blue Mountain separates the region from the Dutch Country's Lehigh and Lebanon Valleys.

Although a few narrow roads scramble over this high ridge wall, primary access is through five stream-carved water gaps: the Delaware, Swatara, Schuylkill, Lehigh, and Wind. In Pennsylvania's Appalachian Mountains, the highways follow the water gaps, the traffic follows the highways, and the diners follow the traffic.

Named after the stream that carved it, Swatara Gap channels I-81 north-south through the Anthracite Region. Heisey's Diner on Route 72 is just a few miles south of the gap. Twenty-five miles to the east, where Schuylkill Gap leads Route 61 through the heart of the coalfields of Schuylkill County, the colonial Schmeck's Diner stands guard on the Dutch Country side of the mountain.

Five more Schuylkill County diners line Route 309, the only main road into the region that traverses Blue Mountain without the aid of a water gap, although the original route passes through Lehigh Gap, the traditional doorway into Carbon County. On a bend in the old road, the Bowmanstown Diner serves those not motoring past on the Route 248 bypass or on the nearby Pennsylvania Turnpike, which enters into the region via the Lehigh Tunnel. Pieces of two vintage diners show through the Bowmanstown's stone facade: a 1952 Fodero and a Silk City graft for a dining room.

Route 33, a limited-access expressway between the Lehigh Valley and the Poconos, crosses Blue Mountain through the partly carved cleft of Wind Gap. One of eastern Pennsylvania's two Gap Diners (the other is just north of the gap through Mine Ridge at U.S. Route 30 and Route 41 in Lancaster County) operates at the southern base of this partial gap. The 1960s diner was recently environmentalized.

The best known of the mountain passes is the Delaware Water Gap, which looks both south toward Philadelphia via Route 611 and east toward New York along I-80. The Delaware Water Gap is the more significant of two eastern gateways into the Poconos. The other is located farther north at Milford-Matamoras, where I-84 crosses the Delaware River into Pennsylvania. Diners cluster at both gateways, which are significant service nodes for

COLLECTION OF BRIAN BUTKO

Joe Caesar helped build diners before buying the Kel-Bert Diner in Wind Gap in 1938. Ten years later, he upgraded to a new Fodero, then added a matching addition in 1951. He followed up with this larger Caesar's Diner (1959 Fodero), a transitional diner between stainless steel and environmental. Joe was also known for his special March of Dimes days, when he'd donate every cent of income (and he took no free supplies). Nothing remains of any of these diners.

COLLECTION OF BRIAN BUTKO

The diner to the right greeted drivers entering Portland, south of Stroudsburg.

the two interstate highways. Up until recently, three diners operated in the Milford-Matamoras area, of which two remain. Just west of the Delaware Water Gap nearly a dozen diners can be found in the immediate Strouds-burg–East Stroudsburg area.

Northeastern Pennsylvania is a region of contrasts. The Poconos include some of the state's fastest-growing counties, while the adjacent coal-rich counties are now characterized by outmigration and deindustrialization. Despite the mountain barriers, the region is historically and geographically tied to both Philadelphia and New York, which has assured a landscape studded with diners. All but four of the region's sixty diners are located in the seven easternmost counties, three of which are Anthracite Region counties (Schuylkill, Luzerne, and Lackawanna) and three Pocono counties (Monroe, Pike, and Wayne). Carbon County straddles the line and contains characteristics of both.

Anthracite is a hard coal found in the region's folded ridges. Until oil and gas took over the market, anthracite was the home heating fuel of choice. Tens of thousands of immigrants poured into the coalfields to live in small, tightly packed cities like Pottsville, Hazleton, and Scranton. Work-ers lived within walking distance of their jobs in the mines, mills, or rail-yards from which trains carried the coal to heat the homes of Philadelphia and New York. The region's first diners operated at the edges of the business districts in pedestrian-oriented towns throughout the coalfields.

Mechanized mines now employ a fraction of what they once did, the mills are shuttered, and the tracks are mostly ripped up, but many of the diners that arrived in the 1940s and 1950s survive. The majority of these are

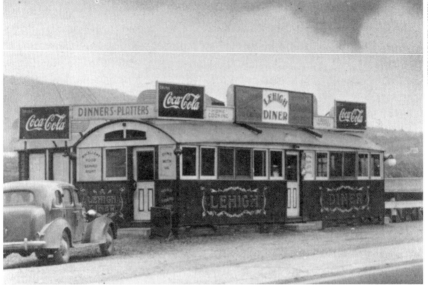

A number of diners opened on the route between Allentown and Scranton, including this one in Lehighton.

edge-of-town or edge-of-business-district diners located in the southern and middle coalfields of Schuylkill County (eleven diners) and the northern coalfield beneath the Wyoming Valley near Scranton and Wilkes-Barre (seventeen diners).

In contrast is the adjacent Pocono Plateau, an expansive upland jutting between the Wyoming Valley and the Delaware River. Pocono diners operate along highways, drawing travelers bound for ski resorts and second homes. The forests, mountain lakes, and waterfalls of the Poconos have drawn nature seekers and skiers from New York and Philadelphia since the coal railroads began building resort hotels in the region at the end of the nineteenth century. With the midcentury shift to automobile travel, a roadside tourist landscape—complete with diners—began to grow along the Poconos' main access roads.

Half a dozen diners are located along Route 6, which meanders across the northern Pocono Plateau, but most of the region's diners are clustered around Stroudsburg and East Stroudsburg, tourist-oriented, urban service centers just beyond the Delaware Water Gap doorway to the region. Stroudsburg (population 5,500) has six strategically placed diners along its major points of entry: three at the edge of town on the main access roads north and west, one at the edge of the business district on the main road south, and one downtown.

Of the sixty diners in the Anthracite Region and the Poconos, only six survive from before World War II, and barely a dozen are newer than 1965. More than half the region's diners were built as modern stainless structures between 1941 and 1964, though many have been remodeled in a later environmental style. Diners in the more economically marginal Anthracite counties tend to be older than those in the Poconos and are less likely to have been remodeled. Virtually all the post-1965 diners are located in one of the three Pocono counties.

In contrast to those of Philadelphia and the Dutch Country, only a couple of diners in northeastern Pennsylvania have undergone significant late-modern or postmodern remodeling, and exaggerated modern diners are practically nonexistent. There isn't a single DeRaffele north of Blue Mountain. What northeastern Pennsylvania does have is Mountain Views—a dozen of them, or 20 percent of the region's diners (more than twice the state's average). It is not known why there are so many Mountain Views in northeastern Pennsylvania, but a manufacturer's list stating the destination of every Mountain View made from 1950 to 1957 shows a definite directional bias in the distribution of the company's product, with the majority being shipped to northeastern Pennsylvania or Metro Philadelphia. Only one was sent to the Dutch Country, currently in business as the Neptune Diner.

Within the Anthracite Region and the Poconos, the Mountain Views are all located in the northern part of the region. The southern part of the region

BRIAN BUTKO

The Olympic Diner, a 1948 Paramount from Wilkes-Barre, was moved 1,500 miles south to Miami Beach and reopened in 1992 as the 11th Street Diner.

The Diamond City Diner (1952 Mountain View #313) in Wilkes-Barre started as the P&M Diner in Exeter. It reopened in 1987 and traded as Joe Palooka's. In early 1999, it was closed with plans to relocate in the Mount Airy section of Philadelphia.

is more like an extension of the adjacent Dutch Country, containing six of northeastern Pennsylvania's seven Silk City diners and nine O'Mahony diners, about one-third of those in the state.

The oldest diners in the Anthracite Region and the Poconos date back to the early days of dinerdom, when restrooms, tile interiors, and "tables for the ladies" were all innovations of diner builder Patrick "Pop" Tierney. Although he died of acute indigestion after eating in one of his diners in 1917, his sons proceeded to build the business into one of the greatest diner manufacturers of the 1920s. Though a diner a day once rolled out of their plant, it wasn't enough to save the company during the Great Depression.

The state's best-known Tierney just departed Stroudsburg. For years, its gray metal exterior touted "Jerry's" in crudely rendered orange paint, named for the previous female owner. It was opened in 1927 by Greek immigrants George Metropoulos and Nick Russpoulos. They ran it as the Lackawanna Trail Diner until 1951. Dinerman Gordon Tindall purchased it late in 1998 and moved it to Lancaster, where he plans to reopen it.

Tierney's biggest competitor for the Mid-Atlantic diner market was the Jerry O'Mahony Company, which churned out hundreds of barrel-roofed dining cars of similar dimensions from its sprawling Elizabeth, New Jersey, plant starting in the 1920s. O'Mahonys poured into Pennsylvania at an even greater rate than Tierneys during the 1920s, many associated with early diner chains. Of the four or so that have survived, one is located less than 30 miles up the old Lackawanna Trail from the Jerry's site. This late 1920s O'Mahony was rescued from a junkyard by Walter Woerhle, then restored and attached to Kay's Italian Restaurant in Daleville as an extra dining room.

Northeastern Pennsylvania has quite a collection of ancient dining cars. A few miles south of Daleville on Route 435 is the Rainbow Inn, a tattered bar past its prime on a bypassed stretch of empty highway. But the Rainbow Inn has an elongated front foyer that is shaped suspiciously like a diner. Completely gutted on the inside, a stuccoed extension has two doors on either end and a profile common to diners that were converted from old interurban cars. Felty's Diner, in the

CURRENT DINER MANUFACTURERS

For those with the resources to buy a new diner, there are still a number of companies making them:

DeRaffele Manufacturing, New Rochelle, NY, (914) 636-6850.

Diner-Mite Diners/Diner Concepts, Atlanta, GA, (404) 237-5221, <www.dinermite.com>.

Kullman Industries, Lebanon, NJ, (888) GO-DINER, <www.kullman.com>.

Paramount Modular Concepts, Oakland, NJ, (201) 337-6146.

Starlite Diners, Ormond Beach, FL, (904) 677-9316.

Sunshine Diners (formerly Musi Dining Car Company), 377 Roosevelt Ave., Carteret, NJ.

USA Diners, Conyers, GA, (770) 922-5105.

crossroads hamlet of Fountain, is an actual dining car that was set against a brick restaurant at the end of an isolated valley in Schuylkill County.

On the old Lackawanna Trail south of Daleville, the stone facade of an abandoned building has fallen away to reveal the word "Diner" and the telltale profile of a rounded roof embedded in the larger structure. Operated as Leo's Diner into the 1970s, the building's altered appearance obscures its origins. The broad curve of its roof is similar to another area diner of muddled pedigree, the Tamaqua Diner, an in-town diner classically located next to a twenties-era corner filling station. The Tamaqua is covered with cream-colored, porcelain-enameled panels that also front the first floor of an adjacent house that was turned into a dining room, a false facade suggesting two barrel roof diners side by side. This is a unique pre-environmental twist on the later remodeling trend that made diners look like houses. Now owned by Bill and Chris Argiros, the Tamaqua spent most of its life as Taylor's Diner.

RICHARD J. S. GUTMAN

Fern's Diner (1946 Silk City #46101) was possibly the original Exton Diner on Route 30 in Exton before it was moved to Ono in 1957. When it closed around 1990, it was called the Windmill. It was then trucked out and refurbished as the Big Dig Diner in Boston. Its vestibule, though, went to Iowa's Clarksville Diner, which was shipped to France in 1998.

It has been suggested that the Tamaqua, and possibly the abandoned diner of Dalesville, were made by the Bixler Manufacturing Company, a Norwalk, Ohio, firm of the 1930s. Bixler specialized in a sectional type of diner that was built in 4-foot-wide slices like a giant loaf of bread and assembled on-site. As a manufacturer, Bixler was a minor player, and

KEVIN PATRICK

The decay of Leo's Diner on Route 435 south of Daleville reveals the Bixler-brand diner within.

Tamaqua Diner, a rare Bixler with an addition in back. The back roofline is only decorative.

although its sales offices were in New York City, it would be unusual if two of these diners survived in northeastern Pennsylvania.

Although now environmentalized with siding and a mansard, the Effort Diner on Route 115 is another unusual barrel roof diner. It is exceptionally long—too long to fit on a railcar or flatbed in one piece. Opened in 1936 (and closed for the war from 1942 to 1945), it may have been built on-site,

The Effort Diner on Route 115 has been remodeled since this picture was taken four decades ago, but the shape of the old dining car remains unmistakable.

although the original structure has a dinerlike end door uselessly perched above the waters of Pohopoco Creek. Owners Mark and Terri Borger say chain restaurants give them stiff competition, but their diner offers real Pennsylvania Dutch cooking. Terri's uncle Dale Feight had owned the diner for fifteen years, and Mark and Terri bought it in 1985 with hopes of carrying on the family's diner tradition. Before that, Dale had opened Allentown's Tom Sawyer Diner, and his brother Pete operated a diner in Breezewood.

Only Metro Philadelphia can compare with the Anthracite Region and the Poconos in the number and diversity of modern stainless diners from the 1940s. Fodero, Mountain View, O'Mahony, Paramount, and Silk City are all represented. Like old cars, many retain elements representative of the design transition from prewar streamline moderne to postwar modern. Eddie's Place, in the Wyoming Valley town of Plains, is an early 1940s O'Mahony with half-moon window ends and a red and stainless facade. Factoryville's Blue Bird II, a late 1940s Mountain View, shows its cow catcher corners and red, fluted porcelain panels beneath a 1970s environmental remodel. Inside, the rounded ceiling, center canopy clock, and cream and maroon tile counter and wall base are all hallmarks of the era. The interior of the 209 Diner north of East Stroudsburg looks like a 1940 postcard, with a brown and blue composite tile floor, curved counter with light and dark blue tile base, and a swoop-ended ceiling profile of the type made by O'Mahony more than a half century ago.

BRIAN BUTKO

Gabe's Diner was redone after a runaway truck wrecked the place. Signs above the counter advertise scrapple and chili. A map in the terrazzo floor pointing out Waco, Texas, is a mystery.

It is the Sunrise Diner, however, that is the region's best preserved modern stainless diner. This blue and stainless O'Mahony has been doing business around the corner from the Carbon County Courthouse in Jim Thorpe since 1951. Its diamond-pattern terrazzo floor and pink-tinged interior (here gracing the ceiling) became common diner design features of that decade.

Pink was rampant in fifties diner decor, also reflected in the interior of Frackville's Dutch Kitchen Restaurant. The bricked-in and mansarded exterior of this Silk City belies its 1959 interior, with its pink and gray tile counter base and floor and pink border of the recessed ceiling.

The same color scheme was used in the Meadowbrook Diner in Brodheadsville, one of the state's most unusual diner grafts. The original pink-and-gray-tiled Silk City was converted to a kitchen when a rehabbed Swingle was placed in front of it in 1974. The original counter is now used for food prep, and the original entryway is behind the counter of the newer diner. Although that diner was environmentalized by Swingle with stucco outside and cross timbers and carpet inside, it retains its original tile wall base, which casts a pinkish hue. In Stroudsburg, the original part of Besecker's Diner, a 1958 Silk City done in pink and blue, is hidden behind the environmental facade of a front addition. This color combination was also used for the Hawley Diner, a 1954 Mountain View run by the Swanick family since 1965.

The diner wave had already crested in northeastern Pennsylvania by the time exaggerated modernity came into vogue, but one manufacturer was ahead of its time. As early as 1954, Kullman was experimenting with the larger visual fronts, flared corners, and broad eaves, which it would perfect

---

BUYING A VINTAGE DINER

If you'd like to own a vintage diner, start by contacting these folks. All three have helped save many diners that otherwise would have been scrapped.

Randy Garbin, *Roadside Magazine,* P.O. Box 652, Worcester, MA 01602-0652, (508) 791-1838, <www.roadsidemagazine.com>. Sells a list of diners for sale.

Daniel Zilka, 110 Benevolent Street, Providence, RI 02906, (401) 461-7932, <dinerdan@aol.com>. Offers restoration and appraisal services and fabrication of vintage parts.

Steve Harwin, Diversified Diners, 2043 Random Road, Suite 302, Cleveland, OH 44106 (216) 229-4003, <www.oh-diners.com>. Specializes in consultation for restoring, operating, and promoting diners, and can supply restoration materials such as flexglass and stainless steel.

The Garfield Diner, a 1954 Kullman in Pottsville, was originally called the Pottsville Diner.

by the end of the decade. One of these Kullmans rode the diner tide into Pottsville as the Garfield Diner.

Pottsville was a densely settled burg of narrow streets, row homes, and mill buildings that was already served by two other diners when the Garfield arrived. Scharadin's Diner, now long gone, had located at the south edge of the Centre Street business district in 1950, and a 1948 Paramount dinette had been set at 14th Street and Market Street. The new diner was located between the two, at the north edge of the business district on Garfield Square.

The 1954 diner was placed sideways on a narrow, urban lot between a pair of three-story brick buildings, one of which was eventually torn down for much-needed diner parking. This twenty-four-hour diner soon became the social hub of Garfield Square, especially after hours. Around 1957, the Garfield was remodeled into an L-shape. The original part was redone in the exaggerated modern style, with horizontal strips of pink porcelain on its exterior, a neon metal box roof sign, a salmon-colored terrazzo floor inlaid with large black diamonds, and a gray boomerang-pattern countertop.

The Anthracite Region and the Poconos also have a few colonial diners, including the Scotrun Diner and the Pioneer Diner on the Route 611 tourist strip west of Stroudsburg. An early example is the Country Squire Diner, a 1960s brick colonial Kullman with adjoining motel on Route 61 south of Schuylkill Haven.

Late modernism reached this mountainous diner enclave in 1984, when Swingle joined a tinted-atrium dining room onto the 1960s Fodero of the Chestnut Hill Diner. Diner postmodernism, with its penchant for nostalgia, has entered the region on the back of the cosmopolitan tourist trade. Hula Hoop's, in downtown Stroudsburg, is a neon-lit assemblage of bar rooms and eateries including a 1948 Paramount set flush to the sidewalk and attached to a second empire house.

Originally stainless on the outside, the diner once sported a stone-covered environmental redo but was restored to its shiny state when converted into a combination pool hall, video arcade, and bandstand. Diner buffs will want to try to find where a later factory-built Fodero addition was joined to the Paramount.

The Yankee Doodle Diner, out U.S. Route 209 near the Shawnee resorts, underwent a major renovation in the summer of 1998 to incorporate mirrored chrome, a waterfall eave line, and other retro diner accouterments. In the Wyoming Valley, Wilkes-Barre's Palooka's Diner opened a decade ago as part of a larger downtown redevelopment project, which included the heritage-oriented reinterpretation of the abandoned Lehigh Valley railyard and the adaptive reuse of the old Stegmaier Brewery. Like the log cabins dragged to outdoor colonial museums in the 1960s and '70s, diners are increasingly becoming set pieces in the industrial heritage projects of the 1990s. Although a natural fit in such pedestrian-focused tourist landscapes, the diners live or die with the fortunes of the larger project. Palooka's, a 1951 Mountain View outfitted with new neon and joined to a cast-off Amtrak railcar, eventually closed, reopened as the Diamond City Diner, and went down again.

Pocono Queen Diner, a 1960s Kullman on U.S. Route 209, was given a postmodern facelift and renamed the Yankee Doodle Diner in 1998.

DINER DRIVES

The Diner Drives of the Anthracite Region and the Poconos, as in other regions, follow the main preinterstate routes of travel. While the pavement still exists, the former preeminence of these routes is overshadowed by interstate highways. One needs only to break out a road map to see that the interstates go the same places as the old roads, just not by the same paths. They're drawn in heavy blue, green, or red lines that boldly slash across the map, while the thinner lines of the old roads fade into the background in a seemingly inconsequential secondary network. The location of diners today is not a matter of where the traffic is, but rather where the traffic was, specifically during the great diner era of the 1920s to the 1950s.

The three Diner Drives of the Anthracite Region and the Poconos, providing an excellent cross section of the region's diner diversity, are the old route of the Lackawanna Trail, U.S. Route 209, and U.S. Route 11 through the Wyoming Valley. There are a few other routes that you may also want to consider driving. Routes 61 and 309 are the traditional main roads into the Anthracite Region from Philadelphia via the Dutch Country and are reasonably well laden with diners. In the 40 miles from the Stadium Diner in Reading to the Mountain City Diner at the edge of the Frackville business district, Route 61 passes nine diners, all projecting an environmental style. Route 309 from Allentown to Wilkes-Barre is the northern extension of

BRIAN BUTKO

The Blue Comet, a 1957 Mountain View, was remodeled in the 1970s with an overwhelming orange roof. When a dining room was added recently, the mansard roof was repainted a soft blue, the roofline was lowered to make room for neon-trimmed chrome, and the vestibule was covered in stone.

Metro Philadelphia's Bethlehem Pike–Route 309 Diner Drive. In the 45 miles from Allentown to the Blue Comet Diner in Hazleton, Route 309 passes five diners, four of them in eastern Schuylkill County in and around Tamaqua. All but the Tamaqua Diner project some form of visual environmentalism. The Blue Comet Diner was established in 1932 and upgraded to a Mountain View in 1957, but today only its pink terrazzo floor hints at its true self; the outside is environmental with a postmodern remodel, and the inside decor shows a Greek influence.

U.S. Route 6, across the top of the region, is also a good Diner Drive, but most of its seven diners are covered by other drives. Milford's Village Diner, the Hawley Diner (uniquely located at the very center of town), Honesdale's houselike Town House Diner, the Six East Restaurant-Diner in Dickson City, and the Blue Bird II in Factoryville are all Mountain Views.

LACKAWANNA TRAIL (ROUTE 611/U.S. ROUTE 11)

Early in the twentieth century, Pocono- and Scranton-bound traffic from New York and Philadelphia funneled into the region through the Delaware Water Gap; the region's earliest roadside diners followed suit. The gap was the eastern terminus of the Lackawanna Trail, the main auto route across the Lackawanna Valley through Scranton. When it opened in the early 1920s, the Lackawanna Trail was described in motor guidebooks as being one of the best paved roads in the east.

The trail was named for the parallel Delaware, Lackawanna, and Western Railroad, which rerouted its line in 1912 to 1915, resulting in the world's largest reinforced concrete arch bridge, the Tunkhannock Viaduct, north of Scranton. Thirty-three miles of abandoned right-of-way between Clark's Summit and New Milford were rebuilt as a graceful, low-grade, concrete highway: the Lackawanna Trail. The diners followed the traffic, with a greater density in the tourist region between the resorts of the Delaware Water Gap and Mount Pocono.

The Lackawanna is a ghost trail now. Its identity was swallowed up in the late twenties by the northern end of what was then U.S. Route 611 (now State Route 611), and a 50-mile stretch of U.S. Route 11. More recently, the entire route was bypassed by pieces of three different interstate highways: I-80, I-380, and I-81. Because tourism is still alive and well in the Poconos, however, the old trail continues to be a local diner mecca. In its first 15 miles, the road passes nine diners—a diner for every 1.6 miles.

Diner devotees doing this drive follow Route 611 north into Stroudsburg and past Compton's Pancake House and Hula Hoop's on Main Street. On the other end of town, the old Lackawanna Trail Diner sat adjacent to a 1920s garage on the left side of North 9th Street until 1999. At the edge of

ANTHRACITE REGION DINERS

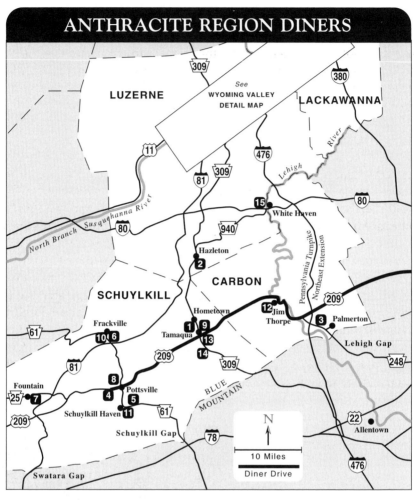

LUZERNE

See WYOMING VALLEY DETAIL MAP

LACKAWANNA

Lehigh River

North Branch Susquehanna River

White Haven

Hazleton

CARBON

SCHUYLKILL

Hometown

Jim Thorpe

Palmerton

Frackville

Tamaqua

Lehigh Gap

Fountain

Pottsville

Schuylkill Haven

BLUE MOUNTAIN

Schuylkill Gap

Allentown

N

10 Miles
Diner Drive

Swatara Gap

Pennsylvania Turnpike Northeast Extension

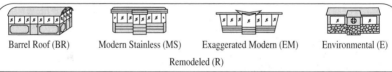

Barrel Roof (BR) Modern Stainless (MS) Exaggerated Modern (EM) Environmental (E)

Remodeled (R)

1 Beacon Diner: Hometown (R)
2 Blue Comet Diner: Hazleton (R)
3 Bowmanstown Diner: Bowmanstown (R)
4 Charlie's Pizza & Subs: Pottsville (MS)
5 Country Squire Diner: Schuylkill Haven (E)
6 Dutch Kitchen Restaurant: Frackville (R)
7 Felty's Diner: Fountain (railcar)
8 Garfield Diner: Pottsville (EM)
9 Just Us Crafters: Tamaqua (R)

10 Mountain City Diner: Frackville (R)
11 Paradise Family Restaurant:
   Schuylkill Haven (R)
12 Sunrise Diner: Jim Thorpe (MS)
13 Tamaqua Diner: Tamaqua (BR)
14 White Diner: Tamaqua (R)
15 White Haven Family Diner:
   White Haven (MS)

town, Route 611 passes the Arlington Diner, a 1940s Silk City with a unique facade made up of potato-size cobbles, which, when coupled with the mansard roof, would seem to date the remodel to the 1970s. The cobblestone coverup is almost as old as the diner, however, making it perhaps the earliest example of a stone-faced stainless steel diner in existence—and proving that owners have long looked for ways to upgrade their diners.

The 611 tourist strip runs from Stroudsburg to the top of the plateau at Mount Pocono, the lower half of which parallels I-80. Four diners are crowded into this 10-mile stretch. The Diner at Tannersville is just off Route 611 at the Route 715 interchange with I-80. Billy's Pocono Diner is a board-and-batten-clad Kullman from the early 1950s with an adjoining ice cream stand. The Scotrun Diner is a cupola-topped colonial, and the Pioneer Diner at Mt. Pocono is a colonial without a cupola. North of Tobyhanna, Route 611 disappears into the fast lanes of I-380, but pavement of the old Lackawanna Trail continues through the forests and upland swamps of the Poconos. For the next 10 miles, the road is four lanes wide but carries virtually no traffic. This one-time main road to Scranton was replaced by the interstate in 1970, leaving the buildings to rot in the woods, like the trolley-fronted Rainbow Inn, and Leo's Diner south of Daleville.

Now marked as part of Route 435, the old Lackawanna runs past Kay's Italian Restaurant, with its O'Mahony add-on, before dropping into the Lackawanna Valley and past the formstone facade of Chaplin's Diner, hard against

Chaplin's is seriously altered, but its classic diner lines underneath are evident.

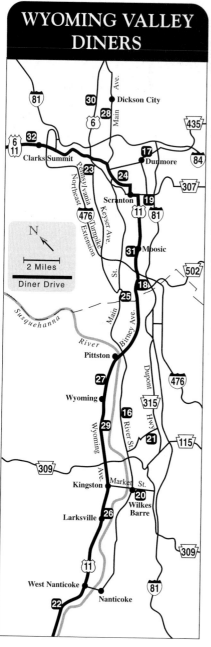

WYOMING VALLEY DINERS

16 Andy's River Road Diner: Plains (MS)
17 Chaplin's Family Restaurant: Dunmore (R)
18 Charge's Diner-Restaurant: Moosic (MS)
19 Chick's Diner: Scranton (MS)
20 Diamond City Diner: Wilkes-Barre (MS)
21 Eddie's Place: Plains (MS)
22 Flamingo Diner: West Nanticoke (MS)
23 Gabe's Diner: Scranton (R)
24 Glider Diner: Scranton (MS)
25 Home Plate Diner: Moosic (R)
26 Lark Diner: Larksville (MS)
27 MD Sporting Goods: West Pittston (R)
28 Mid-Valley Diner: Dickson City (MS)
29 R&J Family Diner: Wyoming (R)
30 Six East Restaurant-Diner: Dickson City (MS)
31 Skyliner Diner: Moosic (MS)
32 Topper's Diner: Clarks Summit (MS)

the sidewalk at the end of the Dunmore business district. Chaplin's was once a classic diner, but new owners remodeled the inside when they bought it in 1988 and redid the outside about six years later. Inside, only the clerestory above the counter reveals its diner pedigree, perhaps a Ward & Dickinson. For years it was Loop's Diner, named for a Mr. Loopia, the owner. Prior to that, it was Pompey's and a 1947 menu from its early days offered such sandwiches as bacon and peanut butter for 50 cents. Mr. Pompey still helped out until 1998, when ill health slowed him down.

The Lackawanna Trail links up with U.S. Route 11 in the northern neighborhoods of Scranton. Just off U.S. 11, on Keyser Avenue, sits Gabe's Diner. It appears to be a small Kullman, but it's hard to tell, as a runaway dump truck led to a remodeling in 1995. A further mystery is a map of Texas highlighting Waco in the terrazzo floor.

Topper's (circa 1954 O'Mahony) was once a popular diner in Clarks Summit. Now it sits abandoned north of town.

U.S. 11 climbs out of the valley past the Clarks Summit interchange, which marks the northern terminus of the Pennsylvania Turnpike's Northeast Extension. This stretch of the Lackawanna Trail, which also overlaps the old Roosevelt Highway (U.S. Route 6), has been a congested commercial strip since the completion of the turnpike in 1957, early enough to encourage Constantinos Pirpinias to open a 1955 O'Mahoney called Topper's Diner. Closed for years, it now lies abandoned a couple miles north. Another Clarks Summit diner that's moved out was a blue-trimmed 1949 Mountain View owned by John Martin.

The 1950s four-lane to Factoryville crisscrosses the old railroad grade followed by the Lackawanna Trail. The highway leads right to the Blue Bird II Diner, easily visible on a curve in a wedge of land at the angled junction with Route 107. It's on the outskirts of town, a classic highway location from the postwar era. Turning north into a low range of hills known as the Abington Mountains, the Lackawanna Trail parallels the tracks of the old railroad, passing through the shadow of the massive Tunkhannock Viaduct. In New Milford, Betty Bennet's Trail Diner, an early 1950s Mountain View, honors the venerable old road. The drive ends near the New York border with Beaver's Restaurant in Hallstead, a red and stainless O'Mahony owned by Brian Hinkley.

U.S. ROUTE 209

U.S. Route 209 is a great Diner Drive through the southern and eastern edges of the region. It's a long road, and most of it is two lanes, stretching 100 miles from Pottsville in Schuylkill County to Matamoras at the borders of New York and New Jersey. The route is a sampler plate of fifteen diners, representing multiple ages and types. Nine of these are in Monroe County,

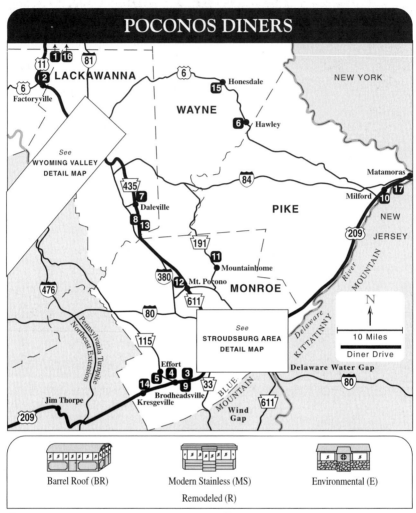

POCONOS DINERS

Barrel Roof (BR)   Modern Stainless (MS)   Environmental (E)
Remodeled (R)

1 Beaver's Restaurant: Hallstead (MS)
2 Blue Bird II: Factoryville (R)
3 Chestnut Hill Diner: Brodheadsville (R)
4 Edy's Bistro: Brodheadsville (MS)
5 Effort Diner: Effort (R)
6 Hawley Diner: Hawley (MS)
7 Kay's Italian Restaurant: Daleville (BR)
8 Leo's Diner: Daleville (R)
9 Meadowbrook Diner: Brodheadsville (R)

10 Milford Diner: Milford (E)
11 Mountainhome Diner: Mountainhome (E)
12 Pioneer Diner: Mount Pocono (E)
13 Rainbow Inn: Daleville (R)
14 Sunset Diner: Kresgeville (R)
15 Town House Diner: Honesdale (R)
16 Trail Diner: New Milford (MS)
17 Village Diner: Milford (MS)

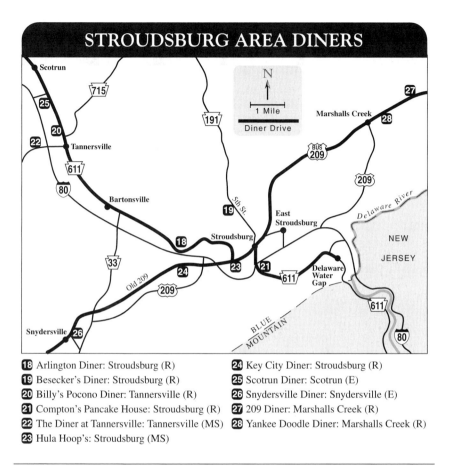

STROUDSBURG AREA DINERS

18 Arlington Diner: Stroudsburg (R)
19 Besecker's Diner: Stroudsburg (R)
20 Billy's Pocono Diner: Tannersville (R)
21 Compton's Pancake House: Stroudsburg (R)
22 The Diner at Tannersville: Tannersville (MS)
23 Hula Hoop's: Stroudsburg (MS)

24 Key City Diner: Stroudsburg (R)
25 Scotrun Diner: Scotrun (E)
26 Snydersville Diner: Snydersville (E)
27 209 Diner: Marshalls Creek (R)
28 Yankee Doodle Diner: Marshalls Creek (R)

the tourist center of the Poconos. Route 209 crosses Route 611 in Stroudsburg, forming a big X that reaches most Poconos attractions.

Philadelphians have been coming into the region via the Turnpike's
Northeast Extension (now I-476) since 1957. But with that route well to the
west of Monroe County, travelers use U.S. 209 as a connector. In the 80
miles of U.S. 209 from the turnpike southwest to the Susquehanna River,
there are four diners, and in the 30 miles of U.S. 209 between the turnpike
and the Pocono resorts near Shawnee, there are nine.

The south end of this Diner Drive is anchored in the Schuylkill County
seat of Pottsville, where two unique diners still operate. At 14th and Market,
Charlie's Pizza & Subs dishes out pies from a 1948 Paramount dinette, the only
one in the state. Although this shortened version of a diner only offers take-out
service, the building is little changed from the day it arrived. Just a few blocks
down Market Steet toward town is the exaggerated modern Garfield Diner.

KEVIN PATRICK

The original Meadowbrook Diner (left) now serves as the kitchen to a newer Swingle (right).

After passing through a string of coal towns, U.S. 209 becomes Broad Street in Tamaqua, passing a block north of the Tamaqua Diner and immediately south of a triangular piece of land at Broad Street, Mauch Chunk Street, and Center Street that holds a gift shop called Just Us Crafters. This brick and mansard building used to be a magic shop, and it was the Feed Store Restaurant before that, but beneath it all is the old Five Point Diner, a 1940 O'Mahony. The only exterior diner remnant is the front door.

Is it only a coincidence that the Sunset Diner at the edge of Kresgeville is just up U.S. 209 from Jim Thorpe's Sunrise Diner? Unlike the Sunrise, with its unmistakable O'Mahony characteristics, the Sunset is a large, rambling restaurant that is anything but dinerlike. It arrived in 1958 from New Jersey, where it had been abandoned. A small annex was added in 1966, and it was remodeled and expanded in 1986. Robert and Sandra Cherry bought it in 1983 and now employ nearly fifty people.

Because of the large volume of through traffic, Brodheadsville, a village of fourteen hundred, supports three diners, all operating at the edges of town. Edy's Bistro is on Route 115 just north of its intersection with Route 209. Environmentalized on the outside and remodeled on the inside to suit a café-bistro format, the original building is a 1950s Silk City, likely the site of the old West End Diner. At a curve in the road on the other side of town lies the Meadowbrook Diner graft. Beyond it is the Chestnut Hill Diner's Fodero-Swingle combination. Six miles east is another Swingle called the Snydersville Diner.

Al Besecker bought the Snydersville from its original owner in the 1950s. (The OK Diner had been at the location since 1930.) Al was trading up in the diner world from a reconditioned Silk City he had run on the Lackawanna Trail since 1940—the old Bartonsville Diner, possibly today's Arlington Diner. The Snydersville Diner did well until 1969, when the restaurant was gutted by fire; Al died a few months later. By 1970, Swingle had rebuilt the Snydersville in the colonial brick and mansard style of the day. Longtime employee Bill Kasperski purchased the Snydersville in 1974 and is celebrating his twenty-fifth successful year, proof of a positive reputation that is even more impressive when considering that the diner was bypassed by the relocation of U.S. 209 in the early 1960s.

The Besecker name is very common in this area. Robert Besecker and his wife, Phyllis, run Besecker's Diner on North 5th Street in Stroudsburg. They too traded up from a smaller diner in the 1970s—the Lackawanna Trail Diner. Though Bob Besecker is no relation to Al, he once worked for him at the Snydersville. Two other Beseckers, Jim and Dave, once ran diners on South Courtland Street in East Stroudsburg and on Route 6 in Delaware, New Jersey. And Jim and Charlie Besecker once operated the Pocono Diner, now Billy's in Tannersville.

Hula Hoop's marks the crossing of U.S. 209 and Route 611 in downtown Stroudsburg. Beyond East Stroudsburg, U.S. 209 enters the Delaware Valley and becomes the main road through the Delaware Water Gap National Recreation Area. Shawnee, at the southern end of the recreation area, has been a major resort since the turn of the century. Second homes, ski slopes, and attractions are scattered throughout the region, and here U.S. 209 is the gas, food, and lodging tourist strip that serves them all. The recently remodeled and enlarged Yankee Doodle Diner operates across the

KEVIN PATRICK

The 209 Diner, a remodeled 1940 O'Mahony south of Bushkill on U.S. Route 209, remains intact inside. Muller's Diner, across the street, was built on-site.

street from a popular flea market. Just up the road, the 209 Diner and Muller's Diner face each other on opposite sides of the road. The 209 Diner spent the first thirty-five years of its life in New Jersey before being brought to the Poconos by its original owner in the 1970s. Its current owners, Mr. and Mrs. Katsiamdes, emigrated from Cyprus to New York, then moved to the Poconos when they bought the 209 Diner in 1985. Mrs. Katsiamdes's brother bought Muller's, a truck stop located across the street. Although he eventually sold the restaurant, he still works as its head chef. The site once held a 1959 diner, but a fire in 1979 destroyed it.

Another U.S. 209 commercial node stretches between Milford and Matamoras where I-84 surmounts the Pocono Plateau. At the edge of the Milford business district, the Milford Diner overlooks the junction of U.S. 209 and U.S. 6 as a longstanding town and family institution. Various members of the Musselwhite family have been involved with three diners at this site: a 1927 Ward & Dickinson, a 1950 Mountain View, and the current 1972 colonial-style Manno. On the outskirts of town is the Village Diner, a 1956 Mountain View set next to a motel of similar age, which the Musselwhites also established. Across the street from this vintage roadside ensemble is a mountain of fill on which the traffic of I-84 thunders by. Between the two diners is Myers Motel, with both old and new tourist cabins in a pleasant U-shaped setting.

Graham Musselwhite stands at the till in his new 1950 Milford Diner, while behind the counter, relative Viola Ogrodnik waits on customers.

Within sight of the bridge to New York, a 1949 Paramount Roadking, outfitted in stainless steel with burnished circles, long operated as Matamoras Diner. In the early 1990s, it was banished to a field in New York, until diner entrepreneur Jerry Berta found it in 1993. The classic Paramount was shipped to Berta's Dinerland assemblage in Rockford, Michigan, but eventually ended up as the West Bay Diner in Grand Marais.

U.S. ROUTE 11

U.S. Route 11 has traditionally been the main road through the Wyoming Valley, carrying the lion's share of the street-level, noninterstate traffic between Wilkes-Barre and Scranton. The route has shifted from one road to another since it was first marked in 1926, but its current alignment through West Nanticoke, Kingston, Pittston, and up Birney Avenue through Moosic and Scranton has essentially been the same since the 1930s. U.S. 11 stretches from New Orleans to Canada, but nowhere along its route are the diners thicker than in this western outpost of megalopolis. Five modern stainless diners from the 1950s currently line 25 miles of older urban and suburban commercial strip. No diners remain on U.S. 11 as it follows the Susquehanna River towards Wilkes-Barre, but at one time, the stretch between Bloomsburg and Berwick had two: the Zephyr (a 1947 O'Mahony) and the Majestic (a 1950s Mountain View).

Today, the first diner northbound is the Flamingo of West Nanticoke. Its edge-of-town setting is typical of the postwar roadside. The old road into West Nanticoke passes behind the diner and is flanked by houses that predate the automobile. The diner sits on the outside of a curve and is adjacent to a U-shaped motel court. The Garden Drive-in Theater is just down the street. The modern diner is steel-clad, painted cream with green trim, and has rounded, glass-block corners. Although the Flamingo has changed little over the years, its appearance does not conform to the stock models used by any of the major manufacturers; it most resembles a Paramount.

The Lark Diner in Larksville, with its distinctive corner scrolls, is a 1950 Mountain View. The Lark sits in an older commercial strip that contains a number of nondiners, and at least one used-to-be diner. Even with its formstone base and mansard roof, Uncle Pat's M.D. Sporting Goods shows the definite lines of a modern stainless diner. More than likely it is a mid 1950s O'Mahony. Across the North Branch of the Susquehanna in Plains, a 1956 Silk City is in service along the original U.S. 11 alignment as Andy's River Road Diner.

Just off the diner drive in Moosic is the Home Plate Diner, across the road from the Lackawanna River. Inside the diner, a black and white marble counter with blue and white tile base remains.

Tony's Diner, a circa 1948 Paramount, lives on in West Nanticoke as the Flamingo.

The U.S. 11 roadside also serves motorists coming off I-81. Just south of this exit, at the corner of Birney Avenue and Spring Brook Avenue (Route 502), Charge's Diner-Restaurant is a 1955 Mountain View that retains the recessed ceiling, diamond-patterned terrazzo floor, and centered canopy

The Home Plate in Moosic retains some of its original 1940s O'Mahony interior.

clock, but came without corner cowcatchers. Charge's has a racing theme and sponsors car shows every Sunday. It serves foods such as potato pancakes and pierogies.

Just north of the interchange is an interstate service strip for those exiting into the southern suburban fringes of Scranton. Gas, food, and lodging establishments have long lined the route. Terry's Diner, a 1956 O'Mahony, was lightly remodeled in 1987 with woodgrain counters and other environmental touches, but it was destroyed by fire in early 1999. It was #2294, one of the last O'Mahonys. The founder's son, Terry Holmes, Jr., is replacing it with the Skyliner Diner, a 1955 O'Mahony from Pittston.

Scranton, cut up by railroads and bisected by the Lackawanna River, isn't the easiest coal and mill town to navigate, and U.S. 11 has been routed through the city in different ways over the years. The North Scranton Expressway now carries northbound traffic that in the 1920s and 1930s went through Providence Square by way of Providence Road, or Lackawanna Street and Main Street, or Wyoming Street and Green Ridge Street. By the 1950s, northbound U.S. 11 followed Pittston Street to Moosic Street, and north on Harrison Street toward Dunmore Street, then west on Green Ridge (Lackawanna Trial). This route caused Moosic Street to carry both north-south valley traffic and the traffic accessing the city over the Pocono Highway (Route 307). But despite this labyrinth of street routes, diner proprietors knew where to find hungry travelers.

Chick's Diner has graced the outer end of Moosic Street since 1951, operating next to a corner Texaco station one lot in from Meadow Street in the fashion of an urban diner. When I-81 was constructed in the sixties, Chick's, located next to the Central Scranton Interchange, continued to benefit. Chick's is a red and stainless Mountain View without cowcatchers. The corner and vestibule panels are quilted, and the diner retains its original squared-off eave. Yet another early 1950s red and stainless Mountain View, with the same counter-and-booth floorplan and the same centered canopy clock, but with cowcatcher corners, operates on Providence Road as the Glider Diner. The diner is named for the original restaurant opened by Charles "Chappy" LeStrange and Eugene Cosgrove, who bought a couple of gliders in 1945. They sold the planes but used the packing crates to build a diner, as materials were scarce after the war. Chappy still runs the current diner. Just up Main Avenue in Dickson City (not on U.S. 11) is the Mid-Valley Diner, another red and stainless Mountain View; this 1950 model also has cowcatcher corners. It is currently for sale, to be replaced by a bank. No doubt about it, this is Mountain View country.

KAY'S ITALIAN RESTAURANT

CIRCA 1920 O'MAHONY

Route 435, Daleville

FEATURED DINER

KEVIN PATRICK

When Walter Woehrle saw the dining car rotting in a junkyard not 5 miles from his family's Italian restaurant in 1983, he had a vision. When he finally bought the thing, people told him he was crazy.

It took thirteen months of family togetherness—replacing oak studs, refinishing woodwork, repairing the old Kelvinator—but now it's the pride of Daleville. The diner originally came with a 38-foot white marble counter and nineteen stools (two originals are in the waiting room).

Most of the food is Italian—all homemade, of course—hero sandwiches; stromboli; appetizers, such as buffalo shrimp, mussels, and antipasta; pasta, including ravioli, gnocchi, ziti, and lasagna; a variety of pizzas, such as white with broccoli and ham and cheese; and entrees of shrimp parmigiana, stuffed eggplant, and scallops and chips. Desserts range from cannoli and brownie à la mode to apple crisp and rice pudding.

BEACON DINER
1941 PARAMOUNT, REMODELED
Routes 54 and 309, Hometown

KEVIN PATRICK

For those familiar with Route 309, the Beacon Diner is synonymous with Hometown. It's hard to tell Hometown from Hazleton or Tamaqua, but there's no missing the Beacon, set back and slanted to the corner of Routes 309 and 54 for maximum visibility. To the uninitiated, the beige, stuccoed building with the cedar shake mansard appears to be like any other road-side restaurant, but a few telltale signs mark the Beacon as a genuine diner. The restaurant's dimensions, window spacing, and pylonlike, metal-box sign on the road proclaiming The Beacon in neon obviously predate the building's environmental style. The curved glass-block corners not only hint at a diner pedigree, but they tag it as a Paramount.

The Beacon is in fact the last prewar diner brought to the Anthracite Region that still stands. It was trucked to the site in two 60-by-14-foot sections and pushed onto a predug, stone-walled foundation. On May 28, 1941, Ernest Taylor opened the diner.

By the time the Beacon was remodeled in 1969, stainless steel was passé, so the owners embraced environmentalism: woodgrain table tops, diagonal plank counterbase, and spindle-top booth dividers in the dining room.

Control of the diner passed on to George E. Taylor, Ernest's son. In 1982, he bought the Route 443 Diner in nearby Lehighton. That diner had been moved near the junction of Routes 443 and 209 in the early 1960s and then was remodeled in 1968. It now operates as the Beacon 443.

The menus at both Beacons are large and eclectic: seafood, steaks, chops, Cajun food, and, especially, Greek food. Being Greeks themselves, the Taylors know their spanakopita from their tieropita. You can get both, as well as pastitso, moussaka, shish kebab, a variety of other dishes wrapped in grape leaves, and desserts made of phyllo dough.

CHICK'S DINER
1951 MOUNTAIN VIEW #289
1032 Moosic Ave. (Route 307), Scranton

KEVIN PATRICK

Chick's Diner is the kitchen of Scranton. Situated next to a corner Texaco station on one of the old roads into the city, this down-home place has all the characteristics of a typical northeastern Pennsylvania diner. The atmosphere is informal and friendly, and the time-honored local tradition of "going to Chick's" has institutionalized the diner as an indispensable part of the community.

In the preinterstate days, Scranton-bound traffic following the old Lackawanna Trail up from Stroudsburg took a left fork south of Daleville (now Route 307) and came over Moosic Mountain into the city on Moosic Street. Chick's is located where the base of the mountain met the edge of the city. As luck would have it, when I-81 was constructed in the 1960s, it followed the same geographic break, with a new interchange at the diner's doorstep. So thanks to the whims of the highway planners, Chick's is alive and well after two generations of owners and five decades of service.

The original Chick's was opened in 1946 by Vince Chickillo and Walter Swanick. Remembered as a "railcar," it was likely a railcar-inspired Ward & Dickinson from before the war, which was the diner of choice in the region then. Five years later, that diner burned down, so Vince and Walter bought a Mountain View diner, a brand popular in the region after World War II. In 1951, the new red-and-stainless Chick's with a dark bluish gray interior opened. It was enlarged in 1959, but little has been altered since. That's a big part of its appeal; after all these years, Chick's has retained the look, feel, and atmosphere of an authentic 1950s diner.

The continuity extends to the diner's ownership, now the responsibility of Ron Chickillo and Jim Swanick, the sons of the founders. In 1965, Jim bought the Hawley Diner to the north, which he still runs with his wife, Carol. Chick's is open twenty-four hours and the diner is best known for its late-night servings of French fries and gravy. Some folks are even convinced that Chick's originated the dish.

CHARLIE'S PIZZA & SUBS

1951 PARAMOUNT

1401 W. Market St., Pottsville

FEATURED DINER

KEVIN PATRICK

Charlie's Pizza & Subs is a pristine 1951 Paramount dinette, a compact style popular among manufacturers just before and after World War II. The low price of smaller diners was a selling point during the Depression, and after the war they appealed to returning vets who were unable to afford a standard diner. Dinettes were made for short order cooking, but as owner Tony DiCello can attest, the workmanship was still top-notch.

After a half century of service, there is virtually no deterioration to either the inside tile or the outside stainless steel. The floor is the original brown-and-beige, octagonal mosaic. The lower walls and counter base are white ceramic with a row of light blue tiles that match the white and blue recessed ceiling. The twelve-stool counter runs half the length of the diner; the other half holds booths. Centered above the stainless steel backbar is a sharp Paramount clock, still ticking.

Charlie's began serving Pottsville's west end as the 14th Street Diner, but was also known as Alfred's Diner, after original owner Al Joulwan. It served a neighborhhood crowd. Locals Ted and Christine Angst remember walking to the diner for Sunday night meatloaf dinners back in the early 1960s.

Characteristic of diner families, other Joulwans were in the business. In 1953, Al's uncle Tom Joulwan opened the nearby Garfield Diner, which garnered enough business to warrant an L-shaped expansion a few years later. He also opened a second diner on Route 61, which later burned down. When Tom retired, he sold the Garfield to his cousin Joe Thomas.

In 1963, Al sold the 14th Street Diner and retired to Florida. Two years later, Charlie DiCello and his son Tony relocated their pizza business from 17th Street to the old dinette. The thirty-five-year stint of Charlie's is a testimony to Paramount's uncompromising craftsmanship, the neighborhood's stability, and most importantly, the DiCellos' fine pizza.

THE DINER AT TANNERSVILLE
1960S FODERO/1982 SWINGLE #1182DKLVR
Route 715 at I-80, Tannersville

FEATURED DINER

KEVIN PATRICK

The Diner at Tannersville is an example of the role the Delaware Water Gap played in the geography of diners in northeastern Pennsylvania. The stainless steel diner is easily seen high on a hill overlooking the ceaseless stream of traffic on I-80. A rooftop neon sign makes it even more noticeable. The

Tannersville is centered in the westernmost diner oupost of I-80. To the east of the gap, the highway cuts right through the megalopolitan heart of Dinerland USA, but as it tracks west of Stroudsburg, it becomes a diner dead zone. Diners are absent for hundreds of miles.

Built by Fodero in the 1960s, the restaurant opened as the Bayway Diner in Elizabeth, New Jersey. Years later, it was traded in to Swingle, reconditioned in 1982, and shipped to Tannersville, where Dick and Sarah Brown ran it as Dick's Country Kitchen. Around the same time, Jim Schlier opened Schlier's Truck Towing and Repair on the same hilltop, creating a multifunctional, interstate service plaza. While the diner went through a number of name and ownership changes, Jim held title to the land. In 1995, he bought the restaurant and renamed it the Diner at Tannersville.

The Tannersville's style is a hybrid between the exaggerated modern diners of the early 1960s and the environmental diners of the 1970s. The top half of the exterior is covered with stainless steel, but the base is made of a pink-colored stone. The interior layout is balanced by a counter, cut in the center, with booths along the front windows and to the left and a dining room to the right. Woodgrain, instead of ceramic tiles, lines the counter base. Floral patterned tiles cover the back wall—a typical late-diner alternative to stainless steel.

Hot turkey and beef platters with mashed potatoes and gravy are popular, but the diner is best known for its homemade soups, especially the New England Clam Chowder on Fridays. Homemade rice pudding is a favorite dessert.

DINER DIRECTORY

BOWMANSTOWN

Bowmanstown Diner
642 White St.
(610) 852-2752
1952 Fodero, Silk City dining room
added 1960.
*American food; crab patties, hot roast beef
sandwiches, french fries with gravy.
Open 24 hours.*

BRODHEADSVILLE

Chestnut Hill Diner
Rt. 209 (Star Route)
(570) 992-3222
Circa 1964 Fodero (formerly Penny's
Diner, East Norwalk, CT), redone by
Swingle in 1984 as #584DKVU.
*American and Greek food; gyros, lamb
and duck (Sun.); homemade cakes.
Open daily, 5 A.M.–11 P.M.*

Meadowbrook Diner
Rt. 209
(570) 992-5205
1974 Swingle #1274DVR. Rehabbed
(formerly Grand Diner, Rahway, NJ,
#567DVDR). Kitchen is a 1950s Silk City.
*Pennsylvania Dutch food; breakfast all day;
cream dried beef, roast turkey; homemade
desserts, apple dumplings.
Open Mon.–Thurs., 6 A.M.–3 P.M.;
Fri.–Sun., 6 A.M.–9 P.M.*

Edy's Bistro
Rts. 115 & 209
(570) 992-9944
Mid-1950s Silk City.
*Fine dining; sautéed dishes.
Open Mon.–Fri., 11:30 A.M.–9 P.M.; Sat.,
11:30 A.M.–10 P.M.; Sun., 11:30 A.M.–7 P.M.*

CLARKS SUMMIT

Topper's Diner
Rts. 6 and 11
Circa 1954 O'Mahony
Closed.

DALEVILLE

Kay's Italian Restaurant
Route 435
(570) 842-6226
Circa 1920 O'Mahony.
*Open daily, 11 A.M.–11 P.M.
For more information, see page 152.*

Leo's Diner
Route 435
1930s Bixler
Closed.

Rainbow Inn
Route 435
1930s.
Part of a bar.

DICKSON CITY

Mid-Valley Diner
1601 Main St.
1950 Mountain View #268, "Streamliner" model.
Closed.

Six East Restaurant-Diner
1611 Rt. 6 (Scranton-Carbondale Hwy.)
(570) 489-8974
1949 Mountain View, remodeled. Originally in Clark's Summit, moved 1963
and called Parrish's Diner.
*American, German, Irish, Italian, Polish,
Russian food; rice pudding.
Open Tues.–Sun., 8 A.M.–10 P.M.*

DUNMORE

Chaplin's Family Restaurant
223 E. Drinker St.
(570) 961-2328
1940s, extensively remodeled. Formerly
Loops Diner.
Home-cooked American food.
Open Mon.–Thurs., 7 A.M.–7 P.M.;
Fri.–Sat., 7 A.M.–midnight;
Sun., 7 A.M.–3 P.M.

EFFORT

Effort Diner
Rt. 115
(610) 681-4212
1936 remodeled.
Homestyle Pennsylvania Dutch food;
breakfast all day; apple dumplings.
Open daily, 6 A.M.–10 P.M.

FACTORYVILLE

Blue Bird II
Rt. 6 and 11
(570) 945-7686
Circa 1948 Mountain View #231.
Formerly Red Chanticler Diner.
American food; meatloaf, chicken; home-
made pies, muffins and cheesecake.
Open Mon.–Sat., 6 A.M.–9 P.M.;
Sun., 6 A.M.–3 P.M.

FOUNTAIN

Felty's Diner
Rt. 25 (near I-81 Hegins)
(570) 682-9850
Former railcar.

FRACKVILLE

Dutch Kitchen Restaurant
433 S. Lehigh Ave. (Rt. 61)
(570) 874-3265
1959 Silk City #5903, remodeled.
Pennsylvania Dutch and Eastern European
food; roast turkey over Dutch stuffing, pot
pie, chowchow; rice pudding, cheesecake.
Open daily, 7 A.M.–10 P.M.

Mountain City Diner
10 W. Oak St.
(570) 874-3039
1950s, remodeled.

HALLSTEAD

Beaver's Restaurant
Rt. 11
(570) 879-4373
Circa 1956 O'Mahony.
Originally in Nicholson.
American food; daily specials;
homemade pies, rice pudding.
Open Mon.–Fri., 7 A.M.–9 P.M.;
Sat., 7 A.M.–8 P.M.

HAWLEY

Hawley Diner
302 Main St. (Rt. 6)
(570) 226-0523
1954 Mountain View #398.
Hot and cold buffet; waffles,
strawberry shortcake.
Open 6 A.M.–7:30 P.M.;
Fri.–Sat., 11 P.M.–4 A.M.

HAZLETON

Blue Comet Diner
45 S. Church St.
(717) 454-7010
1957 Mountain View #488, remodeled.
American and international food; sautéed
dishes, mussels marinara, pasta, chicken
français; cheesecake, bread pudding.
Open 24 hours.

HOMETOWN

Beacon Diner
Rts. 54 and 309
(570) 668-1340
1941 Paramount, remodeled.
Open daily, 6 A.M.–10 P.M.
For more information, see page 153.

HONESDALE

Town House Diner
920 Main St. (Rt. 6)
(570) 253-1311
1957 Mountain View #508, remodeled.
Originally Steve's Diner.
American food; char-broiled hamburgers.
Open daily, 7 A.M.–9 P.M.

JIM THORPE

Sunrise Diner
3 Hazard Sq.
(570) 325-4093
1951 O'Mahony. Originally Steve's
Diner.
American and Polish food; homemade
pierogies, halupki (stuffed cabbage), soup,
roast turkey; homemade cakes and pies.
Open Sun.–Thurs., 5 A.M.–8 P.M.;
Fri.–Sat., 24 hours.

KRESGEVILLE

Sunset Diner
Rt. 209
(610) 681-4482
1930s, extensively remodeled.
American food; daily specials; pork and
sauerkraut, grilled liver, spaghetti, haddock.
Open daily, 6 A.M.–9 P.M.

LARKSVILLE

Lark Diner
650 E. Main St. (Rt. 11)
1950 Mountain View.
Closed.

MARSHALLS CREEK

209 Diner
5139 Milcourt Rd. (Rt. 209)
(570) 223-1144
1934 or 1940 O'Mahony #1090,
remodeled.
Greek food; gyros, shish kebab, spinach pie,
Greek salads; homemade dessert.
Open daily, 6 A.M.–9 P.M. (in summer
until midnight)

Yankee Doodle Diner
5000 Milford Rd.
(570) 223-7272
1960s Kullman, postmodern remodel.
Formerly Pocono Queen Diner,
originally Park West Diner.
Homemade American food; pasta,
garlic chicken.
Open daily, 6 A.M.–9 P.M.

MILFORD

Milford Diner
301 Broad St.
(570) 296-7033
1972 Manno.
American food; rice pudding.
Open Mon.–Thurs., 6 A.M.–9 P.M.;
Fri.–Sat., 6 A.M.–10:30 P.M.;
Sun., 7 A.M.–9 P.M.

Village Diner
Rts. 6 and 209
1956 Mountain View #462.

MOOSIC

Charge's Diner-Restaurant
4700 Birney Ave. (Rt. 11)
(570) 457-8949
1955 Mountain View, possibly #404,
remodeled.
Italian and American food; lasagna with
sausage; homemade pies, rice pudding.
Open daily, 6 A.M.–6 P.M.

Home Plate Diner
2 Lonsome Rd.
(570) 457-4944
Circa 1940s O'Mahony. Formerly
Judy's Diner.
American food; homemade desserts.
Open Mon.–Tues., 5 A.M.–2:30 P.M.;
Wed.–Fri., 5 A.M.–8 P.M.

Skyliner Diner
4118 Birney Ave. (Rt. 11)
1955 O'Mahony. From Pittston.
Closed.

MOUNT POCONO

Pioneer Diner
508 Belmont Ave. (Rts. 611 and 940)
(570) 839-7620
1968 Swingle #568DL.
Greek food; breakfast all day.
Open daily, 6 A.M.–9 P.M.

MOUNTAINHOME

Mountainhome Diner
Rt. 191
Possible 1953 Mountain View,
remodeled.

NEW MILFORD

Trail Diner
Rt. 11
Circa 1950 Mountain View #266.

PLAINS

Andy's River Road Diner
335 N. River St.
(570) 829-9444
1956 Silk City #5607. Formerly
Plains Diner.
Home-cooked American food; pot pie,
sautéed dishes, lobster, steaks, meatloaf.

Eddie's Place
577 Fox Hill Rd.
(570) 823-1990
Circa 1941 O'Mahony.
Homemade American food; breakfast
all day; roast beef, meatloaf.
Open 24 hours.

POTTSVILLE

Charlie's Pizza & Subs
1401 W. Market St.
(717) 622-3609
1951 Paramount.
Open daily, 10 A.M.–10 P.M.
For more information, see page 155.

Garfield Diner
402 W. Market St. (Rt. 209)
(570) 628-2199
1954 Kullman. Originally the
Pottsville Diner.
American food; breakfast all day; pork and
sauerkraut, roast turkey, broiled haddock;
homemade puddings, milkshakes.
Open 24 hours.

SCHUYLKILL HAVEN

Country Squire Diner
300 Rt. 61 S.
(570) 385-3559
1960s Kullman.
American food; breakfast all day; chicken
à la king; London broil, haddock, stir fry.
Open Mon.–Sat., 7 A.M.–9 P.M.;
Sun., 7 A.M.–8 P.M.

Paradise Family Restaurant
Rt. 61 S.
(570) 385-0314
1950s Silk City. Environmental
remodel. Formerly Manheim Family
Restaurant.
American food; breakfast all day; beef liver;
homemade pies, cakes, puddings, baklava.
Open 24 hours.

SCOTRUN

Scotrun Diner
Rt. 611
(570) 629-2430
Circa 1970.
American, Italian, and Greek food;
sirloin steaks; many desserts.
Open daily, 7 A.M.–10 P.M.

SCRANTON

Chick's Diner
1032 Moosic Ave. (Rt. 307)
(570) 344-4156
1951 Mountain View #289.
Open 24 hours.
For more information, see page 154.

Gabe's Diner
1680 N. Keyser Ave. (at Rt. 307)
(570) 347-1294
1950s, probably Kullman remodeled.
American food; stuffed chicken,
pigs in a blanket.
Open 24 hours.

Glider Diner
890 Providence Rd.
(570) 343-8036
1951 Mountain View #302.
American food; hot roast beef sandwich,
Glider burger, Wimpy BBQ sandwich.
Open 24 hours.

STROUDSBURG

Arlington Diner
834 N. 9th St. (Rt. 611)
(570) 421-2329
1940s Silk City, remodeled.
American food; daily specials; spaghetti,
fish fry, pork and sauerkraut, haddock,
chicken stir fry.
Open Mon.–Thurs., 6 A.M.–10 P.M.;
Fri.–Sat., 6 A.M.–11 P.M.;
Sun. 7 A.M.–10 P.M.

Besecker's Diner
1427 N. 5th St. (Rt. 191)
(570) 421-6193
1958 Silk City #5806.
American food; breakfast all day; liver and
onions, salads, pickled beets; homemade
pies and cakes.
Open daily, 6 A.M.–10 P.M.

Compton's Pancake House
105 S. Park Ave.
(570) 424-6909
1948 Paramount and 1950 Fodero,
remodeled.
American food; breakfast all day; lunch
menu; specialty toppings on pancakes.
Open Sun.–Thurs., 6 A.M.–3 P.M.;
Fri.–Sat., 6 A.M.–8 P.M.

Hula Hoop's
745 Main St. (Bus. Rt. 209)
(570) 424-1950
1948 Paramount/1950 Fodero addition.

Key City Diner
1947 W. Main St. (Rt. 209)
(570) 421-5903
1970s environmental.
Homemade American food; breakfast
all day; soups; homemade rice pudding,
bread pudding.
Open Sun.–Thurs., 6 A.M.–9 P.M.;
Fri.–Sat., 6 A.M.–10 P.M.

Snydersville Diner
Bus. Rt. 209
(570) 992-4003
1970 Swingle #1270DU. Originally
Marty's Diner, a circa 1955 Mountain
View (#450) from Wappinger Falls, NY,
with 1971 dining room #271DR. Barrel-
roofed OK Diner originally at site; formerly Besecker's Diner (fire destroyed
earlier diner at site, which included
Swingle #468DVU).
American foods; daily specials;
homemade baked goods.
Open 24 hours.

TAMAQUA

Just Us Crafters
12 Mauch Chunk St.
(570) 668-0219
Remodeled. Formerly Magic Touch.
Originally Five Point Diner, a 1940
O'Mahony.
No food served.

Tamaqua Diner
39 Center St.
(570) 668-3540
1930s Bixler. Formerly Taylor's Diner
and J. B.'s Diner.
*Pennsylvania Dutch, Greek, and Italian
food; seafood, steaks; homemade pastries.
Open 24 hours.*

White Diner
Rt. 309 S.
(570) 386-4333
1950s environmental remodel.
*American food; breakfast all day;
soft ice cream.
Open daily, 5 A.M.–7 P.M.*

TANNERSVILLE

Billy's Pocono Diner
Rt. 611 (just N. of Rt. 715)
(570) 629-1450
1950s Kullman, remodeled.
*American food; breakfast all day; seafood,
steaks, pork chops; homemade soups, gravy,
spaghetti sauce; hard and soft ice cream,
homemade tapioca and rice pudding.
Open daily, 6 A.M.–10 P.M.*

The Diner at Tannersville
Rt. 715 (exit 45 of I-80)
(570) 620-2303
1960s Fodero. Formerly Bayway Diner,
Elizabeth, NJ, redone by Swingle in 1982
as #1182DKLVR. Formerly Diner 45.
Open daily, 6 A.M.–9 P.M.
For more information, see page 156.

WEST NANTICOKE

Flamingo Diner
Rt. 11
(570) 735-6400
Probably circa 1948 Paramount.
Formerly Tony's Diner.
*American food; breakfast all day; sausage.
Open Mon.–Fri., 6 A.M.–6 P.M.;
Sat.–Sun., 6 A.M.–3 P.M.*

WEST PITTSTON

MD Sporting Goods
1320 Wyoming Ave. (Rt. 11)
(570) 655-3521
1950s, probably O'Mahony, remodeled.
No food served.

WHITE HAVEN

White Haven Family Diner
302 Main St.
(570) 443-8797
1950s Paramount. Formerly AJ Diner.
*American food; Sunday breakfast buffet;
big burgers, club sandwiches.
Open daily, 6 A.M.–8 P.M.*

WILKES-BARRE

Diamond City Diner
33 Wilkes-Barre Blvd. (at E. Market)
1951 Mountain View #313. Originally in
Exeter; formerly Palooka's Diner.
Closed.

WYOMING

R & J Family Diner
22 Wyoming Ave.
(570) 693-2864
1953, extensively remodeled. Formerly
Charlie's Supper Club/Wyoming Diner.
*Italian and American food; homemade
spaghetti and ravioli; homemade pastries.
Open Mon.–Sat., 6 A.M.–9 P.M.;
Sun., 6 A.M.–1 P.M.*

CENTRAL PENNSYLVANIA

The mountains of Central Pennsylvania are a diner dead zone. In this twenty-two-county slice through the middle of the state, stretching from the New York border south to the Mason-Dixon Line and from Harrisburg west to the rim of the Alleghenies, there are only twenty-six diners. Several of the counties don't have a single surviving example. In north-central Pennsylvania, extending eastward into the adjacent counties of the Anthracite Region and westward across the state's northern tier, the diner world is particularly bleak. Right in the center of this area is the Wellsboro

Diner, on U.S. Route 6 in the gaslit town of Wellsboro, nearly 100 miles away from the next nearest Pennsylvania diner.

Half of all the diners in the Central Pennsylvania region are in and around Harrisburg. Trucks and trains from across the country funnel through this transportation nexus at the edge of the Appalachians on their way to the big cities of the east. Harrisburg is a western outpost for Dinerland U.S.A., a continuation of the Dutch Country diner belt. Within sight of the city is the same Blue Mountain rampart that separates the Dutch Country from the Anthracite Region and the Poconos. Here, however, it is the boundary between Dinerdom and the diner dead zone.

Just north of Harrisburg, Blue Mountain is the first in a series of Appalachian ridges cleaved by the Susquehanna River to form water gaps that direct the routes of the highways into this washboard region of folded mountains and valleys. Like the gaps farther east, this one, too, is a diner haven. The Decoven Diner is a few miles beyond Blue Mountain on U.S. Route 11/15, and Angie's is up the road at the edge of New Buffalo. Across the river on U.S. Route 22/322 is the site of the old Riverview Diner, yet another Pennsylvania diner loosed from its roadside moorings in the 1980s and shipped abroad. In the mountains beyond, there are only eight diners.

Throughout the entire Northeast United States, the pattern of diners is broken by the Appalachians. Mountainous northern New England has far fewer diners than southern New England. Western New York has a fraction of the

BRIAN BUTKO

Bill's Diner, a 1939 Silk City, moved out of Hummelstown in the early 1990s.

diners found in the eastern part of the state. And in Pennsylvania, the two western diner regions cover two-thirds of the state but have less than 25 percent of the diners. Some have suggested that the increased transportation cost caused by the irregular topography made the delivery of diners prohibitively expensive. However, Appalachian topography was not much of a factor in railroad freight rates for flatcar-delivered diners, and many places that could be reached by highways through water gaps without the need to climb a single mountain don't have a single trucked-in diner. Not only that, but the same mountains exist in northeastern Pennsylvania, where there are plenty of diners.

The Appalachians themselves are not directly the culprit but have influenced the two factors

Lemoyne Diner in 1941. After it closed in the 1980s, entrepreneurs moved it to Baltimore, but it never reopened and is scheduled for the American Diner Museum in Providence, Rhode Island.

Steelton Diner, which was across from the Bethlehem Steel plant in Steelton, was not only a diner graft, but also a "factory gate" diner. It had no parking lot because it served the steelworkers who could walk to it from across the street. The diner was damaged by fire in the 1960s.

that seem most responsible for the proliferation of diners in the Northeast: population density and proximity to diner manufacturers. Very simply, there are fewer diners because there are fewer people, and this much smaller market is a lot farther from the manufacturers. The towns are also smaller and the rural populations are more agriculturally oriented, limiting the number of hungry patrons wandering around at off hours. Except for weekends—and in some places even then—the streets are rolled up at night. The bulk of the eating-out clientele can be handled by traditional in-town restaurants operating during normal business hours.

A secondary Great Lakes diner-manufacturing region evolved during the early twentieth century to tap the market lying beyond the effective reach of the eastern manufacturers. Ward & Dickinson and Rochester Grills, in western New York, and Bixler and J. G. Brill's Kuhlman Car Company, in Ohio, covered the trans-Appalachian west with their products, but none of these companies survived the Great Depression and World War II. Gradually, their dining cars disappeared from the roadsides and mountain towns of the northern Appalachians, with only the biggest roads and the larger communities getting replacement diners from the east after World War II.

At midcentury, Williamsport had a number of diners, but now they exist in name only, as the word *diner* has been applied to a variety of Williamsport

KEVIN PATRICK

Peggy's Diner on Route 220 in Claysburg is one of many surviving environmental models from the 1970s.

restaurants. One of the real ones was Al's Diner (originally the Modern Diner) on 4th Street, named for owner Albino Ferrari. It was forced to move in 1955, when the town's parking authority bought the land to build a parking lot.

A small handful of the old town diners have survived in Wellsboro, State College, Lewistown, and McConnellsburg. These have been joined by at least three extant examples from the postwar years, but for the most part, diner density is pretty low in Central Pennsylvania beyond Blue Mountain.

Nearly half of all Central Pennsylvania diners are located on highways at edge-of-town locations, and the same percentage are paired with gas stations (some now closed), a higher proportion than in any other region. This is a holdover from the preinterstate era when motorist services hugged the edge of town.

Of all the limited-access highways that now cross the region, only the Pennsylvania Turnpike existed before 1962. The postwar diner wave barely made it this far west and had long since crested by the time the new interstates started to arrive. When the turnpike interchanges opened in 1940, they attracted a few diners but offered too little traffic too far from the eastern manufacturers to attract more operators during the diner surge of the 1950s. In anticipation of the superhighway, Pottie's Diner opened in 1938 on Route 11 between Carlisle and Shippensburg. The Carlisle Diner was downtown, and both Betty's and the Pike Diner (a 1941 Silk City) opened just north of the Carlisle interchange.

Central Pennsylvania has nine modern stainless steel diners, all but three in the Harrisburg area. Few diners in the region have adopted a postmodern look, though Harrisburg's Colonial Park Diner, which was originally built on-site as Uncle John's Pancake House, recently added a stainless steel mansard for a retro diner feel.

The best-preserved barrel roof diner in the state is undoubtedly the Wellsboro, but there is another example whose heritage makes up for what its altered form lacks. Just off the diamond in downtown Lewistown, a location typical of only the oldest diners in the smallest towns, is the unassuming brick facade of the Trolley Car Café. Aside from its curious name and two front doors, nothing about it says *diner*—nothing, that is, from the street. Inside, the restaurant's twin curved ceilings reveal a double barrel roof diner graft. Two barrel roof diners—which account for the two front doors—were set side by side perpendicular to the street, flush against the sidewalk, and flanked by two- and three-story brick row buildings.

One of the best examples of an old diner graft was the Cross Keys Diner on the Lincoln Highway (U.S. Route 30) east of New Oxford, now the site of the Cross Keys Family Restaurant. The Cross Keys Diner was established in 1937 by John George, who joined four barrel roof diners together to form a massive graft that could feed seventy at a time. This roadside wonder was demolished a decade ago, however, leaving the Trolley Car as its closest and sole surviving relative in the state.

Although the interior of the Trolley Car has been as heavily remodeled as the exterior, its original form is still visible. The two grafted diners are of different dimensions. The more mysterious newer half is somewhat Bixlerlike (or maybe it's a Rochester Grill), with the original restrooms to the left of a narrow corridor at the far end of the diner. The older half is narrower and shorter and has a traceable pedigree. It's a 1920s O'Mahony that was shipped from the New Jersey factory to Lewistown on a flatcar and then drayed up the street to its foundation with a team of horses, the standard procedure at the time. It was set up as part of a 1920s diner chain known as Club Diners, Inc., which operated O'Mahonys throughout New York, New Jersey, and Pennsylvania, including the Central Pennsylvania towns of Chambersburg, State College, and Williamsport. Like the one in Lewistown, these were in-town diners set perpendicularly on narrow lots. As a chain of standardized, prefabricated restaurants serving inexpensive, quickly prepared food under a single corporate banner, Club Diners had much in common with the more famous White Castle Chain and other fast-food outlets that would come to rule the roadside.

The Lewistown Club Diner was run by George Watson, Ira Briner, and John Hunter. At some point, the second diner was brought in from parts unknown to expand the operation. After World War II, when Club Diners

---

RUNNING A DINER

Diner owners agree that running a diner is a lot of work. If you want to have a well-run diner with good food and service, it means long hours, even if it's only open one shift. It involves ordering, restocking inventory, cleaning, payroll, maintenence, food preparation, bill paying, and cooking the food. Just trying to order supplies so that food doesn't run out and isn't wasted is a huge task. And at any size diner, the details start slipping when the owner's not around.

At Kuppy's in Middletown, Greg Kupp begins work at 4 A.M. preparing for opening an hour later. His wife, Carol, fills in while he naps from 2 to 4 P.M., but he's back there till 8 at night. They're closed Sundays, but even a half day like Saturday means a twelve-hour shift when setup and cleanup are included. As Carol says, "If someone calls off, we can't call a temp agency. We have great employees, and we all fill in where we have to, no matter what the job."

Greg Kupp, the fourth generation in his family to run Kuppy's Diner, and his wife, Carol.

---

were but a fading memory, Bobby Campbell bought the restaurant and operated it as Campbell's Diner into the 1960s. Its patrons aged and drifted away and its heritage faded, with only its form surviving to fool later generations into thinking it was once a streetcar. The diner was bricked up in the 1980s and was transformed into a bar. It was pretty beat up when the current owner bought it in 1992, but he has worked to bring it back to life as a foodways fixture on the streets of Lewistown.

It's likely that Chambersburg's Club Diner was renamed the B&B Diner, which is listed in the 1929 city directory at 136 Lincoln Way. The B&B was renamed the Lincoln Diner in 1936, then moved west of town in 1948 as the Silver Top Diner. A convenience store is reportedly built around it. A new Lincoln Diner replaced the old one in 1948 and operated till 1978, when it became an optician's office; it was razed in 1998.

At the eastern edge of McConnellsburg is Johnnie's Diner, another barrel roof diner, this one disguised beneath a houselike environmental remodel. Johnnie's sits at a critical junction on the old Lincoln Highway known as the Forks. Before World War II, this was the turnoff to Baltimore and Washington for eastbound traffic following the Lincoln Highway, a junction now located at Breezewood with the intersection of the Pennsylvania Turnpike and I-70. Like that modern motorist services node, the Forks had a cluster of commercial activity that peaked in the 1940s when Johnnie's built a motel, diner, and gas station (now gone) as a roadside tourist service one-stop.

Breezewood was formerly home to the Breezewood Diner, a 1945 Silk City. It was later renamed Pete and Betty's Diner and then moved out in 1968. Denny's Classic Diner, the state's first Starlite, began business there in March 1999. Denny's has been opening these shiny, postmodern, factory-built diners across the country since 1997, and twenty-five more are planned for 1999. The company has recently announced that it plans to convert all of its 1,700 restaurants to diner decor.

State College, with its huge resident pedestrian population of Penn State University students, has been a diner town since the 1920s, with seven different diners operating under a variety of names. (For an excellent overview of State College diners, see John Swinton's "Diner Days in State College," *State College,* February 1994.) Two remain, each a representative of one of the two diner waves that swept across the state. The dining-car concept was introduced to State College by Club Diners, Inc., which brought an O'Mahony to 110 East College Street in 1926. After the chain collapsed in the 1930s, the diner was renamed Boots' Diner after operator "Boots" Ripka. In 1941, the diner was moved to the corner of South Atherton Street and Beaver Avenue and operated as the Electric Diner until its demise in 1965.

In 1930, Russ Adamitz opened the College Diner on East Beaver Avenue but soon moved it to 126 West College Avenue. (The Greeley Diner soon arrived at the College Diner's old location, where it operated into the 1940s.) After slipping his Ward & Dickinson diner onto the new lot sideways, Adamitz commemorated the event by renaming the operation the New College Diner. The diner was profitably positioned right across the street from the university, a location that could easily handle the business of two diners. The

PETE FEIGHT

Above: The Breezewood Diner, a Silk City model, arrived just after the Pennsylvania Turnpike opened in 1940. Pete Feight leased it in 1960 and renamed it Pete & Betty's Diner. The turnpike's realignment in 1968 led to the diner's move north to Hollidaysburg. Below: Pete's nephew Steven Mellott baking pies at Pete & Betty's.

PETE FEIGHT

second arrived at 130 West College Avenue in 1933, a Ward & Dickinson that operated as the Penn State Diner. Separated only by the State Theater, both diners served Penn State's transient student population for the next forty years.

Returning home from the Army Air Force after World War II, Bill Henning, Sr., who also had diners in Huntingdon and Butler, bought the Penn State Diner in 1946. When Russ Adamitz retired in 1973, he sold his New College Diner to Bill Hennings, Jr., who got rid of the old Penn State Diner but gave its name to the diner he had just bought. The new diner was resold in 1980 and renamed the Ye Olde College Diner, then resold again in 1987 to current owners Dan Rallis and Dan Pivirotto. Over the years, the diner was expanded and remodeled beyond recognition, acquiring a brick facade

and a blue awning. In 1995, the wooden tabletops were redone with Formica, covering years' worth of initials and graffiti, and in late 1998, the diner was redone with a postmodern retro look. One thing has remained the same, however—the diner's famous grilled stickies.

In the auto-oriented diner barrage of the 1950s, three more prefabricated eateries came to State College, two of them on the emerging suburban commercial strips at the edge of town. To the east, the stainless steel Turf Club (a circa 1962 Silk City, #7271) operated on Benner Pike (Route 150) near the Star-Lite Theater until 1988, stood for years on ties, then was hauled to McElhattan for restoration and a planned new life in Lock Haven. To the north, Carl Temple brought Harrisburg's Empire Diner to Atherton Street (Business 322) in 1956, where it operated in a strip mall next to another drive-in. It last saw life as Brothers Pizza. The 1994 article quotes one of the owners: "We knew all about the value of old diners by this time, but ours had been gutted and was really worthless, so we demolished it." The remaining diner (a circa 1962 Silk City, #3071) is still in business as Baby's Burgers & Shakes at 131 South Garner Street.

BERNIE HEISEY

Now Angie's Restaurant and Lounge, this Kullman has been partially covered on the outside and an environmental-style cocktail bar has been attached to it.

Several diners were sent to the Harrisburg area during the postwar period, and many of them are still serving food. The Susquehanna River bisects the metro area into what are known locally as the East Shore, where Harrisburg and the suburbs of Dauphin County sit, and the West Shore, with its older collection of inner suburban towns like Lemoyne and Camp Hill, as well as newer developments farther out in Cumberland, Perry, and northern York

MRS. HERBERT BROWN

In 1946, Herbert "Brownie" Brown bought the City Line Diner in Harrisburg, at 20th Street and Paxton Street. A decade later, Brownie tore down the diner and replaced it with a new 100-seat Mountain View (#478), above. The diner was so popular that a cafeteria was added in the basement. After ownership changed and business eroded, the diner was demolished in 1981.

KYLE WEAVER

East Shore Diner, a 1953 O'Mahony on Cameron Street in Harrisburg.

Counties. Most of the diners are on the more urban East Shore side. The four diners across the river are lined up along the West Shore's main north-south arterial, U.S. Route 15, which, before the days of limited-access bypasses, connected the main streets of the oldest towns.

Reflecting these regional divisions are the East Shore Diner and the West Shore Diner. The West Shore, a 1930s Silk City, is the older of the two. It was originally bought used by Erney Beatty in 1945 and opened in Lemoyne next to L. B. Smith's. It was moved twice before coming back to Lemoyne at 1011 State Street. This diminutive, white-paneled diner sits in an austere environment surrounded by parking lot, now off the beaten path. Before traffic was diverted onto the U.S. Route 11/15 (32nd Street) Bypass and the Harrisburg Expressway, however, State Street was the main road south from Harrisburg. Nonetheless, the diner serves a regular crowd and just about everybody knows where it is. The curved ceiling typical of the older Silk Citys is retained, as is the centered hood clock and the diamond border pattern on the ceramic tile counter base—in this case, white on blue.

John Katsifis bought the West Shore in the early eighties as the pioneering member of a Greek diner family that came to run a number of Harrisburg eateries. By 1987, his father, Steve, and brother Bill had acquired an idle diner on Harrisburg's South Cameron Street—a red and stainless early 1950s O'Mahony, with a corner entrance and L-shaped interior, originally

Seybold's Diner and last known as Ray's before the Katsifis purchase. In reference to its West Shore Diner family roots, this diner was christened the East Shore. It's in a classic diner setting. Cameron Street, running parallel to the old Pennsylvania Main Line tracks, was Harrisburg's traditional downtown bypass serving a rail-oriented commercial and industrial corridor. Despite deindustrialization, the place hums during business hours but is desolate at night, which accounts for the East Shore's 3:00 P.M. closing time. For the past three years on Christmas Day, George and Chris Katsifis could be found at the West Shore serving a free breakfast for senior citizens, buses from orphanages, and anyone else looking for companionship. Everyone chips in—family, regulars, even strangers—and any donations go to the Salvation Army. Chris says that they remember the tough times when their family of nine moved here from Greece in 1968, and they want to lend some cheer to those less fortunate. He also says it's a good way to teach his children about the meaning of the holiday.

In 1997, the Katsifis family bought another area diner—Wolfe's Diner, another early 1950s O'Mahony, located on the U.S. Route 15 bypass around Dillsburg. John moved over to Wolfe's and left the West Shore in the capable hands of his brothers Chris and George. Sometime between the West Shore and Wolfe's, John also teamed up with a cousin to run Decoven Diner, yet another early 1950s O'Mahony operating along U.S. Route 15 north of Harrisburg. This venture was eventually terminated and the diner sold.

Another Greek diner proprietor, Angie Navropoulos, established a two-unit chain in the 1980s that includes Angie's Family Restaurant and Lounge (a.k.a. Angie's Brookside Diner), on Eisenhower Boulevard outside Harrisburg, and Angie's Family Restaurant, on U.S. Route 15 at the northern edge of New Buffalo. From the south, Angie's Brookside presents itself as a stone-sided, mansard-roofed cocktail lounge. From the north, however, it is apparent that this more recent addition is wrapped around a 1956 Kullman, one of the few exaggerated modern diners in Central Pennsylvania.

DINER DRIVES

With half the Central Pennsylvania diners clustered in the Harrisburg area, it's not surprising that the region's three Diner Drives radiate from this hub. As in other parts of the state, the diners reveal the routes of the old roads to and through the capital city. These include the Harrisburg Pike from Lancaster, U.S. Route 15 from Gettysburg through Perry County, and the old William Penn Highway.

CENTRAL PENNSYLVANIA DINERS

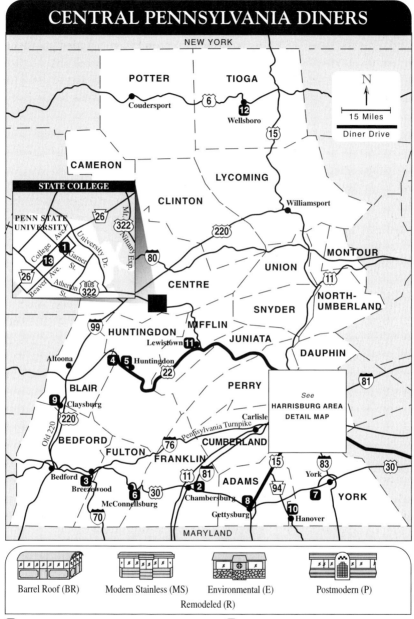

| Barrel Roof (BR) | Modern Stainless (MS) | Environmental (E) | Postmodern (P) |

Remodeled (R)

1 Baby's Burgers & Shakes: State College (R)
2 Chris's Country Kitchen: Chambersburg (R)
3 Denny's Classic Diner: Breezewood (P)
4 Diner 22: Alexandria (railcar)
5 Grubb's Diner: Huntingdon (R)
6 Johnnie's Diner: McConnelsburg (R)
7 Lee's Diner: York (MS)

8 Lincoln Diner: Gettysburg (MS)
9 Peggy's Diner: Claysburg (R)
10 Transport company offices: Hanover (MS)
11 Trolley Car Café: Lewistown (R)
12 Wellsboro Diner: Wellsboro (BR)
13 Ye Olde College Diner: State College (R)

As a Diner Drive, the line of the Lincoln Highway fades the farther west it goes. Eight diners border the route in Metro Philadelphia, and four are spread across the Dutch Country's Lancaster County, but then, with the exception of the new Denny's Classic Diner in Breezewood, the stainless stops with Lee's Diner, west of York, and doesn't pick up again until Pittsburgh, well to the other side of the Alleghenies. Lee's only serves breakfast until 11 A.M., but many Pennsylvania Dutch dishes are offered throughout the day. The 1951 Mountain View has an innovative expansion, which uses stainless from the side to sheath the new section's facade.

HARRISBURG PIKE (ROUTE 230)

Before the Pennsylvania Turnpike was built, there were two main roads to Harrisburg from Philadelphia: U.S. Route 422 through Reading, and U.S. Route 30 to Lancaster, then up the Route 230 spur. The second route was part of the old Pennsylvania Road, which rivaled the more famous National Road as a trans-Appalachian path in the eighteenth and nineteenth centuries. Resuscitated by the automobile in the early twentieth century, the road from Philadelphia became packed with traffic and filled with diners.

Counting the Clearview in Lancaster County, five classic diners still mark the 20 miles of road from Rheems to Harrisburg, even though the route has been bypassed by Route 283 for the last thirty years. The first diner on this drive has been closed for some time. On an empty stretch of road south of Middletown, this late 1950s Kullman, originally Bill Quinn's 230 Diner, was owned for twenty-two years by Stephanie and Jim Arndt, who then bought the Highspire Diner. After they sold the 230 Diner, which had lime green bands above and below the windows, it was redone in the early nineties as the Willowbrook and had much of the stainless covered with stained woods and pastel hues. It last saw business as Demetri's 230 Diner, but plans have been announced to reopen the diner in late 1999.

Harrisburg Pike steps around downtown Middletown, home to Kuppy's Diner. Sitting on a side street at the edge of the business district, Kuppy's could be mistaken for a brick rancher were it not for its vintage neon sign and a stunning wall painting. Behind the brick facade, however, is one of the few still-operating Ward & Dickinson diners in the state, and undoubtedly the best preserved.

North of Middletown, Harrisburg Pike parallels Conrail/Amtrak's Main Line through a series of industrial satellite towns developed when the right-of-way belonged to the Pennsylvania Railroad. The prevalence of factory workers, truckers, and tourists made this strip fertile for diners. After Kuppy's are two more in-town diners that are still in business. Just up the road, the Highspire Diner still looks fresh out of the box after nearly half a century of service. The diner sits snugly among the houses and businesses of

HARRISBURG AREA DINERS

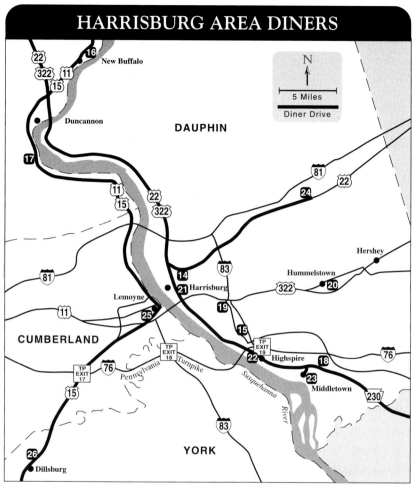

14 American Dream Diner: Harrisburg (MS)
15 Angie's Family Restaurant and Lounge: Harrisburg (EM)
16 Angie's Family Restaurant: New Buffalo (R)
17 Decoven Diner: Duncannon (MS)
18 Demetri's 230 Diner: Middletown (R)
19 Dempsey's American Kitchen: Harrisburg (E)
20 Dempsey's Restaurant: Hummelstown (E)
21 East Shore Diner: Harrisburg (MS)
22 Highspire Diner: Highspire (MS)
23 Kuppy's Diner: Middletown (R)
24 Skyline Family Restaurant: West Hanover (R)
25 West Shore Diner: Lemoyne (MS)
26 Wolfe's Diner: Dillsburg (MS)

2nd Street, the town's main drag. Its interior is a wonderful example of a postwar Silk City, containing a gleaming porcelain ceiling, stainless steel backbar, and diamond-patterned trim along its ceramic tile counter and wall base. Farther north, the road skirts the edge of Bethlehem Steel's much-diminished Steelton tube works, before turning onto Cameron Street and arriving at the East Shore Diner.

The Highspire Diner, a 1953 Silk City south of Harrisburg, was opened by Mr. and Mrs. Carroll Sauder. It's shown here in the early 1990s, when it was called Stephanie's Highspire.

GETTYSBURG PIKE (U.S. ROUTE 15)

During the golden age of the diner, three roads radiated south from Harrisburg. U.S. Route 111 followed the old Susquehanna Trail to Baltimore, U.S. Route 15 was posted over Gettysburg Pike, and U.S. Route 11 angled southwest through Chambersburg and Hagerstown to Virginia's Shenandoah Valley. In the late fifties, U.S. 111 was reincarnated as I-83, one of Pennsylvania's first interstates to be completed. In the early sixties, U.S. 11 was paralleled by I-81. Only U.S. 15 was left to be gradually upgraded, bit by bit, from two-lane to four-lane, from open roadside access to partial access to limited access, from non-divided to dual pavement. Although brutal for motorists, this long-term exposure to roadside development allowed more time for a creeping commercialism that included diners.

Across the Susquehanna from Harrisburg, U.S. 15 joins the old Susquehanna Trail and follows it northward to the New York border and beyond. The nearest interstates going in this direction cross the border 75 miles to the east and 150 miles to the west. While the talk about upgrading U.S. 15 to interstate quality continues, its hodgepodge roadscape of turning lanes, passing zones, and traffic lights, of gas stations, motels, and diners, flourishes much the same as it has since the early days of the automobile.

From Gettysburg in Adams County to New Buffalo in Perry County, five diners still dish up dinners along the braided stream of roadways begot by U.S. 15. A block north of Lincoln Square in downtown Gettysburg, the Lincoln Diner does a nonstop, twenty-four-hour business serving tourists, townies, and students from nearby Gettysburg College. It opened on Carlisle Street (Business Route 15) as Glenn's Varsity Diner, a 1954 Silk City that retains much of its original interior—fourteen stools line a counter with scallops at each setting, and eight redone booths are still in pink.

Being in a tourist town like Gettysburg almost necessitates regular remodelings. During the environmentalism period, the Lincoln was bricked up and mansarded. More recently, the Lincoln was one of the first diners in central Pennsylvania to reflect the shift toward late-modern and postmodern styles and has been re-sided in clapboard stainless and capped with a heavy, squared cornice of chrome, crimson, and neon. The Lincoln Diner is open twenty-four hours, and one waiter said that business only slows between 4 and 5 A.M.—till then, college students keep things busy; afterward, the breakfast regulars show up. Desserts are a specialty and include a variety of cheesecakes, pies, cookies, turnovers, eclairs, ice cream, and Greek pastries.

The four-lane U.S. 15 was extended southward from the Harrisburg Expressway in the 1950s. Circling around Dillsburg, it provided the perfect venue for roadside development. Here, Wolfe's Diner, along with a motel and a gas station, still stands in near-original condition. Though the garage is now a beer distributor, the two-story stucco-sided Resort Motel retains the

KYLE WEAVER

Wolfe's Diner, an early 1950s O'Mahony on Route 15 in Dillsburg.

hard, utilitarian lines of the International Style. A neon metal box sign with an arrow stands before the modern stainless O'Mahony. Even the highway is vintage, still topped with concrete poured in the fifties. The only detractor is the cement barrier between opposing lanes. According to the previous proprietor, it halved the diner's business, effectively walling it off from northbound traffic.

Closer to Harrisburg, U.S. 15 has long since abandoned the State Street route that ran past the West Shore Diner. It now follows a bypass that merges with U.S. 11, reconnecting with the old road north of the Market Street Bridge. It's a rough ride up U.S. 11/15 along the west side of the river, but those who challenge its potholes and no-passing zones are rewarded with the Decoven Diner in Duncannon. Adjacent to a gas station, and set angled to the road on a broad curve for maximum visibility since it was moved here in 1968, the Decoven is a fraternal twin to the East Shore Diner, both corner-entrance, red and stainless, mid-1950s O'Mahonys with L-shaped interior designs. They differ only in the details.

At the north end of the U.S. 15 Diner Drive in New Buffalo is the old Trail Diner, named for the Susquehanna Trail, where it was delivered in the 1950s as part of a diner–gas station combination. Original owners Paul and Marian Rokus were concessionaires in a traveling carnival until 1951, when they brought the Exetor Diner from Duncannon to this spot. In 1954, they purchased a stylish new 1955 Kullman and had it delivered to their 10 acres, where 95 percent of their business was transient. Now called Angie's Family Restaurant, the diner has been significantly altered, the Kullman buried under additions tacked on as the complex evolved into a truck stop. The dark, diamond-studded terrazzo floor marks the diner's original footprint. On the outside, the diner's stone facade is topped with a titanic mansard.

U.S. 15. continues on for miles, its haphazard roadside once the home of many diners including the Mountain Top Diner north of Williamsport, forced to move when the widening of U.S. 15 began in 1991. This pink and blue 1956 Fodero has been restored at the Strong Museum in Rochester, New York. The rest of U.S. 15 seems to have no diners, although some might still be out there behind a false front.

WILLIAM PENN HIGHWAY (U.S. ROUTE 22)

In the 1920s, westbound flivvers from New York could get to Pittsburgh by one of two different trans-Appalachian highways: the Lincoln Highway through Philadelphia or the William Penn Highway through Harrisburg. The William Penn (designated Federal Route 22 in 1926) picked its way through the ridges west of Harrisburg, using the water gaps carved by the Juniata River.

Above: Diner Harrisburg East, a 1955 O'Mahony, sat between a Mobil and the Dairyette on Route 22. It was moved 10 miles north in 1972 and is now the Decoven Diner. Below: Compare the more modern styling of the Decoven with the Highspire (see page 180). This view looks to the L-shaped entrance.

It followed the route of the Pennsylvania Railroad, which followed the route of the Pennsylvania Main Line Canal. Determined by topography, the William Penn Highway stretches from Harrisburg to Hollidaysburg in the shape of a 125-mile-long M. Although longer than the Lincoln Highway, its lower grades made it a favorite among truckers, who kept many a twenty-four-hour diner in business. Only five of these diners are left, spread out over a lot of highway.

By 1960, U.S. Route 22 had been rebuilt as I-78 from Easton to the Lebanon County line near Fredicksburg, where the expressway traffic was routed onto a four-lane highway. Although I-78 was eventually completed into Harris-

burg, U.S. 22 still splits from the interstate at this old terminus, which is a great place for a diner. The Pushnik family, which owned Pushnik's Diner in Lebanon, opened a diner at the first major intersection (with Route 343) on U.S. 22 west of the I-78 terminus. The diner is possibly still there, disguised as a clock shop.

This stretch of U.S. 22 across Lebanon and Dauphin Counties east of Harrisburg is a treasure trove of vintage roadside delights—cabin courts, rusting neon signs, roadhouses, and gas stations in various stages of operation, abandonment, and decay. The only diner still in business here is the Skyline Family Restaurant in West Hanover. Unrecognizable beneath a 1994 Mediterranean remodel is a 1945 Silk City once known as the Blue Diner, a name still discernable on a vertical neon sign by the side of the road.

The original U.S. 22 entered downtown Harrisburg on State Street and left by way of a one-way couplet on Front Street and 2nd Street. The U.S. 22 bypass swung well north of the Capitol Complex, following the current routing over Herr Street and Arsenal Boulevard. At the intersection of these two streets is the American Dream Diner, a 1953 DeRaffele once appropriately named the By-Pass Diner.

The next diner on U.S. 22 is a fair piece down the road. The Trolley Car, like the rest of downtown Lewistown, sits in the Y between the State College–bound U.S. 322 and the southwest-bending U.S. 22. U.S. 22 through Huntingdon County has been somewhat of a diner magnet, bucking the usual trend for the mountainous outlands of Central Pennsylvania. In addi-

KEVIN PATRICK

Grubb's Diner on Route 22 in Huntingdon was the second diner for the Grubb family. This 1964 Swingle was recently redone with vertically ribbed stainless steel.

The Ridge Diner, a 1955 Fodero, formerly Grubb's and Jerry's, was recently moved from its Route 22 Huntingdon home.

tion to some on-site establishments, like Top's Diner and Miller's Diner, the road is served by Grubb's Diner, the railcar-converted Diner 22, and until recently, the Ridge Diner.

Best known is Grubb's, a one-of-a-kind 1964 Swingle attached to the end of a Days Inn. Its most noticeable feature is a two-sided, stainless steel pylon that rises above the door with the diner's name in red neon. Until fall 1998, the diner had the distinctive look of a transitional hybrid, reflecting style elements from both the exaggerated modern and environmental periods. At a time when diner manufacturers were experimenting with new materials, Grubb's was given a smooth, white, ceramic pebble facade with brown highlights, set in a stainless steel building frame. The interior was American colonial with acoustic panel ceiling, false timbers, and a scalloped counter. Although a perfect example of 1960s style trends, it was somewhat behind the times for the dawning of a new millennium. The latest remodel covered the diner in vertically textured stainless steel, polished to a looking-glass shine.

On top of the first big hill west of Huntingdon was a diner–gas station complex that used to pack in the trucks. At the center of a big rig-size parking lot was a modern stainless 1955 Fodero, which, up until its disappearance in the winter of 1998–99, was changing hands a little too often to establish any kind of roadside permanency. It was Grubb's first diner, then Jerry's, then Papa Leone's Family Restaurant, then the Ridge Diner, and now a hole in the ground. After years of service, what appears to be an institution vanished, with no fanfare, no farewell, and no forwarding address. That's life on the ephemeral roadside.

KUPPY'S DINER

1938 WARD & DICKINSON, REMODELED

Brown and Poplar Streets, Middletown

KYLE WEAVER

Kuppy's Diner sits where road meets rail. A pair of tracks runs down the center of Brown Street in front of the diner, occasionally seeing action from switch engines shunting freight cars off and on the nearby Main Line tracks. Although incidental to the operations of the diner, the railroad is not entirely irrelevant to the Kuppy's story. Middletown's compact Union Street business district evolved at a time dominated by steam whistles and engine smoke, when out-of-towners arrived by train and walked to their accommodations in nearby hotels. This way of life persisted into the opening decades of the twentieth century, when Amos Kupp was running the Railroad House Restaurant.

Impressed by the Depression diner boom, Amos's son and grandson, Percy and Karl, paid $7,800 for a Ward & Dickinson in 1933. The diner was placed a block east of the business district at the corner of Brown Street and Poplar Street, better for motorists requiring on-street parking but still within walking distance of downtown. Encouraged by the first day's take of $62, the Kupps were able to upgrade to a new W&D just five years later. In 1939, Percy and Karl opened another W&D—likely their old one—on Market Street in nearby Elizabethtown but sold it to Red Baker after Percy had a stroke the next year. A 1945 flood gave that diner a short ride, so it was relocated to higher ground.

Ward & Dickinson dominated the Pennsylvania diner trade during the interwar years. Its porcelain-clad, monitor roof diners borrowed freely from railroad dining-car design. The interiors were compact and efficient, with the grill behind the counter within arm's reach of iceboxes, utensil drawers, and food cabinets. Wheel wells were an intrinsic part of the structures, even though the wheels were used only to drag the diners to their operating sites.

Kuppy's initially thrived as the only diner between Lancaster and Harrisburg, then was helped by the World War II construction of nearby Olmstead Air Force Base. Originally a twenty-four-hour diner, Kuppy's began closing at midnight in the early fifties after Percy's death. To help out, Karl, Jr., entered the business after graduating from high school in 1954. A dining room was added to the 12-by-45-foot car in 1960, and in 1963, diner gentrification caught up with Kuppy's when it was encased in brick and topped with a gable roof. Typical of many remodelings, the interior of the diner remains virtually untouched.

International media beat a path to the diner's door during the Three Mile Island nuclear incident in 1979. Although well within the danger zone should a catastrophic meltdown occur, the diner stayed open extra hours, serving as a de facto base of operation for reporters.

Since 1991, Kuppy's has been captained by Karl, Jr.'s, son Greg, who's spent most of his forty-some years at the diner. He and his wife, Carol, have

KUPPY'S DINER

Kuppy's is prepped for a brick facing in 1963.

done a lot of upgrading inside since taking over. But the wooden cabinetry is original, as are the eleven counter stools, and a lot of grill action still takes place on the backbar.

Kuppy's oyster pie—a milky mixture of oysters, potatoes, and eggs baked between layers of pastry—draws raves and crowds. Carol says it's so much work that they only offer it every other Friday (preparation starts on Monday). And it's only available in the "r" months—September through April. Breakfast offerings include scrapple and creamed chipped beef on toast. Sandwiches, meats, and seafood are available, as are regular specials such as chicken corn chowder soup on Saturdays and Mondays, and a wide selection of pies are baked on-site. Much of the menu is the same as sixty-five years ago, and recipes are unchanged.

DINER 22

1919 RAILROAD DINING CAR, REMODELED

Route 22, Alexandria

CAROL INGALD

Although Diner 22 isn't a factory-built diner, it represents a significant period in diner history. The beige-sided building with its rear-slanted shed roof looks like a typical 1960s-era roadside restaurant, but a front row of windows suggests something else. The core of this building is a 1919 dining car from the Huntingdon and East Broad Top Railroad. With the rise of the automobile in the twenties and the decline of the economy in the thirties, the nation's shrinking rail networks no longer had use for hundreds of railcars, electric interurbans, and trolleys. A few of these railcars were bought for very little from the scrapyards and reincarnated as diners. That the design of early diners borrowed from the prestigious dining cars, which in some cases—like Diner 22—later became diners is what led to the common belief that old diners were originally railroad dining cars.

This 1919 dining car first plied the roadside trade on 4th Street in Huntingdon, then in nearby Smithfield. When U.S. 22 was being rebuilt in 1946, the railcar was moved a third time, to the new bypass around Alexandria. According to local lore, it somehow fell off the truck before it reached its destination and has operated at that location ever since. The diner was passed on to Agnes Bilich in 1972, who ran the place until 1989, when her daughter and son-in-law, Gloria and Ed Wilt, took over.

Since its arrival, a kitchen and two dining-room additions have been linked to the original railcar, which is just inside the vestibule and to the left. The monitor-roofed railcar is outfitted with a lengthwise counter and backbar.

FEATURED DINER

WELLSBORO DINER
1938 STERLING #388
19 Main Street (Routes 6 and 287), Wellsboro

CAROL INGALD

Like a porcelain jewel, the Wellsboro Diner sits against the sidewalk at the edge of Wellsboro's business district. It's not just the diner that is well preserved—the entire town is a living model of when most people conducted their business downtown by walking from place to place. Assisting the town's leaders in maintaining this desirable quality is the fact that the town acts as the tourist gateway to the state's largest expanse of recreation-oriented upland forest. Woods, mountains, state parks, fishing streams, hunting habitats, and hiking trails lie just beyond this natural wonderland's showpiece, the Grand Canyon of Pennsylvania, which is just down the road from Wellsboro.

The Wellsboro Diner is a Sterling built by the Judkins Company of Merrimac, Massachusetts. Although it opened in 1939, its car number 388 marks it as the eighth diner made by Judkins in 1938. It predates the more famous streamlined Sterlings of the 1940s and therefore projects the more traditional diner form of the early auto era. Its barrel roof is a legacy of the old lunch wagon days, and instead of stainless steel (the material of modernity), its flanks are covered in a cream-colored porcelain enamel trimmed in a green pinstripe pattern common for the period.

Inside, cream-colored porcelain panels sheath the curved ceiling, and the counter is topped by a glass case filled with pies and pastries. Few glass counters survive, but they were typical for the time. While patrons ate their meals, they were reminded of dessert, tantalizingly positioned beneath their dinner plates.

The Wellsboro is Pennsylvania's only surviving example of a New England barrel roof diner, and that it is in such pristine shape borders on the astounding. Pennsylvania has always been the home territory of the Mid-Atlantic diner manufacturers, although a number of Sterlings did break into the market—most notably, Philadelphia's Penguin Diner, the Penn State Flyer in Allentown, and the Streamliner in Ellwood City, all long gone.

Established in 1939 by Louis Meier and his brother-in-law, Walter Schanaker, the sixty-eight-seat diner was first called Schanaker's. In 1941, Walter left to open a new Schanaker's in New York, and by 1950, Louis had the Wellsboro diner for sale. It remained unchanged until 1994, when an adjacent house was converted into a dining room. The annex carries over the diner's alternating red and white diamond floor pattern and is decorated with murals of other diners.

The Wellsboro is now owned by Nelle Rounsaville-Prevost, who says, "We have a reputation for good home-cooked meals." The diner is known for its prime rib dinners and prime rib sandwiches, and its desserts are made fresh daily. The baker, Holly Everitt, who has been working at the Wellsboro for sixteen years, arrives every day at 4 A.M. to make the pies and pastries, which are always devoured by customers before the end of the day.

BABY'S BURGERS & SHAKES

CIRCA 1962 SILK CITY, #3071, REMODELED

131 S. Garner St., State College

FEATURED DINER

CAROL INGALD

Baby's is another example of the Silk City style that continues to defy identification. These Pennsylvania survivors all look alike—zigzag quilted stainless highlighted by three vertical red stripes, thin corner windows, angular ceiling, and a serial number ending with 71. All factors point to their having been built between 1962 and 1964, but rumor has it that they arrived before then.

Some say that this one is a 1949 Silk City set down at 131 South Garner Street in 1950; others maintain that it indeed arrived in the sixties. Post-1966 photos show it as the Char Pit (a Kentucky Fried Chicken franchise). Then it was a Weiner King and Pedro's before an investor group rethemed it as Baby's Burgers & Shakes in 1987. The location is in the shadow of student high-rises in this pedestrian-packed town that's home to Penn State University.

Baby's brought diner retromania to State College, being outfitted less like a diner of the early sixties and more like a fifties restaurant as interpreted today. Postmodernism ignores authenticity, even when the setting is authentic, and Baby's, which caters to a younger crowd, has all the classic

CAROL INGALD

Baby's interior is a mix of circa 1960 styling and a 1990s interpretation of the 1950s.

clichés. A red neon sign hangs on its bronzed aluminum mansard, with "Baby's" written in stylized slanted script. A neon "Eat" sign hangs in the vestibule window. Checkered black tiles line the white tile counter base and the cream tile wall of the kitchen, which is visible through a cutout in the backwall. Records decorate the wall, as do messages such as "Home of the Whimpy" and "Next to home . . . this is the place to eat meatloaf." An adjoining dining room is a minishrine of fifties paraphernalia bathed in the neon glow of another sign that reads, "Famous since 1987."

One profile article said that employees were encouraged to wear gaudy lipstick, put their hair in ponytails, crack gum, and wear buttons like "Eat and get out." Employees complained that the pressure to be cute was sometimes too intense, but that didn't hinder success, and plans are under way to expand to other states.

Obviously, classic diner food is served at Baby's—huge burgers and malted milkshakes, as the diner's full name suggests, and also fried chicken, cheesesteaks, macaroni and cheese, club sandwiches, and ice-cream sundaes.

Restaurants like Baby's may not re-create the decor of the 1950s, but they do a pretty good job of representing the current nostalgia-laced infatuation with the fifties diner experience. The kitschy decorations, despite being yesterday's fads, serve to convey to the buying public that all-important roadside message that the establishment is up-to-date.

AMERICAN DREAM DINER

1953 DERAFFELE

1933 Herr St., Harrisburg

FEATURED DINER

KYLE WEAVER

If the American Dream Diner is a fairly rare DeRaffele, it's also one of the most beautiful, employing the exterior elements that most people associate with diners and wrapping them in a classic, curvy way. D. L. Cronin and J. Levin had an older diner here when they upgraded in 1953. The new diner came in two sections: a green, gray, and pink 17-by-45-foot dining area and a slightly smaller kitchen. They named their new place the By-Pass Diner for the U.S. 22 bypass around downtown Harrisburg, which ran on Herr Street and Arsenal Boulevard. The diner sat right at the intersection of the two roads but was moved half a block west in 1964 to make room for a Mobil station. The diner switched hands a number of times, and business slipped.

When Fred and Linda Jenkins bought the By-Pass Diner in 1988, they set about cleaning the place and attracting customers. They also changed the name to the American Dream Diner. The new name embodies the positive feelings that many people are once again associating with diners.

Inside, the white marble-print Formica counter is surrounded by bluish green floor, trim, and booths. Fred re-covered the booths and stools in 1990 with a sparkly vinyl reminscent of sixties kiddie rides and banana bike seats.

The By-Pass Diner has barely changed since it arrived in 1953.

The ceiling is pink and the backbar is stainless steel. The bluish green terrazzo has three inlaid beige diamonds.

With its location in the state capital, politicians are among the diner's patrons, and the governor has even signed legislation there. Fred says lots of people stop by to take pictures; he figures the out-of-staters must have gotten off at the wrong exit looking for Hershey. Fred does all the cooking during the eight-hour breakfast and lunch shift. Accounting for an amazing 25 percent of business is a foot-long, half-pound pork sausage called the Rope. It's sold in various ways, such as a breakfast platter, on a sub roll with onions, and as a lunch plate with mashed potatoes and a vegetable. Also popular is a four-egg omelet with ham, cheese, peppers, and potatoes. And outside in summer is a trailer selling barbecue on Friday evenings.

DINER DIRECTORY

ALEXANDRIA

Diner 22
Rt. 22
(814) 669-9094
1919 railroad dining car, remodeled.
Open daily, 5:30 A.M.–9 P.M.
For more information, see page 188.

BREEZEWOOD

Denny's Classic Diner
Route 30
(815) 735-3918
1999 Starlite.
American food; breakfast all day; variety of huge burgers, steak, pork, chicken, pot roast, turkey; shakes and malts.
Open 24 hours.

CHAMBERSBURG

Chris's Country Kitchen
1329 Lincoln Way E.
(717) 263-6088
1950s. Extensively remodeled: orange roof, brick facade. Formerly Conrad's, Burkholder's and Five Points Diner.
American and Italian food; seafood, omelettes, hoagies, triple-decker clubs, homemade soups; homemade desserts (whole pies available).
Open Mon.–Thurs., 5:30 A.M.–9 P.M.;
Sat., 5:30 A.M.–10 P.M.;
Sun., 7 A.M.–8 P.M.

CLAYSBURG

Peggy's Diner
Rt. 220
(814) 239-2196
1970s environmental.
Homemade American food; ham pot pie, spaghetti; homemade pies, apple dumplings.
Open daily, 5:30 A.M.–9 P.M.

DILLSBURG

Wolfe's Diner
625 Rt. 15 S.
(717) 432-9924
Early 1950s O'Mahony.
American food; breakfast all day; daily specials; scrapple, smoked sausage, chicken and waffles; homemade pies, rice pudding.
Open Mon.–Sat., 5:30 A.M.–10 P.M.;
Sun., 7 A.M.–10 P.M.

DUNCANNON

Decoven Diner
1913 State Rd. (Rts. 11/15)
(717) 834-4677
1955 O'Mahony. Originally Harrisburg East Diner.
American food; sandwiches and subs, meatloaf, ham, country crisp chicken; homemade pies and cakes, hand-dipped ice cream; car shows and fifties nights in summer.
Open Mon.–Fri., 5 A.M.–7:30 P.M.;
Sat.–Sun., 6 A.M.–7 P.M.

GETTYSBURG

Lincoln Diner
32 Carlisle St. (Rt. 15)
(717) 334-3900
1954 Silk City #5481, remodeled.
Originally Glenn's Varsity Diner.
American food; breakfast all day; home-
made soups, triple-decker sandwiches,
seafood; steaks, deluxe burgers; wide
variety of homemade pies, cakes, cookies,
tarts, turnovers.
Open 24 hours.

HANOVER

Transport company offices
1477 Carlisle Pike (Rt. 94 N.)
Circa 1958 Silk City, remodeled. Former
Hanover Diner.
No food served.

HARRISBURG

American Dream Diner
1933 Herr St.
(717) 234-5480
Open daily, 6 A.M.–2 P.M.
For more information, see page 193.

Angie's Family Restaurant and Lounge
1360 Eisenhower Blvd.
(717) 939-0417
1956 Kullman, remodeled. Also known
as Angie's Brookside Diner.
American and Greek food; scrapple, steaks,
chicken and waffles, ham steak, lump
crabcakes; homemade cheesecake.
Open 24 hours.

Dempsey's American Kitchen
800 Eisenhower Blvd.
(717) 939-1266
1980s DeRaffele.
American and Pennsylvania Dutch food;
breakfast all day; scrapple, mashed sweet
potatoes, meatloaf; homemade pies.
Open 24 hours.

East Shore Diner
711 S. Cameron St. (Rt. 230)
(717) 232-2010
1953 O'Mahony. Formerly
Seybold's Diner.
American food; breakfast and lunch only;
sausage, chicken pot pie.
Open Mon.–Fri., 5 A.M.–3 P.M.;
Sat., 6 A.M.–1 P.M. (breakfast only).

HIGHSPIRE

Highspire Diner
255 2nd St. (Rt. 230)
(717) 939-5366
1952 Silk City #5213.
American and Pennsylvania Dutch food;
daily specials; scrapple, Dutch omelet,
Dutch fries with onions, apple and corn
fritters, beef liver with onions, boneless
pork chops, salmon cakes; homemade pies.
Open Mon.–Thurs., 5 A.M.–9 P.M.;
Fri., 5 A.M.–Sun., 8 P.M.

HUMMELSTOWN

Dempsey's Restaurant
1128 E. Main St.
Park Village Plaza
(717) 566-8069
1966 and 1978 Swingle #1178DVU
(formerly Red Oak Diner, Hazlet,
New Jersey, #466DV).
American and Pennsylvania Dutch food;
breakfast all day; scrapple, mashed sweet
potatoes, meatloaf; homemade pies.
Open 24 hours.

HUNTINGDON

Grubb's Diner
4th St. and Rt. 22
(814) 643-3934
1964 Swingle #364D.
American food; homemade soups,
Brutus salad, garlic salad.
Open Sun.–Thurs., 6 A.M.–10 P.M.;
Fri.–Sat., 6 A.M.–11 P.M.

LEMOYNE

West Shore Diner
1011 State Rd.
(717) 763-0324
Late 1930s Silk City.
Homemade American food; breakfast all
day; sausage, chipped beef on toast, chicken
pot pie; homemade rice pudding.
Open Mon., 5 A.M.–3 P.M.;
Tue.–Fri., 5 A.M.–8 P.M.;
Sat., 5 A.M.–3:30 P.M.;
Sun., 7 A.M.–3 P.M.

LEWISTOWN

Trolley Car Café
15 E. Market St.
(717) 248-9085
Circa 1926 O'Mahony, remodeled, plus
another circa 1940. Originally Club
Diner, and formerly Campbell's Diner.
American food; steak, seafood,
chicken and waffles.
Open daily, 7 A.M.–10 P.M.

McCONNELLSBURG

Johnnie's Diner
709 Lincoln Way E.
(717) 485-4116
1920s, extensively remodeled.
Homemade American food; buffet; home-
made rice pudding.
Open Mon.–Sat., 6 A.M.–9 P.M.;
Sun., 7 A.M.–8 P.M.

MIDDLETOWN

Demetri's 230 Diner
Rt. 230
1950s Kullman.
Closed.

Kuppy's Diner
Brown & Poplar Sts.
(717) 944-5122
1938 Ward & Dickinson, remodeled.
Open Mon.–Fri., 5 A.M.–7 P.M.;
Sat., 5 A.M.–2 P.M.
For more information, see page 186.

NEW BUFFALO

Angie's Family Restaurant
U.S. Rts. 11/15 N.
(717) 834-5797
1954 Kullman (but 1955 model),
extensively remodeled. Formerly
Trail Diner.
American and Greek food;
breakfast all day; baklava.

STATE COLLEGE

Baby's Burgers & Shakes
131 S. Garner St. (at Calder Way)
(814) 234-4776
Circa 1962 Silk City #3071, remodeled.
Open Sun.–Thurs., 7 A.M.–10 P.M.;
Fri.–Sat., 7 A.M.–midnight.
For more information, see page 191.

Ye Olde College Diner
126 W. College Ave.
(814) 238-5590
1920s, extensively remodeled.
American food; cheesesteaks, macaroni
and cheese; grilled stickies.
Open 24 hours.

WELLSBORO

Wellsboro Diner
19 Main St. (Rts. 6 and 298)
(570) 724-3992
1938 Sterling #388.
Open Mon.–Sat., 6 A.M.–7 P.M.;
Sun., 7 A.M.–7 P.M.
For more information, see page 189.

WEST HANOVER

Skyline Family Restaurant
7510 Allentown Blvd. (Rt. 22)
(717) 652-1780
1945 Silk City, extensively remodeled.
Formerly Blue Diner.
American food; scrapple.
Open daily, 5:30 A.M.–9 P.M.

YORK

Lee's Diner
4320 W. Market St. (Lincoln Hwy.,
Rt. 30)
(717) 792-1300
1951 Mountain View #301.
American and Pennsylvania Dutch food;
steaks, hot beef sandwiches, chicken pot pie,
sausage and potatoes; cruise nights.
Open Mon.–Sat., 5 A.M.–7:30 P.M.;
Sun., 6 A.M.–4 P.M.

WESTERN PENNSYLVANIA

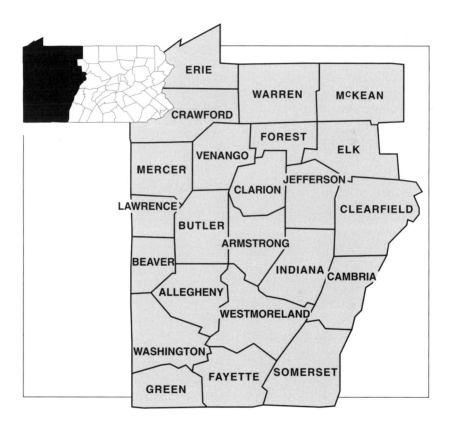

ounded to the east by the high backbone of the Allegheny Mountains, Western Pennsylvania is farther from the megalopolitan core of Dinerland than any of the state's five diner regions. As a result, diner densities are low by eastern standards, but because Western Pennsylvania contains two large industrial cities, Pittsburgh and Erie, there are more diners here than in Central Pennsylvania. Western Pennsylvania's thirty-one diners average out to 1.3 per county, just above Central Pennsylvania's 0.8.

Western Pennsylvania is a big place, but nearly three-quarters of its diners are located in the four metropolitan counties that surround Pittsburgh, Erie, and Sharon. Thirteen diners are located in Pittsburgh's Allegheny County and

DINOR VERSUS DINER

For some strange reason, many diners in northwest Pennsylvania are spelled *dinor*, but no one seems to know why. This misspelling has continued for so long that the answer is only conjecture now: a German variant? an advertising gimmick? a mistake run rampant?

The odd spelling didn't spread far, but it was quickly adopted in Erie and nearby towns like Conneaut Lake, Franklin, Meadville, Oil City, Warren, Wesleyville, and Conneaut, Ohio. In 1930, three of five diners in Erie's city directory were spelled *dinor*, and by 1958, it was nineteen of twenty-one. The immediate Erie area still has five *dinors*—Girard, Haggerty's, Park, Peninsula, and Russ's. Three more survive in nearby Edinboro, Greenville, and Union City, and a twice-remodeled *dinor* is found in Weirton, West Virginia, 100 miles to the south.

Note: Peninsula, Russ's, and Greenville are not factory-built diners.

suburban Westmoreland County to the east. Sharon's Mercer County has three, and there are five in Erie County. Those who have driven through miles and miles of farmland in Mercer County may balk at calling it metropolitan, but the U.S. Census designation is based on the characteristics of its population and not the appearance of its landscape.

In the four counties south and west of Pittsburgh, no diners remain, and only a couple are known to have ever existed: the barrel-roofed Quitsie's Diner, a half mile west of Washington on Route 40, and Jane Ann's Restaurant (Swingle #1177DKV), delivered to New Stanton in 1977.

Most other counties in Western Pennsylvania have only one diner each, with two exceptions: Butler County has two diners, and McKean County has three. Compared to Metro Philadelphia or the Pennsylvania Dutch Country, a county with three diners hardly sounds amazing, but in Western Pennsylvania, only Allegheny and Erie Counties have more. So what accounts for this spate of diners in a rural county way up on the New York border, 100 miles from the nearest city, where the largest town has a scant 11,000 people? The answer to that question cuts to the very essence of what Western Pennsylvania's diner geography is all about.

Compared to diners in the rest of the state, those in Western Pennsylvania are older and more likely to have been manufactured in New York. More than half of Western Pennsylvania's thirty diners were built before World War II. In contrast, it's one quarter in Central Pennsylvania and only three out of seventy-five in Metro Philadelphia.

In the early twentieth century, a secondary diner-manufacturing region evolved around the eastern Great Lakes to serve the growing industrial cities

Bob McKendrick sold diners for Ward & Dickinson of Silver Creek, New York. When the Depression found him laid off, he bought the Boston Diner, a 1920s Ward & Dickinson on Peach Street in Erie, a block from Gannon College. He upgraded to this new Silk City in 1948, which lives on as Haggerty's Bar & Dinor on West 26th Street.

of the Midwest. Manufacturers like Ward & Dickinson and Rochester Grills, of western New York, and Bixler and Kuhlman, of eastern Ohio, dominated the trans-Appalachian diner market.

Nineteen percent of the region's diners came from New York, including at least five from the western part of the state: three Ward & Dickinsons and the state's only Rochester Grill and Mulholland. All five of these diners are within 20 miles of the New York state line.

By midcentury, the Great Lakes diner manufacturers were gone, and the industry concentrated around New York City, where the remaining manufacturers offered larger sectional diners to a megalopolitan market. Western

MRS. BETSY JONES

Leo Reinhardt owned numerous diners—all named Reinhardt's Diner—in Erie. This one was at 2607 Parade Street.

Pennsylvania is far enough out of this market that there has been little trading up to the giant environmental diners after 1965. The older, smaller diners of Western Pennsylvania were big enough to serve their more modest customer base and continued to be competitive. Also, small-town, nonmetropolitan diners tend to have a higher survival rate because in a stag-

WARREN COUNTY HISTORICAL SOCIETY

A view inside Riche's Dining Car in Youngville, near Warren, in 1937. It was still there in the 1960s, but had been renamed the Blue Star Diner.

The Eldred Dinor, shown in 1945, was moved to Eldred from the Scranton area. It sits half a block east, remodeled as Cappy's Diner, but is now closed. Manufacturers of diners of this age are difficult to determine—this could be a Sorge Brothers, Mulholland, or the more common Ward & Dickinson.

nant or slow-growth scenario, with no drastic changes in population or the economy, what's around tends to stay around.

Many of Erie's prewar diners, however, have disappeared, including a chain of Reinhardt's Diners. Leo Reinhardt opened one of city's first dining cars around 1920 on East 14th Street. In 1929, a second diner was delivered to 2607 Parade Street. His daughter, Betsy Jones, believes that he owned a couple of other diners, but she's not sure where they were. After Leo's death in 1944, his wife leased out the diner on Parade Street, which was renamed the Marvintown Dinor.

Leo's three brothers also had diners: Carl's Diner (later Dinor), at 1403 Peach Street; Dave's Diner, on West 13th Street near Peach Street; and George's Diner, at 5th Street and State Street. Betsy recalls that her dad and Carl also squeezed a diner between buildings on State Street near 14th. "They all made a good living," she says, "even during the Depression."

All four diners in McKean, a rural Western Pennsylvania county on the New York border, were constructed by western New York firms before World War II. The Ward & Dickinson factory in Silver Creek was a mere 50 miles away.

Cappy's Diner in downtown Eldred is believed to be a W&D. It's been moved at least once, and like so many of Western Pennsylvania's prewar diners, its exterior has been remodeled.

The Smethport Diner was the Milroy from 1953 to 1966. The insulbrick and a later mansard have been removed and a dining room and caboose-shaped vestibule added.

Smethport—the "Hub of McKean County" and the county seat—is the home of the Smethport Diner, which is itself the home of the half-pound Hubber Burger and Hubber Dog. Although John and Linda Keith, owners of this local institution since 1993, have turned up evidence that the diner was built locally in 1937 and transported to the site in three sections, it has the

Smith's Dining Car was brought to 13th Street in Franklin in the 1920s (that's William Smith and cook William White). It was turned perpendicular to the street about 1930, renamed Anderson's Diner in the 1940s, and stuck around town until the 1960s.

same dimensions and telltale monitor roof as a 1930s W&D. The Keiths have added a fifty-six-seat dining room and a caboose-shaped vestibule, drawing on the visual link between the look of the old diners and the railcars they mimicked.

The two remaining McKean diners, in nearby Bradford, no longer operate as restaurants but stand as noteworthy examples of rare prewar designs. Canted across a corner lot at the edge of the East Bradford business district is a Ward & Dickinson whose exterior is largely intact. A large wooden vestibule and a squat mansard roof obscure part of the building, but still visible are the steel body panels and original green stained-glass windows in the upper sashes. The diner last saw restaurant action as Chu Lee's Chinese Garden, which moved up the street to a larger building, leaving the W&D to Kan's Meat Market, a business that has also closed.

Downtown, half a block off Bradford's Main Street, there sits a very rare diner. Now functioning as a flower shop named Bloomer's, it was made in Rochester, New York, by Rochester Grills around 1940. Few Rochester Grills diners are known to exist, and this one is remarkably well preserved. Typical for its vintage and location, the barrel roof diner sits endways on a narrow lot. The entrance is through a side vestibule accessed from the alley. A decorative fascia caps either end of its rounded roof, and the diner is huge for its type. Like Bixler, Rochester Grills constructed diners in cross sections that were assembled end-to-end like a giant loaf of sliced bread. In this way, the

This rare Rochester Grills diner in Bradford is now Bloomer's, a flower shop.

The distinctive shape of a barrel roof extends onto the sidewalk at the Girard Dinor.

diner could be wider than a conventional barrel roof diner that had to conform to the width of a flatcar or truck trailer and it could be as long as the customer wanted it. The seams visible in the diner's steel skin show that it was assembled in thirteen sections. It stretches half a block from Congress Street to the back alley. Even though the aroma of breakfast has been replaced by the scent of roses, Bloomer's still retains the original counter, stools, and a couple of booths.

Beyond the borders of McKean County, the diner story is similar. Most of Western Pennsylvania's oldest diners are in small towns scattered across the rural northern part of the region. The Girard Dinor may be the oldest prefabricated diner still operating in the state. Of unknown origins, but reportedly opened in 1913, the diner is set sideways in downtown Girard. The original counter section is beneath the vaulted barrel roof, adjacent to a later booth-filled addition. Another barrel roof diner, dating to the 1930s, is found in Franklin at the edge of the business district. Long known as Diner's Delight, it was recently reopened as Cauvel's Diner.

On the north end of the Union City business district, on a corner in the shadow of the old Hotel Congdon, is the Union City Dinor. Hidden behind its pink painted bricks is Pennsylvania's only known Mulholland diner. Headquartered in Dunkirk, New York, the Mulholland Company had a product history not unlike other early diner manufacturers, characterized by ongoing diversification to keep up with changes in the marketplace. The company started with vehicle springs in 1881, then expanded into wagons, buggies, automobile bodies, and in the 1920s, diners.

On a back street in downtown Clearfield is the 1930s-era Clearfield Diner. This long-term, local social institution has been re-sided, but its size and barrel roof suggest that it may be another sectional Bixler. Old menus offer T-bone steak dinners with bread and butter, potatoes, and a drink for

$1.50, and homemade pies and cakes for a dime a piece. Other interesting selections included tongue and sardine salads and sandwiches.

The challenge of detecting the original diner beneath the remodeling carries over to Mercer County, where the Grove City Diner and the Middlesex Diner are certainly much older than their environmental remodelings. The Middlesex Diner, north of West Middlesex, is reportedly the original Mercer Diner from 1922, but only the counter area hints that a factory diner could be underneath the modern decor. The menus bear the story of owner Demetrios Vournous, who in 1972 jumped off a Greek cargo ship plying Lake Erie and went ashore in Toledo, Ohio. He spoke no English and had only $120 in his pocket. Demetrios knew only one family in America, the Hionas family, and he became a dishwasher at their restaurant. He later married their daughter Maria. Two years later, the couple purchased their first restaurant, and two years after that, the diner. "Only in America," Demetrios says, "can a kid who washes dishes take a giant step and reach up and touch the stars."

There can be no doubt about the origins of Edinboro's Crossroads Dinor and Fredonia's Coach Diner, both trolley diners from a time when America was sending hundreds of streetcars to the scrap heap. Some were converted into restaurants, but few trolley diners like these survive.

The large, electric interurban cars that ran between towns were the most likely to be converted into diners. Before settling at the corner of Meadville Street and Plum Street, the car that would become the Crossroads Dinor was hauling day-trippers to Conneaut Lake, milk to Erie, and coal to the Edinboro State Normal School. Car 103 was built by the Niles Company in 1913 and served the Northwestern Electric Service line before its 1929 reincarnation as the Crossroads, which was then run by Andy Mukina for the

The Union City Dinor began as the Corner Diner in 1926, one of the few P. J. Mulholland Company cars ever made by the Dunkirk, New York, firm.

The Coach Diner in Fredonia is one of the few trolley cars converted to food service.

next forty years. The diner, expanded well beyond the original streetcar, is now owned by James and Sharyn Gillette.

Fredonia, a rural hamlet of 700 people well off the main highways, is an unlikely place for a diner. But before World War II, the village aspired to be something more, offering to lease a piece of borough land for ninety-nine years at $5 per year to any diner operator who would come to town. What arrived in 1940 was a rehabilitated interurban car from the New Castle line. The Coach Diner, now painted a fire-engine red, has been serving the town of Fredonia ever since.

No longer serving Meadville, this diner at 863 Park Avenue was also known as Gawne Brothers Diner, KJ's Diner, and Kessler's Dinor.

A handful of prewar diners survive in the Pittsburgh area, but as a larger metropolitan environment, the commercial landscape is much more ephemeral. Diners first appeared in city directories in 1927—Kuhn's Dining Car at 107 Seventh Street downtown and the Nixon Dining Car on Penn Avenue in East Liberty—but there were probably diners before then. Proving the quirkiness of the diner business, Kuhn's was called a restaurant the next year, and the Nixon had moved far across town to West Liberty Avenue.

Only two prewar diners still operate close to downtown Pittsburgh. Pip's stone facade makes it look like anything but a diner, but the interior leaves no doubt. The rounded ceiling, marble counter, and ceramic tile wall and counter base are little changed from when the diner rolled out of the Tierney factory in the 1920s. It opened in the West End neighborhood in the 1950s, but no one can remember where it came from. When the Lackawanna Trail Diner left Stroudsburg in April 1999, Pip's was left as the only operating Tierney in the state.

Pittsburgh's other prewar model is on Penn Avenue near Wilkinsburg, a small, steel gray monitor roof diner named Charlie's, the only extant National-brand diner anywhere. National was founded by Joe Fodero in 1939 and was closed by the war, so it built diners for only two years. This one first showed up as the Downtown Diner on Strawberry Way in downtown Pittsburgh. It was run by Thomas Scott and his four sons, who moved it in 1947 to Penn Avenue. It was Scotty's until 1993 and has been Charlie's since then.

Scotty's many diners served Pittsburgh for half a century. It all started where Charlie's is today at 7619½ Penn Avenue, a couple doors from Brad-

The Streamliner (1940 Sterling #4011) first served the hungry of Warren, Ohio. Years later it moved to Ellwood City under the same name. Restorer Steve Harwin took it back to Ohio in 1987, and it now awaits final restoration in Minnesota.

University of Pittsburgh students will recognize Scotty's Diner (1948 O'Mahony), above, as the current site of Forbes Quad, just around the corner from old Forbes Field. The first Scotty's sat here on the other side of the Mobil, against the four billboards and perpendicular to the road. It was moved to 15th Street and Penn Avenue in Pittsburgh's Strip.

dock Avenue. Local diner entrepreneur William Ritter opened a diner there in 1934. Thomas Scott was pumping gas across the street when he bought out Ritter in 1942 and renamed the car Scotty's. Ritter had opened a second diner in 1939 near Forbes Field in Oakland; Scott bought that one too, then moved it to Pittsburgh's Strip District in 1948 and replaced it with a new O'Mahony.

Scotty's opened Swingle #1059DV on Route 8 in Etna in 1959. Swingle records show one of the old Scotty's was traded in then, rehabbed as Swingle #560DU, and reopened in Hollidaysburg as Ray's Diner. The final Scotty's was a 1979 Swingle on Route 22 in Monroeville, now Jaden's. The Scotts also ran a couple of Red Barn chain restaurants, and one son built the diner look-alike Eastwood Diner on Frankstown Road.

When age caught up with the elder Scott, his sons sold off the diners. The Route 8 and Frankstown Road locations were replaced by supermarkets in the 1980s. Charles Huwalt took over the Wilkinsburg location in 1993, after managing it for twenty-three years (and another ten before that at Route 8). He's helped by his wife, Michelene, whom everyone calls Evelyn. Just before the 1993 sale, the booths and floors were updated, and jukebox wallboxes pulled, but otherwise, Charlie's has changed little in its half century. It retains its light gray and blue tile wall and counter base, glass block around the end door, original wood trim, art moderne designs on the interior walls, and a striking stainless steel winged clock. Best of all, much of the cooking is still done on the backbar grill below a sunburst stainless steel backwall. One specialty is Lyonaisse potatoes—home fries with onions—served any time.

As the central industrial metropolis in a galaxy of mill towns, Pittsburgh was made for diners. Steel-mill towns like McKeesport, Homestead, and Johnstown were similar to the textile-mill towns of New England, with the same need for twenty-four-hour working-class eateries within walking distance of home, work, and town. As diners aged, the cities cast them off to surrounding burgs or to some distant field to rot. Morgan's Eastland Diner in Butler and the Yakkity-Yak Diner in North Apollo both started life closer to Pittsburgh.

A 1940 Kullman now sits in a weedy patch south of Blairsville, windowless and wide open to the elements. Some of the rusted sheet metal on the diner's barrel roof has fallen away to reveal the wooden planks, but the cream-colored, fluted porcelain panels are still intact, as are some of the cream and blue ceramic wall and counter base tiles. This was Dick's Diner of McKeesport, a booming steel town at midcentury able to support two diners a few blocks apart on Lysle (then Jerome) Boulevard. Dick's was opened in 1941 as Bill's Diner by A. William Platt, another local diner entrepreneur. Joe

THE DAILY NEWS, MCKEESPORT

Bill's Diner (1941 Kullman) opened in 1941 on Lysle Boulevard in McKeesport. It was renamed Dick's a few years later.

Dick's Diner was displaced by the urban-renewal frenzy of the early 1970s and ended up in this roadside rut south of Blairsville on Route 217. Just south of here, the Dreamliner Diner (1941 Sterling) opened in Derry on South Main Street in 1941.

Serro's Diner (1938 O'Mahony #1015) was torn from its foundation and set aside after the arrival of a new Mountain View in 1957.

Dick, a gas station operator, bought the diner in 1945. He remembered the difficulties of the diner business. "We used to be most crowded at night when the bars let out," he later recalled. Late-night revelers, who, when not passing food out the bathroom window, would play the jukebox all night. "The song they played was 'Nickelodeon.' You know, 'Put another nickle in.' That song drove me crazy." In the late 1960s, McKeesport embarked on an urban renewal plan, and by 1972, both of its diners were gone, Dick's having been replaced by a muffler shop.

In contrast to the forgotten Dick's Diner, Serro's has been preserved as a museum artifact. In 1938, when work started on a Route 30 bypass around Irwin in anticipation of the Pennsylvania Turnpike's western terminus, two Serro brothers purchased O'Mahony #1015, a diner with white porcelain enamel outside and orange tile inside. All the papers survive from the purchase, even a letter from O'Mahony explaining how to return the wheels the diner rolled on after leaving the Irwin train station.

When the Serros traded up to a modern stainless Mountain View in 1957 (#522), the old O'Mahony was shipped to U.S. Route 119 south of Greensburg, where John and Lillian Rolka remodeled it to resemble a train station, renaming it Willow Diner Station. In 1992, the Rolkas retired, and the Historical Society of Western Pennsylvania purchased the diner for its

In 1960, John and Lillian Rolka bought Serro's, which had been moved south of Greensburg, and renamed it the Willow Diner. After running the diner for more than 30 years, they closed it down after serving breakfast on August 15, 1992. It was then purchased by the Historical Society of Western Pennsylvania for future restoration.

DINER MODEL KITS

About a half dozen firms produce diner model kits. Jim Sacco's City Classics offers the Route 22 Diner, a circa 1950 stainless steel–style model for $18. The HO-scale kit, approximately 4 by 6 inches, has a kitchen annex, freestanding sign, and painting tips on how to achieve a realistic stainless steel finish. Best of all, the directions are written in a clear and friendly manner. And to prove it's a true Pennsylvania dining car, "Dinor" decals are included.

You can find Jim Sacco's diner kit at hobby stores or write to City Classics, P.O. Box 16502, Pittsburgh, PA 15242.

new museum, the Senator John Heinz Pittsburgh Regional History Center. The diner now sits in a warehouse awaiting reincarnation as a museum showpiece.

The Serros sold their Mountain View in 1968 to Zig Barton, who renamed it the Norwin Diner. It was replaced in 1976 by a three-section Mediterranean modern Kullman, and the shiny Mountain View was moved to Butler, where it's served since as Morgan's Eastland Diner, though the Serro's name can still be found in its beige and black terrazzo floor.

In 1969, Lou Serro went back into business when he bought Marie's Diner in downtown Greensburg. Coincidentally, thirteen years earlier, he'd seen and even filmed this 1957 Mountain View (#525) being built while he was visiting the Mountain View factory to see the Serro's Diner under construction. In 1985, Lou lost his lease and moved his Greensburg diner to a hillside overlooking the Pennsylvania Turnpike. It was eventually moved to Seaford, Delaware, where it is now Seaford Diner.

Many prewar diners survive in Western Pennsylvania, and so do several examples from the second wave of diner building that occurred after World War II. With the East Lakes manufacturers gone, new diners came from the major firms around New York City. Only Paramount is missing from the list of surviving postwar diners in Western Pennsylvania.

Diner manufacturers of the late 1940s suffered the same dilemma as automobile manufacturers. Demand for their product was generating a flurry of orders, but in the wake of wartime production, it took time to retool old plants, build new ones, secure scarce resources, and design new product lines. Both sectors scrambled to meet the demand by reworking prewar designs. For diners, that meant the final hurrah for the passé barrel and monitor roofs.

The Summit Diner on U.S. 422 east of Butler shows that DeRaffele was still selling barrel roof diners as late as 1949. From the windows up, the Summit is silver-sided stainless, but the base is clad in vertical navy blue porcelain panels. Paired up with a Texaco station on a lonely stretch of highway, the ensemble functions as a truck stop.

The Summit originated in Pittsburgh, when Terry and Alice Feiler opened it on Baum Boulevard. The Feilers visited the DeRaffele factory in 1949 with Forrest and Virginia Early. Each couple ordered a new diner, both salmon, yellow, and blue inside. The Feilers' diner was the last of DeRaffele's old style. It cost $23,000 and was slid off the delivery truck using Fels Naphtha soap.

Forrest and Virginia Early's diner was different. It was the first DeRaffele ever to feature the company's new waterfall-style roof and all-stainless exterior. Their Hilltop Diner opened that July in Pittsburgh's Greenfield neighborhoood. When the Earlys lost their lease in 1973, the diner was auctioned off and was rumoured to have been moved north to Route 19 near Erie.

Just a hint of monitor roof can be detected on postwar O'Mahonys like the recently restored Gatto's Cycle Diner in Tarentum. Postwar Silk Citys still featured monitor roofs, as seen in a pair of 1948 models in Erie: the former Boston Diner from Peach Street, which in early 1999 was being rehabilitated as part of Haggerty's Bar & Dinor on Erie's West 26th Street, and the Park Dinor, a pristine red, white, blue, and stainless diner set sideways at the end of the Lawrence Park business district.

A modern monitor roof appears in old photographs of Tops 1, a 1948 Fodero that was once at Walnut Street and Conemaugh Street in Johnstown. There was no need for one on Tops 2. When owner Louis Segal decided to expand, he ordered a diner that could be incorporated into an existing building. Fodero built the diner on-site at Main Street and Market Street in 1952 for $160,000, twice the cost of Tops 1.

Another immediate postwar purchase was Paul's Diner on Pittsburgh's Saw Mill Run Boulevard, the main route from downtown to the southern suburbs. George Paul opened a diner in the thick of this congested strip in 1948. The Pauls also ran a second diner in State College for four years. In 1973, Paul's Diner was sold and moved to just outside Pittsburgh's Liberty Tunnels, where it lasted only a few months. It was then moved east to near Blairsville, where it was renamed the Double Deuce, then Kelly's. It burned in the 1980s.

By 1950, the modern stainless diner was the standard, and owners of out-of-style prewar models began trading up. In Mercer, Leo McMonagle had sold his home in 1945 to buy the Mercer Diner, a 1922 model. In 1952, he upgraded to O'Mahony #2241 and reopened the old diner in West Middlesex. The Mercer Diner operated until 1996, when it was bought over the phone by Bernd Richter, who had purchased two other diners for shipment to Europe in an attempt to satisfy the fascination with American popular culture. But first it was shipped to the Jim Diner Company in Cranford, New Jersey, for restoration.

Just like McMonagle or the Serros in Irwin, this pattern of postwar upgrading was followed by the Dean family. By 1940, there were five Dean's Diners

Above: A new roof and dining room were added to McKeesport's Club Car Diner (1946 O'Mahony) in 1958. The peaked roof behind is the B&O station. Locals rejoiced when urban renewal in the early 1970s eliminated the bothersome tracks and rundown businesses, but the concrete-walled inner-city mall that rose here failed to bring back shoppers. Below: Waitresses and cooks celebrate the holidays at the Club Car in 1958.

throughout western Pennsylvania. The only one to survive long after the war was one in downtown Blairsville. But when a four-lane bypass was constructed in the early 1950s, a modern stainless Dean's was opened on the new road.

Closer to Pittsburgh, the location of a number of modern stainless diners was influenced by the early 1950s construction of two limited-access expressways: the western extension of the Pennsylvania Turnpike, from Irwin to the Ohio border, and the Penn-Lincoln Parkway, connecting Pittsburgh with Monroeville in the east and suburbs in the west. The combination of the new Monroeville turnpike interchange and the parkway shifted the way easterners entered Pittsburgh; instead of using the Lincoln Highway via Irwin, the preferred choice became the William Penn Highway (U.S. 22), where it joined the parkway.

The opening of the Monroeville interchange spawned a new diner, the Parkway Diner, founded by Fred Jameson in 1951. Five years earlier, Fred had opened McKeesport's Club Car Diner, an O'Mahony with just sixteen stools and four booths; the closest restrooms, however, were across the train tracks at the B&O station. Jameson sold the Club Car in 1950 to a partnership of managers, then bought a hotel on Route 22 in Monroeville and renamed it the Parkway. The next year he added the Parkway Diner, a 1951 O'Mahony. In 1955, he sold it to the partners who had bought the Club Car. They renamed it the Red Coach, around the time when the Penn-Lincoln Parkway was extended east to the turnpike, bypassing Monroeville and the diner.

But suburban development only increased on old Route 22, and by 1956, the partners had opened a third diner just down from the Red Coach called the Gateway. It was another O'Mahony, but with that manufacturer on the ropes, it took some legal wrangling to retrieve the diner. In 1959, the

The Red Coach, a 1951 O'Mahony, in front of its adjoining hotel and dining room on Route 22 in Monroeville. The site now hosts a Red Lobster and Chi Chi's.

partners ordered a fourth diner for Somerset, 50 miles southeast on the Pennsylvania Turnpike. With O'Mahony now out of business, this diner was ordered from Swingle. Don Bailey, a son-in-law of partner Walt Estep, had been managing the other diners and was called on to open the Summit.

Don has blueprints from early 1960 showing revisions that illustrate the rising tide of environmentalism. Two examples are the addition of false timber ceiling beams and the switching from sixteen round stools 24 inches apart to fourteen square stools with backs 27 inches apart. The Summit is thoroughly clad in stainless steel, with alternating strips of gold and a touch of exaggerated modernity in the unusual steel pylons that rise from its corners. The inside captures diner styles in transition: The bluish green terrazzo floor hints at the exaggerated modern, but the wagon wheel chandeliers, wood paneling, and acoustic ceiling tiles suggest the approaching environmental style. Instead of patterned stainless steel, the backwall is covered with small blue-green ceramic tiles. The copper-faced center clock is incorporated into a formstone hood with abstract dashes for numbers, and counter- and tabletops are surfaced with wood-grain Formica. The blueprints note that the color scheme was based on that of Swingle's Frontier Diner in Plainfield, New Jersey, and the booths were modeled after those of Swingle's Tamarack Diner in Somerville, New Jersey.

Don managed the Summit for six years after its opening in 1960, then returned to the Club Car. But times had changed, and McKeesport was falling to urban redevelopment. The Club Car closed in 1972. Monroeville's Route 22 strip had also changed, going from semirural to always crowded. The Red Coach closed in 1977 to make way for a Red Lobster and Chi-Chi's.

Venus Diner, a 1957 Fodero, shown here in 1990, after green postmodern awnings were added.

The diner was moved near the Volkswagen plant in New Stanton, but it never reopened and was apparently scrapped.

The Gateway closed at the end of 1978 to make way for a Burger King; the equipment was auctioned and the diner sold for $100, but it almost met its death when the mover took too long and the developer put a bulldozer blade against the front door. The diner reopened in Vandergrift as a video store before being resurrected as the Yakkity-Yak Diner in North Apollo.

The Summit is now the only diner between Pittsburgh and Breezewood, and Don Bailey is the most active of the partners. It still has a full-time meat cutter plus twenty-eight other employees. Manager Larry Baughman has worked there for all but one of the diner's years. In a nod to tradition, the Summit still makes its hotcakes one order at a time, just like the Club Car and its cousins once did.

CHUCK BIDDLE

Chuck Biddle is a Pittsburgh artist who has been photographing and drawing neon signs and roadside architecture for the past fifteen years (see page 25).

"My interest in this area of American history originated with my experiences growing up near the roadside in western Pennsylvania. My parents owned a 1950s Italian restaurant called The Gondolier, complete with boomerang-pattern Formica countertops, blond wood furnishings, and a neon sign in the parking lot.

"My earliest memories of the sign lit at twilight continue to manifest themselves in my work to this day.

"I consider my images to be an attempt to preserve, in a compelling way, structures from the mid-twentieth century that display both creativity and originality in their design and appearance."

Two exits west of Monroeville, the turnpike's Butler Valley interchange was graced by the arrival of the Venus Diner in 1957. A green and stainless Fodero, the Venus is a younger brother to Dean's, but its lines are slightly exaggerated, with more flare to the corners. The name is a play on the nearby town of Mars, and when the Venus landed, there wasn't much this far out the William Flinn Highway (Route 8). Acres of farmland have since succumbed to housing developments, and the popularity of the Venus has grown with the suburban population of Richland Township. Its homemade pies are legendary, and its neon sign is a treasured landmark.

If the Venus and the Summit wrapped up the second wave of diners, a much curtailed third wave brought full environmentalism. The Western Pennsylvania diners most representative of this period were brought into the Pittsburgh metropolitan area in the 1970s. In Irwin, the replacement of the Norwin Diner with a new Kullman in 1976 brought Mediterraneanism to the area. The outside is dominated by a colonnade of arched windows

Park Classic Diner, introduced by Eat'n Park Restaurants in Jeannette in 1999, is a converted on-site restaurant.

and a mansard roof, and the inside is a mix of dark red, black, and wood grain. Swingle likewise adopted the new trends, and the design changes initiated at diners like the Summit were complete when Scotty's Diner was shipped to Monroeville in 1979. Now called Jaden's, its Mediterranean modern form belies its origins as a prefabricated diner.

The same can be said about Dick's Diner just east on U.S. 22 in nearby Murrysville. The original car was a 1946 O'Mahony, but Dick's has undergone two dining-room expansions. A counter area remains, but only the outlines of the old diner survive, not the actual pieces. Like many southwestern Pennsylvania diners, Dick's is known for its wide selection of pies.

Perhaps the most stylish of the environmental designs was Fodero's Mediterranean modern stock model used for the 1976 replacement of Ritter's Diner on Baum Boulevard in Pittsburgh. The red and stainless 1951 DeRaffele was then moved to Station Square, a collection of railroad buildings renovated into a shopping area. Arrayed around the old Pittsburgh and Lake Erie terminal hotel and shopping mall is a collection of mementos from Pittsburgh's industrial past: a Bessemer converter, a stern-wheeler paddle, assorted railcars, and Ritter's Diner, now home to a sightseeing company.

The newest diners opening in Western Pennsylvania are an outgrowth of a family restaurant chain. Like Denny's, Eat'n Park has tapped the nostalgia eating market. The Park Classic Diner in Jeannette is a former car hop–coffee shop on Route 30 that has been converted into a postmodern diner, complete with barrel ceiling and CD Wurlitzer. A proposed second location in Monroeville will be factory-built. The company's aim is to open diners in locations that are too small for Eat'n Park's regular restaurants.

DINER DRIVE

LINCOLN HIGHWAY (U.S. ROUTE 30)

Before the recent opening of Denny's Classic Diner in Breezewood, there wasn't another diner on the Lincoln Highway east of Irwin until Johnnie's in McConnellsburg, 110 miles away on the other side of the mountains. In contrast to the relative rarity of diners to the east, the 20 miles of Lincoln Highway between Irwin and Pittsburgh's West End has four diners, with two more just off the route.

The Lincoln Highway from the old western turnpike terminus at Irwin west to Pittsburgh has become one long suburban strip. Although fast-food outlets now dominate, the Norwin Diner survives as the Mediterranean-style flagship restaurant of this stretch. Closer to Pittsburgh, a late 1950s Silk City once operated as the Blue Dell Diner in the neighborhood of Stewartsville. It was part of a popular recreation spot that included the Blue Dell Drive-In Theater and the Blue Dell Swimming Pool. In the 1960s, it was leased by Jerry Athans, who renamed it Jerry's Diner. The diner moved out two decades ago but lives on farther along this drive as Laverne's in Pittsburgh's West End. The pool was recently obliterated, but a few remnants of the long-closed drive-in remain.

The next surviving diner isn't until Charlie's, a few feet into the Pittsburgh city limits from Wilkinsburg. The transcontinental Lincoln Highway

BRIAN BUTKO

Laverne's Diner, a remodeled 1959 Silk City in Pittsburgh's West End, first served on Route 30 in North Huntingdon east of Pittsburgh as the Blue Dell Diner, along with a pool and drive-in theater.

WESTERN PENNSYLVANIA DINERS

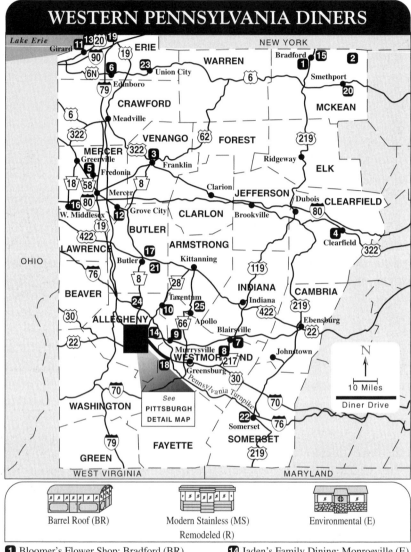

Barrel Roof (BR)   Modern Stainless (MS)   Environmental (E)
Remodeled (R)

1 Bloomer's Flower Shop: Bradford (BR)
2 Cappy's Diner: Eldred (R)
3 Cauvel's Diner: Franklin (BR)
4 Clearfield Diner: Clearfield (BR)
5 Coach Diner: Fredonia (streetcar)
6 Crossroads Dinor: Edinboro (streetcar)
7 Dean's Diner: Blairsville (MS)
8 Dick's Diner: Blairsville (BR)
9 Dick's Diner: Murrysville (R)
10 Gatto's Cycle Diner: Tarentum (MS)
11 Girard Dinor: Girard (R)
12 Grove City Diner: Grove City (R)
13 Haggerty's Bar & Dinor: Erie (MS)

14 Jaden's Family Dining: Monroeville (E)
15 Kan's Meat Market: Bradford (BR)
16 Middlesex Diner: West Middlesex (R)
17 Morgan's Eastland Diner: Butler (MS)
18 Norwin Diner: Irwin (E)
19 Park Dinor: Lawrence Park (MS)
20 Smethport Diner: Smethport (R)
21 Summit Diner: Butler (BR)
22 Summit Diner: Somerset (MS)
23 Union City Dinor: Union City (R)
24 Venus Diner: Gibsonia (MS)
25 Yakkity-Yak Diner: North Apollo (MS)

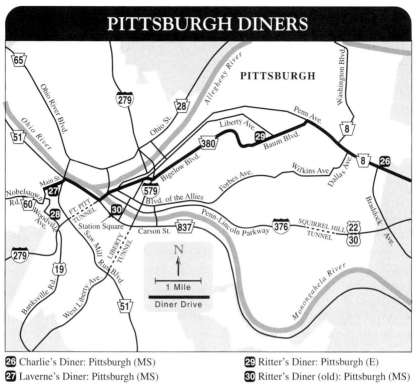

PITTSBURGH DINERS

26 Charlie's Diner: Pittsburgh (MS)
27 Laverne's Diner: Pittsburgh (MS)
28 Pip's Diner: Pittsburgh (R)

29 Ritter's Diner: Pittsburgh (E)
30 Ritter's Diner (old): Pittsburgh (MS)

once joined the William Penn Highway in Wilkinsburg, before the advent of the Penn-Lincoln Parkway. The route followed Penn Avenue through East Liberty to Baum Boulevard and Bigelow Boulevard into downtown Pittsburgh. In the 1920s and '30s, this became the city's premier automobile row, a corridor of gas stations, auto showrooms, garages, and diners. Gone is a Feiler's Diner in downtown Wilkinsburg, another Feiler's Diner a few blocks west of Charlie's, Britt's/Smarz Bros. Diner across from the East Liberty Nabisco plant, and yet another Feiler's Diner, first at the Nabisco site, then moved a mile west to 4914 Baum Boulevard in Shadyside, and now in Butler as the Summit Diner. This was the type of neighborhood that nurtured the monitor roof National-brand diner long called Scotty's and now known as Charlie's.

Ritter's Mediterranean modern diner is at Baum and Powhattan, across the street from the site of Ritter's original DeRaffele that was moved to Station Square.

On the other side of the Golden Triangle, the Lincoln Highway Diner Drive passes Station Square and the old Ritter's, then ends at Laverne's on Main Street in the West End. In preparkway days, the Lincoln Highway came across the now-demolished Point Bridge, through the West End, and out the Steubenville Pike toward Ohio. In 1938, when the highway still directed traffic through the West End, Lester Jacob opened Lester's Diner at 101 South Main Street. Within a year it became Launie's Diner, which it stayed for the better part of a generation.

Laverne Yorkgitis bought the old barrel roof diner in 1973, by then called the Truk Stop Diner. When she wanted to upgrade, she bought the Blue Dell in Stewartsville and had some truck-driving customers haul it from Route 30 to a spot behind her old diner. But one week before opening, the new one burned, forcing a year's repair. That's why this 1959 Silk City has a drop ceiling and no jukeboxes. The rounded corner windows have been replaced by stained-glass mosaics that splash a rainbow of color across the diner's interior when sun is at the right angle. The on-site location for a number of commercials and films requiring diners, Laverne's carries on a sixty-year tradition of a diner at this spot. A few blocks away is Pip's Diner, a 1920s Tierney, but the next diners on the Lincoln Highway are a pair in Lisbon, Ohio, 50 miles away.

PIP'S DINER

1920S TIERNEY, REMODELED

1900 Woodville Ave., Pittsburgh

KEVIN PATRICK

Pip's is Pittsburgh's oldest diner, dating to the 1920s. Since arriving in Pittsburgh's West End about 1954, the diner has gone by a number of names—Eve's, Franny's, Bell's, Bell-Ray, Marie's, Palumbo's, and Irene's. No one recalls where it came from—it was likely somewhere else in Pittsburgh, perhaps the old Scotty's from the Strip District or Smarz Bros. from East Liberty. Its rock-covered facade was added in the 1970s partly to thwart burglars by making the windows smaller.

Despite local scuttlebutt, the diner is not a train car but a factory-built restaurant, identifiable as a Tierney by the patterned tile walls, marble counter, and skylights. A skinny marble counter once ran beneath the front windows. The diner has fifteen four-leg chrome stools facing the short-order grill, which was also updated recently, and a tiny addition holds four booths.

Customers are always in and out, and most seem to know each other, but first-timers are warmly welcomed. Cars park anywhere they can in the gravel lot, but order somehow prevails.

One constant since 1976 has been Dutzer, the cook. (Don't ask her if that's her first or last name or even a nickname; she won't tell you.) Dutzer

BRIAN BUTKO

Until about 1990, Pip's Diner had a counter beneath the windows that matched the main marble counter.

arrives every day before 5:30 A.M. to prepare the day's specials and open the doors. She pokes out of the kitchen every so often, and like everyone here, she fills in where needed.

The food and service are among the best you'll find, but don't be surprised if a regular serves your drink if the diner is busy.

Two handwritten menu boards list the specials, or a small menu is available if you ask. One of our favorite days is Friday, when the specials include such Eastern European staples as pierogies and haluski (buttered noodles and cabbage), as well as huge fish sandwiches, macaroni and cheese, and hamburgers. Breakfasts are made to order anytime. Desserts include pies and cakes—best on Mondays or Wednesdays, when they are baked.

DEAN'S DINER
1953 FODERO
Route 22, Blairsville

KEVIN PATRICK

Dean's Diners were spread across Western Pennsylvania for decades, but only one remains, a shiny stainless model north of Blairsville. It's been run for decades by Darrell Dean, but it was his grandfather Harry P. Dean who started the chain in 1927. That first Dean's was a Ward & Dickinson in Indiana, Pennsylvania, on the corner of 7th Street and Philadelphia Street, moved to 533 Philadelphia in 1936.

In 1934, Darrell's father, Emerson Dean, opened another W&D at 178 East Market Street in downtown Blairsville on the route of the William Penn Highway (U.S. 22). Two years later, Emerson opened a third W&D at the junction of U.S. 22 and U.S. 119, east of Blairsville. Emerson's brother Rodney opened a fourth Dean's in 1941 on U.S. 30 in Forest Hills, and a fifth Dean's opened even farther away in New Castle. (Another Dean's appeared on U.S. 22 in Huntingdon, but it was owned by a Dean cousin, Bill Henning, who used the Dean's name because of its good reputation.)

The Forest Hills Dean's was sold in 1944 when Rodney decided to devote his full attention to his job as a school principal; the diner was renamed Dennis's Diner. The Indiana Dean's went out of business soon after Harry died in 1948. Finally, only the downtown Blairsville Dean's remained, but it was threatened by a four-lane U.S. 22 bypass.

DARRELL DEAN

Rodney Dean at the Indiana Dean's, after its retirement.

Like countless in-town proprietors facing the devastating effects of high-way realignment, Emerson Dean moved to the new road. When the bypass opened in 1953, he was ready with a new stainless steel Fodero trimmed in green flexglass. It cost $45,000 and was one of the last diners built in one section. Business was good enough to add a matching dining room in 1957, but it was made by a Pittsburgh firm, not Fodero. Business at the downtown diner dropped off, and it was closed in 1960.

Steady business on the bypass led to the replacement of the vintage dining room in 1988. Despite the additions and expansions, only the booths have been changed in the original diner. The color scheme is light green with plenty of stainless rising from a pink terrazzo floor containing a dozen green diamonds.

Darrell, who has run the diner since the 1950s, says that three-fourths of his customers are transients, though many are regular transients.

Two of Dean's best-sellers are Swiss steak and the double-decker hamburger platter, but pies are the specialty, including such unusual ones as apricot, raisin, graham cracker cream, and peanut butter cream. Darrell sums it up this way: "It's good food served promptly—but not fast food."

RITTER'S DINER
1976 FODERO
Baum Boulevard, Pittsburgh

KEVIN PATRICK

Whenever Pittsburgh news stations want to poll the man in the street, they take their news vans to Ritter's Diner. Most diner owners brag that they serve a mix of people, but Ritter's is one of the few that really does so regularly. Families, bikers, frat kids, the up-and-coming, and the down-and-out. And always the politicians. No one hesitates to visit, because they know Ritter's is always open.

Bill Ritter sold this diner decades ago, but in Pittsburgh, his name is synonymous with *diner*. Ritter owned a number of local diners in the 1930s and '40s, including one at Forbes Field, one at the site that's now Charlie's near Wilkinsburg, and another three blocks from that. Ritter opened a new DeRaffele-built diner in 1951 across the street from the current location. That red and stainless diner was bought by Art, George, Perry, and Pete Velisaris in 1968. When they upgraded to the current diner in 1976, the Velisaris brothers donated the shiny DeRaffele to the Station Square shopping and office complex, where it serves as headquarters for sightseeing tours.

The modern Ritter's was built by Fodero. The Golden Sword in Philadelphia is a twin. Both are stylized Mediterraneans with a pebble panel facade topped by angular arches and large windows. The arches are reminiscent of a zigzag roofline from the exaggerated modern fifties, a pattern repeated inside above the backbar. The rest is environmental: the acoustical tile ceiling, brass and tulip-shaded lights, scalloped counter, black and off-white trapezoidal-tile backbar, woodgrain Formica booth dividers, speckled brown terrazzo floor, and dark paneled walls. Seeburg consolettes at window booths offer oldies like Elvis and the Four Tops, but current hitmakers like Tim McGraw and Sheryl Crow are here, too.

Breakfast is served twenty-four hours a day; Ritter's Specialty Breakfast Sandwich is a bagel with ham or bacon or sausage, egg, and cheese. There are a number of Greek offerings on the menu too, including a feta cheese omelette.

PARK DINOR
1948 SILK CITY
Lawrence Park, Erie

KEVIN PATRICK

"I'm living the American dream," says George Gourlias. Born in Athens, Greece, he emigrated with his family to New York City, where his father went into the restaurant business. When George was 10, the family moved to Erie, and by the time he was 21, he was the new owner of the Park Dinor.

Lawrence Park evolved as Erie's most renowned industrial suburb, home to General Electric's sprawling locomotive works. Just down Main Street from the plant is a small business district and at the far end sits the Park Dinor. Aside from George's cheerful paint job of red, white, and blue on its exterior, this Silk City has changed little since the day it arrived in 1948.

BRIAN BUTKO

The Park Dinor is still very authentic inside.

The original owners, Harold and Irene Curtis, named it the Lawrence Park Diner and had it positioned with its side to the street in front of their home. Typical of Silk Citys of this vintage, the diner's interior has a counter-aisle-booth arrangement, laid out lengthwise beneath the vaulted gloss of a curved porcelain panel ceiling, with restrooms off a narrow hallway at the far end of the diner. The color scheme, light blue trimmed in beige, is carried by the wall and counterbase tiles.

In their first year, the Curtises counted 202,910 customers, who ate 12 tons of meat and downed 225,000 cups of coffee. The Curtises were charitable with their success and once held a March of Dimes promotion, in which all payments for meals became donations.

George Gourlias has also been successful at the Park, and in 1994 he expanded his operations with his brother by opening the Peninsula Dinor on West 12th Street, near the entrance to Presque Isle State Park.

The Gourlias brothers are especially proud of their Greek sauce, a hamburger puree containing spices. According to George, it was invented at New York's Coney Island as a way of dressing up a hot dog. It can be used on sandwiches or, in a favorite Erie way, over french fries. "Cold American cheese and hot Greek sauce over fries—I must sell forty orders of that a day." Other favorites are the homemade soups, hot roast beef sandwiches, tuna melts, and of course, traditional diner food.

GATTO'S CYCLE DINER
1946 O'MAHONY, REMODELED
Tarentum

YAKKITY-YAK DINER

1956 O'MAHONY #2291, REMODELED
North Apollo

Gatto's and Yakkity-Yak are a pair of Western Pennsylvania diners that had been gutted and nearly destroyed, but the greasy spoon reputation of yesteryear's diners has given way to preservation and restoration. Today, these diners don't look exactly like they did when they rolled out of the factory, but their owners couldn't be more pleased that they've brought a bit of the fifties into the nineties.

Gatto's Cycle Diner had four previous owners. The story starts with Herman Dight, who ran Frampton's Diner in Grove City in the early 1940s, then switched to a used diner in nearby Butler. Business was so good at his location at Washington Street and Jefferson Street that in 1947, he bought a new fifty-one-seater O'Mahony—the one that is now Gatto's.

One of Dight's employees, William Morgan, bought the diner in 1955 and added a Kentucky Fried Chicken franchise, only the fifth at the time.

Gatto's Cycle Diner.

KEVIN PATRICK

Yakkity-Yak Diner.

Morgan's next venture was a drive-in with what was reportedly Pennsylvania's first Teletray electronic curb service. He also started a chain of Morgan's Wonder Boys, which numbered fifty-two when he sold the chain in 1970.

Morgan's Diner was sold in 1981 to William "Digger" Young and renamed Digger's (there's now a different Morgan's Diner east of Butler). His nickname derived from the family's adjacent funeral parlor. Young ran Digger's Diner for two years, then sold it, but he rebought it in 1986 to acquire the land for parking for the funeral parlor, and the diner was moved across town, where it sat abandoned for years.

The diner looked terrible when George Gatto rescued it about 1990—booths and countertops gone, chunks of paint peeling, outside panels torn off. But Gatto put his metalworking and restoration experience to work. The diner is an unusual but beautiful green, cream, and red outside, and inside the chrome and stainless sparkle. Old pictures and memorabilia combine with new neon in this 1940s diner to re-create the fifties. Patrons can enter by the front door or through the showroom of Gatto's motorcycle business.

The diner serves chili in three degrees: regular; nitro, which comes with a release form that patrons must sign; and super nitro, which comes with a fire extinguisher. Menu items have cycle-theme names, such as Fatboy burger.

The Yakkity-Yak has had a similar rebirth. It once sat on a Route 22 hilltop just east of Monroeville, where it was called the Gateway, named, like the surrounding school district, for the role the area played in funneling traffic in and out of Pittsburgh on the old William Penn Highway. The 1956

O'Mahony was supposedly a show diner, used to advertise the company's newest gadgets, but when the diner closed in 1978, the contents were auctioned. It's a miracle that the diner survived; perhaps the $100 selling price and its conversion to a video store in Vandergrift combined to keep it alive until Debbie Pugsley and friends could save it.

The partners bought the shell for $2,000, and then the hard part began: transporting and restoring it. They moved it to North Apollo and worked long hours to find and fit new stools, booths, and tables; everything needed to be cleaned, repaired, or replaced. The diner opened November 1994 with a couple pairs of big neon lips yakkity-yakking on the roof.

The menu is filled with comfort foods—hot roast beef, meatloaf, spaghetti, liver and onions, corned beef hash, fried chicken, real mashed potatoes, pies, bread pudding, and of course, breakfast. There are blue plate specials, like ham and cabbage, and the Yakkity Yak, a fried stacked bologna sandwich. Drinks are served in curvy Coke glasses, and the jukebox blares oldies. "The fifties were a good time for the country," says Debbie. "People were content with the simple things in life." Her dream was to re-create that atmosphere in a real diner. "My dream came true!"

DINER DIRECTORY

BLAIRSVILLE

Dean's Diner
2175 Rt. 22 W.
(724) 459-9600
1953 Fodero.
Open 24 hours.
For more information, see page 227.

Dick's Diner
Rt. 217 S.
1940 Kullman. Originally in
McKeesport.
Closed.

BRADFORD

Bloomer's Flower Shop
16 Congress St.
(814) 368-1489
Circa 1940 Rochester Grills, remodeled.
Formerly Congress Street Diner.
No food served.

Kan's Meat Market
431 E. Main St.
1920s Ward & Dickinson, remodeled.
Formerly Allen's Diner and
Chun-Lee Gardens.
Closed.

BUTLER

Morgan's Eastland Diner
127 Oneida Valley Rd. (at Rt. 422)
(724) 282-2800
1957 Mountain View #522.
Homemade American food; pastries.
Open daily, 6 A.M.–7 P.M.

Summit Diner
760 Rt. 422 E.
(724) 287-9809
1948 DeRaffele.
Homemade American food; breakfast
all day; homemade pies, including
coconut cream, banana cream, chocolate
peanut butter.
Open Mon.–Fri., 6 A.M.–7 P.M.

CLEARFIELD

Clearfield Diner
207 E. Locust St.
(814) 765-9721
Circa 1930, probably Bixler.
American food; hot sandwiches, homemade
fries and gravy, roast beef, turkey, meatloaf.
Open Mon.–Thurs., 6 A.M.–7 P.M.;
Fri.–Sat., 6 A.M.–8 P.M.;
Sun., 6 A.M.–4 P.M.;

EDINBORO

Crossroads Dinor
101 Plum St.
(814) 734-1912
1913 trolley from Niles, #103,
remodeled.
American food; breakfast all day; Cross-
roads melt burger; homemade pie.
Open Sun.–Thurs., 6 A.M.–9 P.M.;
Fri.–Sat., 6 A.M.–10 P.M.

ELDRED

Cappy's Diner
185 Main St.
1930s. Possibly Ward & Dickinson.
Remodeled. Formerly Eldred Diner and
Cottage Cookery.
Closed.

ERIE

Haggerty's Bar & Dinor
1930 W. 26th St. (at Hampton Rd.)
(814) 454-2777
1948 Silk City #4821. Originally Boston
Diner from Peach Street.
American food; lunch and dinner only;
cheeseburgers.
Open Mon.–Fri., 11 A.M.–11 P.M.;
Sat., noon–11 P.M.

Park Dinor
4019 Main St.
(814) 899-4390
1948 Silk City.
Open Mon.–Sat., 6 A.M.–3 P.M.
For more information, see page 230.

FRANKLIN

Cauvel's Diner
408 12th St.
(814) 437-6518
1930s. Formerly Wheeler's Diner
and Diner's Delight.
Homemade American food; breakfast
all day; homemade rolls, cinnamon
rolls, and pies, including apple and
coconut cream.

FREDONIA

Coach Diner
149 2nd St.
(724) 475-4442
Harmony Short Line trolley car, circa
1910, converted 1948.
Homemade American food; breakfast
all day; homemade mashed potatoes and
french fries; homemade pies, including
graham cracker crumb.
Open Mon.–Sat., 7 A.M.–2 P.M.

GIBSONIA

Venus Diner
5313 William Flynn Hwy. (Rt. 8)
(724) 443-2323
1957 Fodero.
Home-cooked American food;
homemade meringue pies.
Open daily, 5:30 A.M.–8:30 P.M.

GIRARD

Girard Dinor
222 W. Main St. (Route 20)
(814) 774-4888
1913 factory-built, remodeled.
American food; soups, burgers, crisp
chicken; homemade pies.
Open Mon.–Thurs., 6 A.M.–8:30 P.M.;
Fri., 6 A.M.–Sat., 10 P.M.;
Sun., 5 A.M.–3 P.M.

GROVE CITY

Grove City Diner
108 E. Main St.
(724) 458-8030
1930s, extensively remodeled.
Originally The Diner.
Homemade American food; cream chicken
over biscuits; homemade desserts.
Open Mon.–Sat., 6 A.M.–8 P.M.;
Sun., 7 A.M.–8 P.M.

IRWIN

Norwin Diner
10640 Rt. 30
(724) 863-2941
1976 Kullman. Originally Serro's Diner.
American food; sausage, cole slaw, broasted chicken; homemade pies, apple dumplings.
Open 24 hours.

MONROEVILLE

Jaden's Family Dining
4727 William Penn Highway (Rt. 22)
(412) 373-8575
1979 Swingle #879DKV.
American food; homemade soups, sauces, pot roast; wide pie selection; car cruises and bike cruises.
Open daily, 6 A.M.–10 P.M.

MURRYSVILLE

Dick's Diner
4200 William Penn Highway (Rt. 22)
(724) 327-4566
1946 O'Mahony, extensively remodeled.
American food; breakfast all day; Yum Yum cake with creamy icing and pies, including coconut cream, banana cream, lemon meringue, red raspberry, Boston cream.
Open daily, 6:30 A.M.–10 P.M.

NORTH APOLLO

Yakkity-Yak Diner
River Road (Rt. 66)
(724) 478-2472
1956 O'Mahony #2291, remodeled.
Originally Gateway Diner in Wilkins Township.
Open daily, 5:30 A.M.–11 P.M.
For more information, see page 232.

PITTSBURGH

Charlie's Diner
7619 1/2 Penn Ave.
(412) 241-9506
Circa 1940 National. Originally Downtown Diner, then Scotty's Diner.
American food; daily specials; lyonnaise potatoes.
Open 24 hours.

Laverne's Diner
113 S. Main St.
(412) 921-2166
1959 Silk City #5902, remodeled.
Formerly Blue Dell Diner.
American food; meatloaf, chili.
Open daily, 6 A.M.–3 P.M.

Pip's Diner
1900 Woodville Ave.
(412) 922-2900
1920s Tierney, remodeled.
Open daily, 6 A.M.–3 P.M.
For more information, see page 225.

Ritter's Diner
5221 Baum Blvd.
(412) 682-4852
1976 Fodero.
Open 24 hours.
For more information, see page 229.

Ritter's Diner (old)
Station Square, Carson St.
1951 DeRaffele. Nonrestaurant office.
No food served.

SMETHPORT

Smethport Diner
423 W. Main St. (U.S. Rt. 6)
(814) 887-5001
1937 Ward & Dickinson or Liberty, remodeled.
American food; half-pound burgers, Hubber dogs.
Open Mon.–Sat., 6 A.M.–7:30 P.M.; Sun., 7 A.M.–7 P.M.

SOMERSET

Summit Diner
791 N. Center Ave.
(814) 445-7154
1960 Swingle #460DV.
American food; hotcakes; all meat cut and ground on premises; sausage made and seasoned same way since 1960; pies.
Open 24 hours.

TARENTUM

Gatto's Cycle Diner
139 E. 6th Ave.
(724) 224-0500
1946 O'Mahony, remodeled.
Open Mon.–Thurs., 9 A.M.–7 P.M.; Fri., 9 A.M.–5 P.M.; Sat., 9 A.M.–3 P.M.
For more information, see page 232.

UNION CITY

Union City Dinor
48 N. Main St.
(at W. High St., Rts. 6 and 8)
(814) 438-7679
1926 Mulholland, extensively remodeled.
American food; real mashed potatoes, fish fry.
Open Sat.–Thurs., 7 A.M.–2 P.M.; Fri., 7 A.M.–7 P.M.

WEST MIDDLESEX

Middlesex Diner
462 Sharon Rd.
(724) 528-9381
1922, probably Ward & Dickinson, extensively remodeled. Originally Mercer Dinor in Mercer.
Homestyle American food; daily soups and specials.
Open 24 hours.

Lost Diners

Moved Out of State

Pennsylvania has seen a shocking exodus of diners in the past decade. Here's where they were and where they've gone.

METRO PHILADELPHIA

West Chester
Birmingham Grille (1949 Kullman) is now Andy's Truckee Diner in Truckee, California; its annex (1965 Kullman) has joined Ruthie & Moe's Diner in Cleveland, Ohio.

Willow Grove
Willow Grove Diner (1948 Fodero) is now the Blue Water Diner in Bainbridge Island, Washington.

PENNSYLVANIA DUTCH COUNTRY

Columbia
Bob's Diner (1947 Mountain View #237) is in storage in southern Maryland.

Easton
Lafayette Diner (1952 Mountain View) is now the Silver Diner in Waterbury, Connecticut.

Kuhnsville
Peter Pan Diner (1957 Mountain View #498) is now Betsy's Diner in Falmouth, Massachusetts.

Ronks
U.S. 30 Diner (1957 Kullman) is in storage in Kentucky.

ANTHRACITE REGION AND THE POCONOS

Berwick
Zephyr Diner (1947 O'Mahony) is being restored as the Sweet City Diner for Cleveland Heights, Ohio.

Matamoras
Matamoras Diner/Uncle Wally's (1949 Paramount) is now the West Bay Diner in Grand Marais, Michigan.

Wilkes-Barre
Chow Tyme/Suzanne's Diner (1955 O'Mahony) is now Al's Diner in Alpena, Michigan.
Olympic Diner (1948 Paramount) is now 11th Street Diner in Miami Beach, Florida.

CENTRAL PENNSYLVANIA

Harrisburg

Riverview Diner (1940s O'Mahony) became part of the Fat Boys Diner chain (now dissolved) in London, England.

Hummelstown

Bill's Diner (1940s Silk City) is a private hunting lodge nearby.

Lemoyne

Lemoyne Diner (1941 O'Mahony #1104) is in Baltimore, scheduled to move to the American Diner Museum, Providence, Rhode Island.

Mifflintown

Zimmie's Diner/Keith Kauffmann's (1958 Silk City #5810) is now a company lunch room in Macedonia, Ohio.

Ono

Fern's/Windmill/Ono Diner (1946 Silk City #46101) is now the Big Dig Diner in Boston.

Williamsport

Mountain Top Diner (1956 Fodero) is now the Skyliner Diner at the Strong Museum, Rochester, New York.

WESTERN PENNSYLVANIA

Ellwood City

Streamliner Diner (1940 Sterling #4011) is in storage in Duluth, Minnesota.

Greensburg

Marie's/Serro's Diner (1957 Mountain View #525) is now the Seaford Diner in Seaford, Delaware.

Mercer

Mercer Diner (1953 O'Mahony) is reportedly in Stuttgart, Germany.

Munster

Terrace Diner (1937 O'Mahony) is being restored for the Western Reserve Historical Society in Cleveland, Ohio.

Missing

Hundreds of other diners have disappeared from Pennsylvania. Did they remodel? Move away? Get flattened? We wish we knew.

METRO PHILADELPHIA

Abington

A diner (1954 Mountain View) at 1716 York Road

Chester

Boyd's Diner (1948 Fodero) at 10 East 7th Street

Edgemont Diner/Tres-Bon (1957 Mountain View #511) at 12th Street and Edgemont

Jerry's Diner (1958 Swingle #658DKV)

Rainbow Diner (1941 Silk City) at Fourth Street and Morton Ave

A diner (1953 O'Mahony) at 3300 West 2nd Street

Collegeville
College Diner (1941 Silk City) at
   111 Main Street

Croydon
Croydon Diner (1949 Comac)

Drexel Hill
Township Diner (1951 Fodero)

East Lansdowne
Fernwood Diner (1947 O'Mahony) at
   Baltimore Avenue and Beverly Avenue

Eddystone
Peewee's Diner (1952 DeRaffele), near
   Chester

Elkins Park
Cal's Diner (1930s)

Exton
Exton Diner (1950s Paramount) on
   Lincoln Highway (Route 30)

Glenolden
Glen Croft Diner (1940s) at Chester Pike

Glenside
Keswick Diner (circa 1950 Paramount)
   on Easton Road (Alt. Route 611)
Walt's Kenyon Diner (1951 Silk City) at
   2708 Limekiln Pike

Horsham
Runway Diner (1953 Mountain View
   #382) at 3759 Easton Road (Route
   611), Hallowell Township

Media
5-Points Diner (1957 Mountain View
   #517) at Providence, State Road, and
   Sumner Street

Montgomeryville
Bellevue Diner (1940, probably Paramount) at the intersection of U.S.
   202, Route 309, and Route 463

Morrisville
Yankee Clipper Diner (1940 O'Mahony)
   on Old Lincoln Highway (Route 1)

New Hope
New Hope Diner (1955 Kullman)
   at U.S. 202

Norristown
Birkett's Yankee Clipper Diner (1940s
   O'Mahony) at 41 East Lafayette Street
Charley's Diner (1930s probably
   O'Mahony), U.S. 202, three miles
   north of Norristown
Fred's Diner (1955 Mountain View
   #456) at Ridge Pike, Plymouth Town-
   ship, near Norristown

Norwood
Norwood Diner (1953 O'Mahony,
   L-shaped) at 618 Chester Pike

Philadelphia
American Diner (1949 Comac) at 4617
   Girard Avenue
Bridgeton Grille (1941 reconditioned
   Silk City) at 2016 Hunting Park
   Avenue
Century Diner (1940 reconditioned
   Silk City)
Franklin Diner (1954 Mountain View
   #384) at 2200 Whitaker Avenue and
   Hunting Park Avenue
Girard Diner/Nick's Diner (1948
   Fodero), 822 West Girard Avenue
Globe Diner (1953 Mountain View
   #358) at 4800 Germantown Avenue
   and Rockland Road
Grove Diner (1948 Paramount) at 8705
   Germantown Avenue
Passyunk Diner (1941 Silk City, and
   later a 1950 Kullman) at Passyunk
   and 25th
Pen-Mar Lunch (1920s O'Mahony)
Pennsylvania Grill at 40th Street and
   Spruce Street

Robinson's Diner (1951 Fodero)
at 2328 Grays Ferry Avenue
Robinson's Diner (1952 Fodero)
at Buist Avenue at 74th Street
Silver Streak (1950 O'Mahony) at 4233
North Broad Street at Hunting Park
Spring-Ridge Diner (1953 Mountain
View #355) at 12th Street and Spring
Garden Street and Ridge Avenue
Tioga Diner (1952 O'Mahony) at West
Allegheny Avenue
William Penn Grill (1948 Master)
at 1074 then 7425 Frankfort Avenue
A diner (1950 Kullman) on Gray's Ferry
Avenue
A diner (1952 Mountain View #327)
at 7257 Hanford Street
A diner (1953 Kullman) on Lansdowne
Avenue at State Street
A diner (1954 Mountain View #403)
on Washington Lane

Phoenixville
West End Diner (1940 Silk City)

Pottstown
Art's Diner (1948 Kullman) at 225 West
High Street

South Abington
Keystone Clipper (1940 O'Mahony)
on Route 6

Trevose
Golden Arrow Diner (1948 Comac)
on Route 1

Washington Square
A diner (1940 O'Mahony)

West Chester
Squire Diner (1953 O'Mahony) at 305
Gay Street

PENNSYLVANIA DUTCH COUNTRY

Allentown
Dick's Grill (1920s O'Mahony) at
721 Linden Street
Ina's (Ward & Dickinson pair) at
15 South 10th Street
Park Manor Diner (1955 Silk City
#5511) at 4301 Tilghman, South
Whitehall Township

Bethel
A diner (1955 Kullman) on Routes
22 and 83

Bethlehem
The Hearth (1940 Silk City)

Breinigsville
Garden Diner (1940s Silk City) on
Route 222

Boyertown
Boyertown Diner (1930 O'Mahony) at
371 South Reading Avenue (Routes
100 and 562)

Easton
Walt's Diner (1941 reconditioned
Silk City)
Wilson's Diner (1941 National then
1948 Fodero) on U.S. 22

Ephrata
D&B Diner (circa 1940 Silk City) on
Route 222, north of Ephrata

Lancaster
Hyway Diner (probably 1920s Tierney)
on Lincoln Highway East

Lebanon
Lincoln Diner (1940 O'Mahony),
Lincoln Avenue at Cumberland Street
Panorama Diner, 1539 East Cumber-
land Street

Reading
Buttonwood Diner (1940 Ward & Dickinson) at 325 Buttonwood Street

Wyomissing
Queen of the Valley Diner (1954 Kullman) at 1730 Penn Avenue

ANTHRACITE REGION AND THE POCONOS

Bartonsville
Bartonsville Diner (1940 Silk City) on Lackawanna Trail

Bushkill
Olympia Diner (circa 1960 Kullman) on Route 209

Dupont
Silver Coach Diner (circa 1952 Mountain View) on Route 315

Hazleton
Mulrain Bros. Diner (1920s O'Mahony) on East Broad Street
Sunset Diner (1940 reconditioned O'Mahony)

Kingston
Cottage Diner (1930s), a 19-stooler on Wyoming Avenue
Top Hat Diner (1955 Fodero) on Wyoming Avenue, Routes 11 and 115
A diner (1940 Kullman) in Kingston

Mountainhome
Phil & Dom's Diner (1953 reconditioned Mountain View)

Pottsville
Palace Diner (1920s O'Mahony)

Scranton
Yank's Diner (1941 Sterling Streamliner) at 126 Adams Avenue
A diner (1948 Mountain View) in Greyhound Bus Terminal

A diner (1953 reconditioned Mountain View) at West Market Street and Hallow Avenue
A diner (1954 Mountain View #404) run by the National Dining Car Company

South Center
A diner (1952 Mountain View) on Route 11

Wilkes-Barre
A diner (1940 O'Mahony) on River Street
A diner (1949 Kullman)

Wind Gap
Caesar's Diner (1959 Fodero)

CENTRAL PENNSYLVANIA

Carlisle
Carlisle Diner, 10 North Pitt Street

Chambersburg
C-Burg Diner (1941 Silk City), 831 South Main Street

Harrisburg
Paxton Diner, 1200 Paxton Street
Porter's Diner, 3rd and North Paxton
A diner (1940 reconditioned O'Mahony) on North Cameron Street

Huntingdon
Ridge Diner (1955 Fodero), Route 422

Jonestown
Clover Leaf Diner, Route 22
Johnston's Diner, Route 22

Lewistown
Dreamline Diner, Route 22, 1/4 mile east of Lewistown

Middlesex
Pike Diner (1941 Silk City), Route 11, just north of Carlisle Turnpike interchange

New Cumberland

Bridge Diner (1930s), Old York Road in Fairview Township, near New Cumberland

Reading

Mt. Penn Glass Front Diner (1930s barrel roof), Route 422, east end of Lindbergh Viaduct

Steelton

Steelton Diner (barrel roof), Front Street and Swatara Street

York

York Diner (1930s), on U.S. Route 30, 2¹/₂ miles east of York

WESTERN PENNSYLVANIA

Cheswick

A diner (1946, probably Kullman, run by diner entrepreneur A. William Platt)

Derry Township

Dreamliner Diner (1941 Sterling) at South Main Street Ext.

Ebensburg

Hi-Way Diner (1920s trolley) at 215 West High Street (Old Route 22)

Erie

Bill Jones Stadium Dinor (1949) at 26 East 26th Street

Club Diner at 25 West 8th Street

Glenwood Dinor at 3624 Peach Street

Kern's Dinor at 1012 Parade Street

Pullman Dinor at 1315 State

Ross's Diner (1949 Silk City)

Sunshine Dinor (1940s) at 2519 Parade Street

Indiana

Lewis Diner (1920s) at 658 Philadelphia Street

New Castle

Crossroad Diner (1951 Silk City)

Smith's Diner on Routes 224 and 422

New Kensington

Short's Diner at 8th Street

Pittsburgh

Pat's Diner (circa 1930 Ward & Dickinson) at 900 Shore Avenue, end of Manchester Bridge

Royal Clipper (circa 1945 O'Mahony) on Neville Island

Further Reading

BOOKS

Baeder, John. *Diners*. Revised and updated. New York: Abrams, 1995.

Genovese, Peter. *Jersey Diners*. New Brunswick, NJ: Rutgers, 1996.

Gutman, Richard J. S. *American Diner: Then and Now*. New York: HarperPerennial, 1993.

Gutman, Richard J. S., and Elliot Kaufman. *American Diner*. New York: Harper & Row, 1979.

Kaplan, Donald, and Alan Bellink. *Diners of the Northeast*. Stockbridge, MA: Berkshire Traveler Press, 1980.

Kittel, Gerd. *Diners: People and Places*. New York: Thames and Hudson, 1998.

Williams, Robert O. *Hometown Diners*. New York: Abrams, 1999.

Witzel, Michael Karl. *The American Diner*. Osceola, WI: Motorbooks International, 1999.

MAGAZINE

Roadside Magazine. Worcester, MA: Coffee Cup Publishing. *For subscription, write P.O. Box 652, Worcester, MA 01602 or call (508) 791-1838.*

CHILDREN'S BOOKS

Day, Alexandra. *Frank and Ernest*. New York: Scholastic, 1988.

Gibbons, Gail. *Marge's Diner*. New York: Crowell, 1989.

Kraft, Jim, and Mike Fentz. *Garfield and the Haunted Diner*. New York: Grossett & Dunlap, 1989.

Loomis, Christine, and Nancy Poydar. *In the Diner*. New York: Scholastic, 1993.

Mickey's Diner. SL: Mouseworks, 1995.

Moss, Marissa. *Mel's Diner*. SL: Bridgewater Books, 1994.

VIDEO

Pennsylvania Diners and Other Roadside Restaurants. Pittsburgh: WQED Video. *For sale through WQED Video at 4802 Fifth Avenue, Pittsburgh, PA 15213 or (800) 274-1307.*

Index

About the Authors

Brian Butko is the author of *The Lincoln Highway* and a forthcoming history of the Isaly/Klondike ice cream company. He was associate producer of the WQED-TV documentary *Pennsylvania Diners and Other Roadside Restaurants*. Kevin Patrick is a professor of geography at Indiana University of Pennsylvania and editor of the journal *Lincoln Highway Forum*.